AMERICA'S GLORIOUS

QUILTS

America's

QU

EDITED BY

Distributed by Macmillan Publishing Company, New York

Glorious

QUILTS

Dennis Duke and Deborah Harding

HUGH LAUTER LEVIN ASSOCIATES, INC., New York

Printed in Japan by Dai Nippon Printing Company
©1987 Hugh Lauter Levin Associates, Inc., New York
ISBN 0-88363-487-2

CONTENTS

INTRODUCTION   9

AN AMERICAN TRADITION   14

Laura Fisher

QUILTS: AMERICA'S FOLKLORE   62

Deborah Harding

QUILTS: THE ART OF THE AMISH   110

Phyllis Haders

HAWAIIAN QUILTS   134

Lee S. Wild

QUILTS—CRAZY MEMORIES   152

Virginia Gunn

BABY, CRIB, AND DOLL QUILTS 176

Pat Long and Dennis Duke

QUILTS AT AN EXHIBITION 194

Donna Wilder

CONTEMPORARY QUILTS 214

Luella Doss

A QUILT–COLLECTOR'S PRIMER 256

Celia Y. Oliver

LIVING WITH QUILTS 294

Phyllis George Brown

BIBLIOGRAPHY 315

INDEX 318

ACKNOWLEDGMENTS

This book incorporates the combined efforts of many individuals, so that to list each person who made a contribution is impossible. However, we would like to thank the following people who immeasurably contributed to its production: Our publisher, Hugh L. Levin, whose vision it was to conceive a book that would bring together the most exemplary American quilts and who believed that such a publication could be educational as well as aesthetically stimulating; Ellin Yassky, Hugh's associate, who coped with many difficult problems and solved them brilliantly; our editor, Michael Sonino, who smoothed the rough edges with skill and dispatch; and Philip Grushkin, who gave the book a handsome design.

We must also specially thank Jean Ariyoshi, the former First Lady of Hawaii; Karen Berkenfeld; Katy Christopherson; Dr. and Mrs. Dero Dowing; Kei Kobayashi; Gene A. Morin; Madeline Guyon of J. C. Penney Co., Inc.; Julie Silber, curator of the Esprit Collection; Hope Hanley Levy, needlework expert and author; Deanna Nardozzo, quilt collector and lecturer; Peggy K. Silhanek; Mr. and Mrs. Truman Watkins; Roger Tate; Dr. Scott DePass; and Mr. and Mrs. W. B. Duke, who provided support from the very beginning until the book's completion.

Finally, we thank a true folk artist—the American Quilter.

INTRODUCTION

For five days in April 1986, a unique event was held in New York City: the Great American Quilt Festival and Contest, cosponsored by the Museum of American Folk Art and the Scotchgard division of 3M Corporation. The contest offered a previously unequaled $20,000 as its first prize. There were more quilt experts gathered together there than anywhere ever before—as well as quilts for sale, displays of quilts on loan from museums, and specially curated exhibits. There were lectures and quilting workshops. Participants included the country's leading textile designers, authors, teachers, collectors, prizewinning quilters from every state, dignitaries, invited guests, and those who were simply curious.

Among the 25,000 people who attended the festival were the art book publisher Hugh Levin, Atlanta businessman Dennis Duke, and myself. Hugh was there because he was intrigued by the phenomenal growth of this previously taken-for-granted craft and because he was stimulated by the colors and designs created by American quilters of the past and present. Dennis had been in New York for a year and a half as Special Projects Director for the Museum of American Folk Art. He was the director of this impressive and ambitious event and was intimately involved in all aspects of its organization. I attended the event because I am a crafts and needlework editor and I had been given exclusive rights to write a magazine article about the contest and to interview the winning contestants.

Our paths crossed at special ceremonies, press parties, and preview events. However, we were not really acquainted at the time; we knew each other only by reputation, and we had no opportunity to compare our impressions. Nevertheless, we independently came to the realization that quilts had outgrown the crafts-and-hobby stage and had finally attained recognition as artistic masterpieces.

Hugh Levin had recently issued three lavishly illustrated books on Monet, Van Gogh, and Italian Renaissance art. After attending the festival he decided that America's quilts and quilters deserved a similar and long-overdue tribute to their particular art. He got in touch with us, and in July 1986 we met for lunch. Our enthusiasm over the project was immense. We immediately agreed that the book should not be another of those do-it-yourself volumes that have been the most recent trend in publications dealing with quilts—quite the opposite. We wished to present the finest examples this country had to offer in a book that was splendidly illustrated, authoritatively written, and interesting to lovers of the fine arts as well as to quilters.

We discussed whether to limit the work to antique, traditional, and familiar grass-roots examples, or to devote it to more adventurous contemporary compositions. We finally decided that if the book were to be truly representative, it should include the best of all categories from all periods. Our next step was to contact museum curators, collectors, dealers, designers, historical societies, and quilt guild members throughout the country to ask for their opinions and cooperation. Dennis and I mailed thousands of letters and made as many telephone calls. I traveled throughout the country interviewing collectors and designers and listing and photographing hundreds of important quilts. We then selected ten leading authorities and invited them to write essays in which they would share their knowledge so that we could assemble a historical survey of quilts and furnish information on many aspects of the craft.

The opening chapter, ''An American Tradition,'' is by Laura Fisher, a noted dealer and collector of Americana who has lectured widely on quilts. The author of *Quilts of Illusion*, she reviews the history of quilting and defines basic techniques and design categories. Her informative beginning makes the succeeding parts of the book more meaningful and more enjoyable.

In the next chapter, ''Quilts: America's Folklore,'' I explore the myths, superstitions, and stories that inspired the pattern names. Kentucky is singled out as an example of a state that has a rich quilt heritage and that established itself as a role model for documenting native quilts with its ground-breaking Kentucky Quilt Project.

In ''Quilts: The Art of the Amish,'' Phyllis Haders explains the unique character of Amish quilts, which derives from the use of bold, vibrant colors in simple patterns. She also explains why pre-1940 Amish quilts are so highly valued today. Ms. Haders, a leading collector and dealer, has made frequent lecture appearances and is the author of *Sunshine and Shadow*, a book about the Amish and their quilts.

Hawaiian quilts have a grace and romance all their own. Some patterns are so carefully guarded that members of the same family often keep their work secret from one another while it is in progress. Stealing a quilt design is considered equal to stealing a part of someone's soul. Lee S. Wild, in the chapter entitled ''Hawaiian Quilts,'' discusses such taboos, presents a history of the growth and development of quilting throughout the Islands, and investigates the source of uniquely Hawaiian motifs and techniques. She is Special Events Coordinator for the Mission Houses Museum and a Hawaiian Quilt Resources Person for the Bernice Pauahi Bishop Museum, the Honolulu Academy of Arts, the Daughters of Hawaii, and the Lyman House Museum. Ms. Wild helped to create the documentary film ''The Hawaiian Quilt—A Cherished Tradition.''

The chapter ''Quilts—Crazy Memories'' discusses the appeal of crazy quilts to the women of the Victorian era, who personalized them with names, dates, family initials, embroideries of homes and pets, and sentimental scraps of fabric from their wardrobes. Crazy quilts are a collage of memories from a bygone era, with their rich designs and often luxurious fabrics. The author, Virginia Gunn, is Associate Professor of Clothing and Textile Arts in the Department of Home Economics and Family Ecology at the University of Akron and curator of that university's historic costume, textile and Hower House collections. She is on the board of directors of the American Quilt Study Group and has published many articles on nineteenth-century American costumes and quilts.

Antique crib and doll quilts are among the most collectible textiles today. One may pay more for a crib quilt in good condition than for a full-size quilt of the same pattern and date. This and other aspects of miniature quilts and the world of the child are investigated in ''Baby, Crib and Doll Quilts,'' coauthored by Dennis Duke and well-known lecturer and designer Pat Long.

In her chapter "Quilts at an Exhibition," Donna Wilder details the growth of fairs and their importance to quilt makers and also discusses quilts that incorporate images of historic and political events. Ms. Wilder has served as a local, regional, and national quilt judge and is on the advisory board for the annual Quilt National show, as well as the Quilt Festival and Market, both in Houston, Texas.

"Contemporary Quilts" was written by Luella Doss, who is nationally recognized for her award-winning quilt and wearable art designs. She also serves on the board of directors for two well-known folk art shows, "Christmas in the Country," was Midwest judging coordinator for the Great American Quilt Festival, and is working on a book devoted to contemporary quilts and quilters. In her chapter we learn that not all collectible quilts are antiques; there are many contemporary designers whose pieces are owned by museums, galleries, and major corporations. They may follow traditional patterns, or they may create what has come to be known as the "art quilt."

Having researched and documented hundreds of handsome quilts, we wanted to know what makes a quilt really worth collecting and where some of these quilts can be seen. We therefore turned to the resident textile specialist at Vermont's renowned Shelburne Museum, Celia Y. Oliver, who provided "A Quilt-Collector's Primer." The Shelburne houses one of the finest quilt collections in America, and this chapter not only informs us how museums evaluate quilts as potential acquisitions but also offers information of a useful nature.

Finally, we decided to reveal how some people enjoy displaying their quilts in everyday surroundings. We asked Phyllis George Brown to write "Living with Quilts." During her years as First Lady of Kentucky, Mrs. Brown spent much time promoting the quilts and crafts for which her state is famous. "Oh! Kentucky," a display of her state's crafts, was exhibited in a number of major department stores throughout the country. A special appendix added to this last chapter offers valuable practical information on the care and display of quilts plus a list of places that specialize in the conservation and repair of treasured antiques.

My coeditor Dennis Duke and I are proud to have had this opportunity to explore this unique American art form and to present some of this country's most cherished and spectacular quilts, those we consider to be *America's Glorious Quilts*.

Deborah Harding

AN AMERICAN TRADITION

AN AMERICAN TRADITION

by Laura Fisher

The quilting tradition in this country began in the early eighteenth century, as pioneer women sought ways to keep their families warm. Quilts have evolved with this nation's history into a highly personal folk art form entailing craft as well as creativity. Indeed, they are beginning to be recognized as one of the foremost examples of American folk art, characterized by ingenuity, originality, color, texture, and liveliness —even joy.

Quilts were made almost exclusively by women, who took pleasure and comfort in quiltmaking as one of the few creative outlets allowed them. Even in the hands of a member of a somber religious sect or impoverished American family, quilts reflected a spirit and energy that makes them outstanding examples of a national and international folk art. (It is interesting to note that the development of their decorative patterns has no correlation to any other culture or artistic medium.) It was the fortuitous conjunction of bits of fabric out of a practical need and a spontaneous creativity that resulted in this unique tradition.

The ability to design—to manipulate color, harmony, scale, and geometric form—are skills inherent in the best quilt artists. Early quilt makers, presumably, were individuals untrained in sophisticated design with a limited exposure to art and a limited ability to experiment. Yet they succeeded in producing works of art.

An appreciation of quilts can develop from at least two distinct standpoints: they can be regarded as significant reflections of this country's history from the 1700s, their patterns, materials, and subject matter evoking specific eras and pointing up changes in technology and life styles; or they can be enjoyed on their aesthetic merits with no knowledge of their historical context. They are paintings in fabric, collages of color.

PRECEDING PAGE: *Pyramid Tumbling Blocks Amish Pieced Quilt* (detail). c. 1935. Ohio. Cotton. Collection America Hurrah Antiques, New York City. Photograph by Schecter Lee.

While it may interest the historian or collector to know if a specific quilt includes fabric of a certain date or type, or if a design depicts a national event, a political or social celebration, or an episode from the Bible or family history, it is just as fascinating to approach a quilt as a work of art isolated from sentiment or intention. Jean Lipman in her book *Provocative Parallels* states that Amish Center Square quilts have been compared to Minimalist paintings; intricately pieced "postage stamp" quilts with Pointillist compositions; and intriguing nineteenth-century illusionist cube quilts with the works of Vasarely and other 1960s Op Art figures.

"Quilt" is derived from the Latin *culcita*—a stuffed sack, mattress, or cushion. The dictionary defines the word as a bed cover of two layers filled with wool, cotton, or down and held in place by stitched designs. The insulation qualities of layered fabric were known to the Egyptians, the Chinese, and the Turks, who used quilted materials for warmth as well as for cushioning in their armor. Europeans adopted quilted petticoats and undergarments as early as the fifteenth century.

The oldest quilt extant is a Sicilian example from the fifteenth century. Scenes from the legend of Tristan and Isolde are quilted on linen with brown and white linen thread.

While quilting may be found in many areas of the world, it is the Americans who have experimented with, embellished, and developed it. The earliest known American pieced quilt is a geometric design in brocaded silk and velvet. It is believed to have been created in 1704 by Sarah Sedgwick Leverett (wife of John Leverett, Governor of the Massachussetts Bay Colony from 1673 to 1697) and her daughter Elizabeth. The lining is paper and includes parts of the 1701 catalog of Harvard University.

QUILT CONSTRUCTION

As we know them, quilts are composed of three layers: a top, a batting or lining, and a backing. A quilt is often described as a textile sandwich. The *quilting* itself is actually the stitching that holds the three layers together and prevents the filling from shifting.

The *quilt top* is the decorative layer, and it is made first. It is often carefully planned in advance according to a design scheme of pattern shapes and color combinations. The two most popular methods of making quilt tops are piecing and appliqué.

Piecing is just what the word implies: the individual cutting, organizing, placing, and stitching of many pieces of fabric together. Many pieced quilts have a geometric format in which the pieces may be squares, diamonds, triangles, rectangles, or hexagons. A patterned top may be composed of a dozen to hundreds or even thousands of these shapes, arranged in designs with such evocative names as Sunburst, Tumbling Blocks, Log Cabin, Postage Stamp, Mosaic, Birds in the Air, Flying Geese, or Streak O' Lightning.

To appreciate the precision of working with tiny sections, consider that if the measurement of just one edge of one piece is not perfectly aligned, the plan of the entire quilt top can be jeopardized. Paper templates are often used as a lining, or stiffening, to make the tiny pieces easier to manipulate. The paper is basted in place onto the fabric and removed later.

An extraordinary quilt composed of 66,153 pieces is in The Kentucky Museum in Bowling Green: it is aptly titled "Spectrum". Its creator, George W. Yarrall, joined pieces of percale in squares of ⅜ inches and of ¼ inches. He worked on it from July 2, 1933 to December 30, 1935. Mr. Yarrall was a silver engraver who felt that the exercise of working on this quilt would keep his fingers limber.

Of course, not all quilts are pieced with such miniscule elements. Simple square patterns, the straight edges of which are easy to work with, make up the majority of everyday quilts; these were the first types of quilt made in this country.

The more acute the angle, the more difficult the piecing of the pattern, as in Grandmother's Garden or Star of Bethlehem designs. Quilts pieced of elements with curved edges require yet more skill, and among the most familiar patterns of this type are the Double Wedding Ring and Drunkard's Path.

Pieced tops were often "scrap-bag" creations, the components of which were salvaged from remnants or worn-out garments:

> *Portions of discarded uniforms, old coat and cloak linings, brilliantly dyed wool flannel shirts and well-worn petticoats were components of quilts that were needed for warmth. A magnificent scarlet cloak, worn by a Lord Mayor of London and brought to America by a member of the Merrit family of Salisbury, Massachusetts, went through a series of adventures and migrations and ended its days as small bits of vivid color, casting a grateful glory and variety on a patchwork quilt in the Saco Valley of Maine!* (Marie D. Webster, *Quilts, Their Story and How To Make Them*, pp. 66-67.)

These scraps can be difficult to date, since the maker might have collected, saved, and traded scraps for decades before combining them in a top. The most exciting and imaginative pieced quilts combine different geometric shapes that create yet other patterns on the quilt's surface.

The other popular method of quilt construction is *appliqué*. This involves cutting out, layering, and stitching small pieces of fabric on top of larger ones. Because the pieces do not have to fit together, appliqués are not usually geometric in design. Wonderful pictorial elements —flowers, bows, swags, birds, people, and animals—all become subjects in appliqué.

Quilt tops are often designed in blocks of four or more and then joined together. The individual blocks may be separated by bands called *sashing* or *sets*. Patterned blocks may alternate with solid blocks, which allowed for a virtuoso display of quilting stitching. It is not at all unusual to see piecing and appliqué combined on the same quilt top.

Under the quilt top is the middle layer of the quilt, the *batting*. The batting is usually cotton or wool, but it might also have been a worn quilt, rags, feathers, corn husks, newspapers, or any scrap material available. In Colonial times, and in rural areas as late as the early twentieth century, the batting was mostly home grown wool or hand-carded cotton. A home grown cotton batting is sometimes recognizable by the dark hard seed casings that remain in the crudely carded filling, which can be felt or seen through the fabric. Commercially produced battings were available as early as the mid-nineteenth century. Today's battings are made mostly from synthetics, which are lightweight, easily washable, and available in a variety of thicknesses.

The bottom layer of the quilt is the *backing*. It can be a single sheet of fabric or large strips sewn together. Once in a while, a pieced pattern is used to back a quilt. Because the design emphasis is concentrated on the top, a pieced backing will not be as detailed, yet occasionally one is lucky enough to find a reversible quilt.

After the top is completely assembled, it is ready to have the design marked on it with pencil or chalk or by pricking tiny holes in the fabric. Simple overall patterns, such as a grid of boxes or diamonds, or diagonal lines can be measured out with a yardstick. Simple curved patterns might be accomplished by tracing a household item such as a teacup, a saucer, or a pocket watch. For more intricate designs, cardboard or tin templates can be made or purchased. There are templates that one can trace, and there are templates with perforations through which one shakes powder or flour to mark the stitching lines.

When the quilt is ready to be put together, the backing, which is usually cut a little larger than the other layers, is spread out flat and fitted carefully onto a frame. Within the frame two stretcher bars are covered with ticking or muslin; the backing is stitched into place on this. Then comes the batting, and finally the top. All three layers are basted together to prevent shifting. One person can work at the frame, changing positions, or as many as a dozen can gather around a large frame. They stitch as far toward the center as they can comfortably reach. Then the quilt is rolled sideways to one end of the stretcher bars so that any missed areas can be filled in. Some large homes had stationary quilting frames that were valued household furnishings. Others had collapsible frames or frames that could be pulled down from the ceiling on pulleys when needed.

The stitching stage of construction was often the occasion for a quilting bee, when the women of the community gathered to finish quilts and visit with neighbors. A group of experienced quilters could complete several quilts in a day.

The quilting stitches that join the three layers are running stitches. The greater the skill of the quilter, the more even the stitches and the greater their number. Some fine examples have over twenty running stitches per inch.

On pieced quilts, the stitching simply follows the outlines or traverses the shapes of the pieces. But appliqué or whole-cloth quilts serve as virtual canvases for a needlework artist. Their open field "ground" invites a wide variety of stitching motifs: flowers, baskets, vines, waves, feathers, clam shells, hearts, stars, birds, or human figures.

After the quilting is completed, the quilt is removed from the frame. Binding the rough edges to seal the layers is the last step before the quilt "goes to bed." Early binding materials varied from hand-loomed tapes to bias-cut fabric to store-bought binding. In lieu of a separate binding, other options for quilt finishing include overlapping the backing to the top; turning in both top and backing and hemstitching, blanket stitching, or inserting piping; or adding a separate hand-knotted or store-bought fringe or ruffle.

In addition to pieced and appliquéd quilts, there are also whole-cloth quilts, for which the top is essentially a single, large piece of fabric. It may be a solid color, decoratively quilted, or a printed fabric with stitching following the outlines of the pattern in the print.

QUILTING MATERIALS

Understanding textile history can aid in determining the approximate age of a quilt. The earliest were principally composed of homespun rather than commercially produced fabrics. Only the best quilts would have been made from such multicolored printed fabrics as cotton chintz, which was often cut out and appliquéd on a solid ground to enhance the impact. Print fabrics are found regularly in American quilts dating from 1820 on. The textiles most commonly seen in nineteenth-century quilts are cottons (including solids, calicoes, ginghams, muslin, and dimity), wool, and challis.

Block printing was the earliest form of textile-design technology; this was followed by the development of engraved copperplates that produced large-scale designs of birds, scenes, and historical events in single colors; later, roller printing allowed for continuous printing in several colors in a less expensive and faster manner than copperplate printing. The English-born John Hewson, who settled in Gunner's Run, Pennsylvania, owned a bleaching and printing establishment, and between 1778 and 1780 he produced the first cotton print in America, using the discharge or roller-printing method. The prints were called calicoes. Originally, "calico" was the term for a type of handwoven fabric from India, named after the city of Calcutta. It has since become the general term for printed cotton. A dress-goods fabric mostly associated with nineteenth-century American prairie life, many think of calico as a fabric with a small-scale repeating pattern, usually in two colors.

The majority of printed fabrics used in quilts were clothing and furnishing fabrics. The earliest designs included florals, landscape scenes, animals, and Classical motifs such as pillars or urns. After the middle of the nineteenth century, the Far East having long opened to Western trade, Oriental motifs, including paisley designs, abounded.

Eli Whitney's invention of the cotton gin in the early 1790s radically altered the production of cotton; the device simplified the process of removing cotton seeds from the cotton boll. Soon, manufactured cotton fabric and batting became more readily available to the homemaker.

Owing to the scarcity of fine fabrics in frontier regions, quilts from the early years of American expansion reflect a decidedly different hand than do their urban counterparts. Many were constructed of rough muslin or sacking materials for the top, a thick, often uncarded batting, and a coarse backing. Generally, the layers were stitched together in a wide-set parallel quilting or were made into "comforts" or "ticks" tied with knots at intervals rather than quilted. This latter method enabled the quilt maker to untie the knots and remove the batting for cleaning. Among the most familiar comforts are those made with pinstriped wools, serge, melton, or flannel and composed of large, rectangular sample swatches that traveling salesmen left for potential customers.

In the Victorian era, costly, fancy fabrics—silks, brocades, velvets, taffetas, satins—were used in quilts. They were salvaged from ball gowns, waistcoats, draperies, and other furnishings, or they were purchased from textile manufacturers who, in the 1880s, capitalized on the crazy-quilt mania by offering previously worthless scraps for sale.

In the early twentieth century, quilts incorporated printed materials that manufacturers put on feed and sugar sacking. In an interview that appeared in *Texas Quilts, Texas Women*, March 19, 1979, Fannie McIntyre of Driftwood, Texas, testified:

[My husband] smoked Duke's tobacco and it came in little cloth sacks. Back then, now I'm tellin' you, it was hard times and things was scarce. I didn't want to throw all them little sacks away because they was good material—unbleached domestic. So I saved enough of 'em to make a quilt. I had to rip the seams out and wash 'em and iron 'em. And after I dyed 'em I had to iron 'em again. I dyed 'em three colors—pink and green and yellow. There's a bush, algerita, some folks call it, and the roots makes the most beautiful yellow dye you have ever seen. It made a pretty quilt. My husband kept sayin', "Why I wouldn't fool with them things if I was you. That's too much trouble." But after he seen what I had done with 'em, he was kinda pleased about it.

Miss Evelyn Fuqua reports that she used nine hundred tobacco sacks in one quilt. The custom of asking the men to save these little pieces of unbleached muslin is widely reported. The tobacco sack salvage has its analogue in the use of feed sacks for backing. Some feed sacks [were produced] in colorful prints as an added attraction for the home seamstress. Before this trend, however, feed sacks with the label showing were used for utility quilts. Mrs. Ben Harrison of Edmonson County happily showed an example of Acme labels on the backing of one of her quilts. She had another reversible quilt made entirely of patterned feed sacks . . . she also showed a reversible quilt made entirely from salvaged sugar sacks.

(Mary Washington Clarke, *Kentucky Quilts and Their Makers*, p. 23.)

Specialty materials printed to commemorate significant historical events or individuals, as well as political campaign ribbons, prize ribbons, souvenir fabrics, printed kerchiefs, and tobacco premiums, all found their way into nineteenth-century quilts. Some of the tobacco premiums were silk rectangles approximately 2 by 3¼ inches printed with flowers, butterflies, birds, or flags. They were inserted in packs of cigarettes, such as Straights, between 1912 and 1915 to encourage women to smoke. There were also inch-wide silk cigar bands or ribbons with their brand names printed in gold, that were used to tie bunches of cigars together. Pieced together on the diagonal, their printing became part of the quilt's pattern. Another fabric insert was the "blanket," made of flannel and printed with flags, baseball motifs, or American Indian designs.

In addition to the textile content and its patterning, dyes are another clue to the age of quilts. The earliest dyes were made from natural materials: roots, bark, flowers, plants, minerals, shellfish, and insects. In the mid-nineteenth century, the advent of synthetic chemical dyes revolutionized the textile industry, making it possible to produce a broad range of colors. The earlier natural shades and combinations resulting from the overprinting of one color on another (for instance, blue over yellow produces green) gave way to limitless possibilities of directly dyed color. Unfortunately, some of the earliest natural dyestuffs were set with mordants that, over time, became corrosive to the fabrics on which they were printed, making materials brittle and leaving holes where the print once was. These older quilts are now extremely fragile and require educated handling. Susan Stewart in her "Sociological Aspects of Quilting in Three Brethren Communities in Southern Pennsylvania" (*Pennsylvania Folklife*, Spring 1974: p. 25) writes of the process: "The women boiled their brown dyes in a kettle, dissolving enough of the iron to create a black dye. This also released the mordant to make the dye fast, but in doing so caused a more rapid deterioration of black and brown fabrics."

TYPES OF QUILTS

While there are more than two dozen types of quilts, twelve major categories are described below. Several others are accorded chapters of their own.

Linsey-Woolsey

This is generally a whole-cloth quilt and is practically synonymous with the Colonial quilt. The name reflects its composition of textiles—a combination of linen (the wrap) and wool (the weft). These covers, usually made with a coarse wool backing, were valued for their warmth. The dyes were natural, and the colors included blues, reds, oranges, browns, mustards, and greens. Two or sometimes three loom-widths of homespun fabric were used to create the top. The stitching that quilted the layers ranged from simple diamond grids to elaborate curvilinear swirls formed into flowers, wreaths, and plumes (a remarkable technical feat, considering the thickness and lack of suppleness of the linsey-woolsey material). When sometimes these tops are pieced, it is most frequently in blocks or squares.

Calimanco

A finer version of linsey-woolsey is the calimanco spread. The top is a woolen fabric finished to a high shine by rubbing the wool with a smooth stone until it takes on a gloss (much like well-worn serge suiting) or by coating the fabric with an egg white glaze. Such spreads are commonly seen in historic restorations, where they complement bedchambers decorated with crewel-embroided draperies. Calimanco spreads were already popular in the early eighteenth centuries.

Whitework

This, too, is a whole-cloth coverlet on which the top consists of one or two loom-widths of fine white cotton atop a backing of coarser linen. This elegant style was popular in America from 1790 to 1830 but has its origins in seventeenth-century Europe.

Since the materials used were only of one color, the designs were achieved entirely by intricate patterns of quilting stitches. These masterpieces were attempted only by the most proficient needleworkers, who combined superior stitching with an ability to plan an often exquisitely detailed composition. By making very small stitches and placing them close together, they caused the unstitched areas to puff up to become the design elements surrounded by outline or stipple (dotlike) quilting. The effect was a *bas-relief*. These quilts contain very thin batting, or none at all. The classic format was a central medallion design of a cornucopia, a latticed basket of fruit, or an eagle, pineapple, or feather wreath surrounded by borders of grapevines, trailing leaves, or bows and swags. Dates and names were often included in the quilting.

A dramatic form of whitework is the *trapunto* or *stuffed-work* quilt. In these, the designs were developed in high relief by the insertion of soft cotton or cording through fine partings of the backing. When these quilts were washed, the fibers closed over the areas of insertion, resulting in a tightly packed, sculptured effect on the quilt.

Broderie Perse

This term refers to putting appliqué motifs cut from chintz or another printed fabric onto a plain background. Such quilts were not made for warmth, but were show quilts and rarely used. Made in more affluent sections of society (particularly in the South and East), their popularity peaked between 1820 and 1840. Their style was influenced by, and imitative of, imported Indian fabrics. Center designs included Tree-of-Life motifs with peacocks, pheasants, and flowering branches framed by one or more borders. Such designs are always one-directional because the tree must be upright.

Stenciled

Although stenciling is found on many early household items, there are very few examples to be found on quilt tops. Flowers, fruit, and birds were the favored subjects, often requiring many small stencils to achieve a single image. It was sometimes decided to add free-hand detailing as well. These quilts were more prevalent in the Northeast and date from the 1820s and 1830s.

Embroidered

Very small details on quilt tops, such as flower centers and stamens, eyes, feathers, and names, dates, and other lettering, were sometimes embroidered rather than quilted. Pieced and appliqué shapes sometimes were outlined or joined with embroidery. This type of stitchery reached its apex in the Victorian era, with the development of crazy quilts, and displayed a wide variety of embroidery stitches and pictorial elements.

A more subdued and familiar form of embroidered quilt dates to the late nineteenth century and employs one-color thread—frequently red—on a white background. The subjects were often derived from nursery-rhyme characters. Kate Greenaway motifs were favorites, such as boys and girls with pets and toys. The shapes were drawn or printed in outline and sometimes the motto "Sweet Dreams" accompanied the image of a sleeping child, or "Good Morning" the image of a sun or bird. Such motifs were published in ladies' magazines of the era, from which transfer designs could be ordered. Preprinted muslin blocks, which could be combined with an embroidered creation, were also available.

Pattern or Kit

From the 1920s on, patterns and preprinted kits that included fabric sufficient for entire quilts were made available through nationally syndicated newspaper columns, *Good Housekeeping*, and the *Ladies' Home Journal*. Their widespread replication and reinterpretation in the Depression era resulted in buoyant designs in piecework and appliqué that were often surprisingly similar, though they were made in different parts of the country.

Dozens of companies provided patterns for this revival of interest in quiltmaking. Although more commercial, perhaps, than their nineteenth-century counterparts—when patterns circulated principally among friends, family, and community—the more widely disseminated twentieth-century patterns are now also regarded as originals, for their designs originated in the home: they were often submitted by readers, either spontaneously or in response to the thousands of quilt contests sponsored by newspapers and companies like Sears, Roebuck; or they were created by women like Marie Webster and Rose Kretsinger, who began small, local quilt-design businesses in the Midwest, and soon became sought after and nationally published as professional designers.

Representational

People, animals, houses, trees, baskets, ships, and scenes were as popularly depicted in cloth as in oil paint, watercolor, and pastel in the nineteenth century. Most quilts of this type repeat an image a dozen or more times across the surface of the quilt, almost like Pop Art's multiple-image manipulations in the 1960s.

Commemorative, Patriotic, and Thematic

Memorable events prompted special-occasion quilts, the subject matter (and sometimes coloration) of which reflected the maker's feelings. In the nation's first two centuries, there were few ways more appropriate for Americans to show their love of country than to decorate everyday household objects with national motifs. The quilt became a canvas on which the needleworker expressed patriotic pride; thus quilts serve as social documents illustrating political sentiments. Occasions such as the admission of a state into the union, the election of a candidate, or the promulgation of a political cause became subjects for patriotic quilts.

Whether political, religious, historic, or personal, such commemorative quilts are rarer within the broad range of quilts produced. A young man reaching maturity might have received a "freedom" quilt; the occasion of Lindbergh's flight might have spurred a pictorial or scenic quilt; most recently, the Centennial of the Statue of Liberty inspired thousands of quilts commemorating that celebration.

Album

The practice of incorporating many separate design blocks within a single quilt has resulted in a fascinating legacy of album quilts. Such works were usually prepared in the appliqué technique, either by a single individual who desired a collection of images on fabric, or by a group, each of whom contributed a block to the total composition.

Baltimore Album quilts are the exemplars of this style. They are

prized for their unusual designs, exquisite craftsmanship, and striking beauty representing floral motifs, ships, churches, Baltimore monuments, and historic events. These designs in printed cottons have been appliquéd to individual cloth squares, measuring 16 to 18 inches, which are then sewn together in series to form quilts as large as ten feet square. It is the assembling of these blocks, many of which are inscribed with the contributor's name, that led to the appellation "album quilts," since each quilt square is similar in spirit to the page of an autograph album. The most distinguishing characteristic of the finest of these quilts, made in Baltimore between 1846 and 1852, is the imaginative manner in which printed cottons were pieced together to suggest texture, shading, and contour.

(Dena S. Katzenberg, *Baltimore Album Quilts*)

Sampler

Similar to album quilts, sampler quilts bring together separate designs arranged in block form, but they are usually made up of differing pieced patterns rather than appliqué motifs. They too were created either by a single individual who wished to try her hand at favorite quilt patterns without having to make an entire quilt of one design, or by several individuals (friends, relatives, a church or community group) who made a quilt usually to present as a token of remembrance or fellowship.

Friendship, Autograph, Signature, Charity, and Tithing

It would have been helpful if all quilt makers had signed their work, but names and places seem to have been considered important to record only in friendship quilts made to give as gifts. The blocks either were made, or signed, by an individual, a family, or a group. In autograph quilts, contributors often paid for the privilege of having their names inscribed on the quilt either in India ink or in thread. Such a quilt might then have been raffled or auctioned to raise additional revenue for a particular group or organization. On such quilts have been found signatures ranging from those of schoolboys to leading political figures.

THE VALUE OF QUILTS

Some quilt historians feel that the peak period of American quiltmaking extended from 1775 to 1850, but fine examples are being discovered from all periods, including the present, with the stimulating work of today's designers, such as Michael James and Nancy Crow, being collected by museums. Therefore, it seems limiting to place a date on the value or growth of this constantly evolving craft.

"Interest in collecting quilts began in the 1920s. At first, specialists focused on the quality of the needlework, but in the 1960s, the emphasis shifted to an aesthetic appreciation of quilts as collectors began to value examples that could be related to modern art." (Robert Bishop, *Quilts, Coverlets, Samplers, Hooked Rugs*) Interest in quilts has been escalating since the 1971 exhibit *Abstract Design in American Quilts* held at the Whitney Museum of American Art in New York. The Museum of American Folk Art in New York reports that its best-attended exhibitions are those that feature quilts.

Handmade American quilts of the past centuries—and decades—are an increasingly attractive investment. From their humble beginnings as bedcovers, created most often from discarded scraps, quilts have currently acquired broad international appeal. Designs as diverse as nineteenth-century appliqué album quilts and bold Art Deco pieced works of the Depression years are much sought after by present-day exhibitors and collectors.

Luckily, many antique quilts have been cherished by generations of descendants or given to museums where they have been preserved and put on display for our enjoyment and enlightenment, rather than subjected to the daily hard use for which they were originally intended.

The growing awareness of the artistic worth and investment value of quilts is evidenced by recent auction prices. Skinner's in Massachusetts set a record in October 1984: $30,800 for a pictorial appliqué quilt made by Sarah Ann Wilson of New Jersey in 1854 and purchased by Kate and Joel Kopp of America Hurrah Gallery in New York. In January 1986, Sotheby's nearly matched this price, selling to the same astute purchasers Martha Hewitt's 1856 kaleidoscopic star with people and American flags for nearly $30,000. Undoubtedly, quilts have sold for more on the *private* market, although such records are generally not disclosed. Thomas K. Woodard claims to have established a record for twentieth-century quilts with his firm's recent purchase, for about $9,000, of a 1930s appliqué quilt done in the manner of the nineteenth century with superb needlework. Although some quilt prices are now topping six figures, their price rise in no way approaches the escalating prices for other types of Americana. However, experts believe that antique quilt prices have not yet peaked. As with any art form, "the general trend is that anything of good quality, of superior design and condition, will continue to go up and up and up," according to Nancy Druckman, American folk art specialist at Sotheby's. Evidence of this was forthcoming when in January 1987 a Baltimore Album quilt made by Sarah and Mary J. Pool around 1840 was sold at Sotheby's for $176,000, thus establishing a record price at time of writing.

These high prices are remarkable, even ironic, if one considers that in the nineteenth and early twentieth centuries, quilts were finished by groups or individuals charging only for the spools of thread needed to stitch them; depending on the size of the stitches, each quilt averaged 2½ spools (albeit larger than today's), at a cost of fifty cents per spool!

Today it is hard to pick up a magazine without reading about quilts; seeing quilt patterns adapted to fashions; finding how-to-quilt directions; or learning how they decorate a celebrity home or a corporate environment. Major corporations, hotels, and even banks employ art curators who acquire quilts for their board rooms, lobbies, and executive offices.

At the same time as collectors and investors are stockpiling antique quilts, quiltmaking in America is alive and well, flourishing as widely now as it was during the Victorian quilt mania. There are quilt shops, quilt classes, over 2,000 quilt guilds, competitions, and exhibitions. The industries that supply fabrics, batting, pattern books, sewing machines, and special publications are a big business.

For five days in April 1986, almost 25,000 people from all over the world attended the Great American Quilt Contest and Festival in New York, jointly sponsored by the Scotchgard division of the 3M Corporation and the Museum of American Folk Art. There were old and new quilts to buy, special displays, lectures, and classes.

There is an annual event in Houston, Texas, held every October: the Quilt Market and Quilt Festival. Manufacturers exhibit and sell their newest products to shopowners. The event comprises over a week of exhibits, demonstrations, seminars, classes, contests, shopping trips and tours, quilts to buy, fashion shows of quilting clothing, and special breakfasts, luncheons, and dinners. Thousands of quilt enthusiasts attend, including teachers, students, designers, dealers, authors, magazine editors, decorators, and museum curators. What draws them together are the same things that attracted their ancestors: a chance to meet with other quilters, exchange ideas and patterns, work together, make new friends, hear about new products, or simply to socialize, catch up on the news, and have a good time. The only difference is that instead of carrying a sewing basket to attend a neighborhood bee, riding there in a horse and buggy, today's quilters arrive on jets, carry portable electric sewing machines, and may even purchase their instructions on video cassettes.

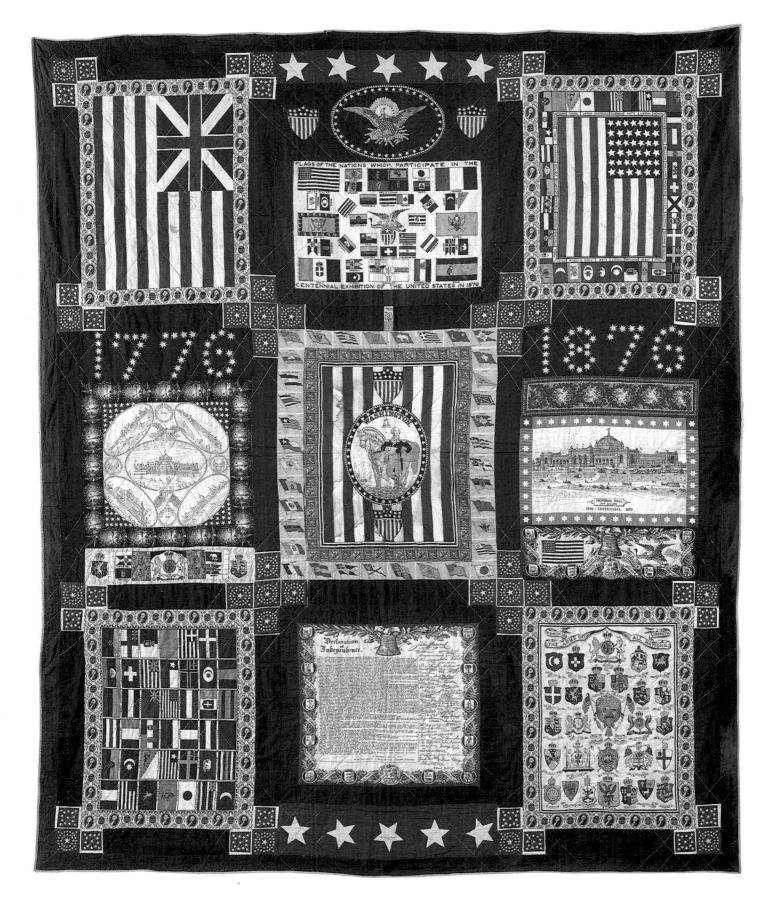

![icon] 1

Pieced and Appliquéd Centennial Quilt. c. 1876. Union, Maine.
Cotton, 104 × 84″. Collection Laura Fisher Quilts and Americana, New York.

This quilt is composed of nine cotton kerchief squares printed with patriotic and historical motifs for the Philadelphia Centennial Exhibition. The subjects include the Declaration of Independence (bottom center); George Washington on his horse against a red-and-white-striped ground (middle); Memorial Hall in Philadelphia (center right, below the date 1876); Memorial Hall Art Gallery in Philadelphia (center left, below the date 1776); the British and American flags; and a panel printed "Flags of the Nations which Participate in The Centennial Exhibition of the United States in 1876." The sashing seems to be made of printed cotton; blue and white stars are organized according to dates commemorating the Centennial (1776 and 1876) and in firework-like motifs to corner and jauntily frame the kerchiefs. The piece is lightly batted and backed with muslin in a natural color. The machine-stitched quilting is simple and is composed of large diamonds criss-crossing the surface.

🌀 2

Sarah Ann Wilson. *Black Family Album Quilt*. 1854. New York or New Jersey. Cotton, 85×100".
Collection Stephen Score. Collection America Hurrah Antiques, New York City. Photograph by Schecter Lee.

This is an unusual quilt because all of the figures are executed in black fabric. Another quilt made by the same woman, illustrated in the *Index of American Design*, includes the same people, which indicates that they were probably members of Sarah Ann's family. Pictorial quilts are rare; the fact that in the present example each block is different, that each exemplifies a clean, folklike design, and that all the figures face the viewer adds to its overall greatness. Motifs include three houses and many birds and animals, including a lion, a boar, a deer, and a swan and fish in a pond. The familiar heart-and-hand motif is in the last block. The sashing between the appliqué blocks is pieced. Note the superior and intricate stitching in the quilting, and the unique double-scalloped border with appliqué details, and the beautiful bias binding on each of the scallops.

🌀 3

Log Cabin Mennonite Pieced Quilt Windmill Blades Variation. c. 1880.
Lancaster County, Pennsylvania. Cotton, 72×90″. Collection Phyllis Haders.

In the example shown here, there is the sense of constant movement in the center design and in the beautifully striped border of triangles.

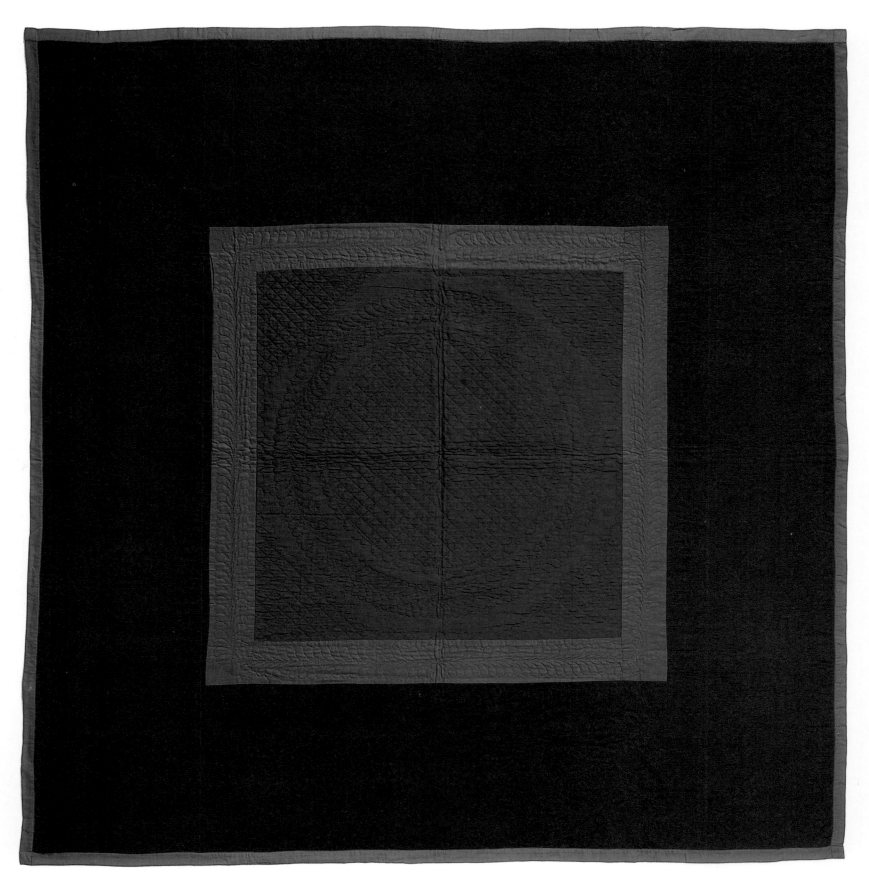

4

Square Within a Square Amish Pieced Quilt. c. 1900. Lancaster County, Pennsylvania.
Wool, 77 × 77". The Esprit Collection, San Francisco.

This work typifies the Lancaster County quilt in its purest form. It is within such a framework that
the Diamond, Bars, and all their variations were developed. It bears a strong resemblance to the
works of the abstractionist Josef Albers.

 5

Diamond in a Square Amish Pieced Quilt. c. 1920. Lancaster County, Pennsylvania.
Wool, 81×80″. Collection America Hurrah Antiques, New York City. Photograph by Schecter Lee.

This example is notable for its handsome colors. Note especially the concentric circles of quilting within the diamond.

6

Pyramid Tumbling Blocks Amish Pieced Quilt (detail). c. 1935. Ohio. Cotton, 108 × 94″.
Collection America Hurrah Antiques, New York City. Photograph by Schecter Lee.

This quilt incorporates superb architectural design elements; it is a brilliant accomplishment.

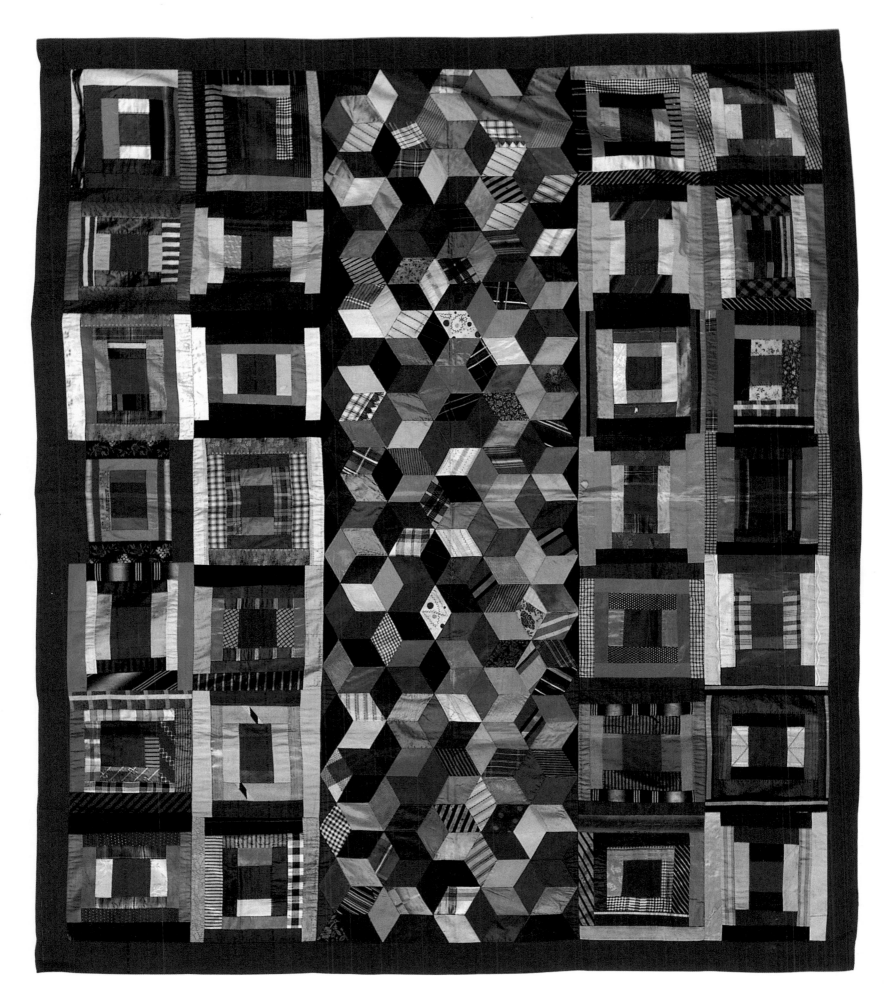

7

Tumbling Blocks and Log Cabin Pieced Quilt. c. 1890. New York.
Silk, 63×63″. Private collection. Photograph by Steve Mitchell.

It is unusual to see these two patterns combined, especially when they are executed in such
delicate fabrics. The Tumbling Blocks are in the center, and a column of Log Cabins is on each
side. The red border holds the whole work together. This spectacular quilt is like a contemporary
work of art.

✿ 8

Log Cabin Pieced Quilt, Streak O' Lightning Variation. c. 1880. Massachusetts. Wool, 74×78″. Collection America Hurrah Antiques, New York City. Photograph by Schecter Lee.

The illusion of diamond shapes in this stunning quilt is accomplished by the placement of minute strips of light and dark fabrics.

✿ 9

Log Cabin Pieced Quilt, Barn Raising Variation. c. 1880. New York. Wool challis, 70×71″. Collection Phyllis Haders.

The interesting aspect of this Barn Raising variation lies in the fact that the light-and-dark pattern sections are arranged on the square rather than in the usual diamond format.

🐢 10

Log Cabin Pieced Quilt, Barn Raising or Sunshine and Shadow Variation. c. 1890. Kentucky.
Cotton, 80½ × 64¼″. Collection The Kentucky Historical Society, Frankfort, Kentucky. Photograph by Nathan Prichard.

Barn Raising and Sunshine and Shadow are Log Cabin variations. Although very little is known about this quilt, it is included because of its dramatic use of color. The treatment of the red and black in the center in this type of quilt is unique.

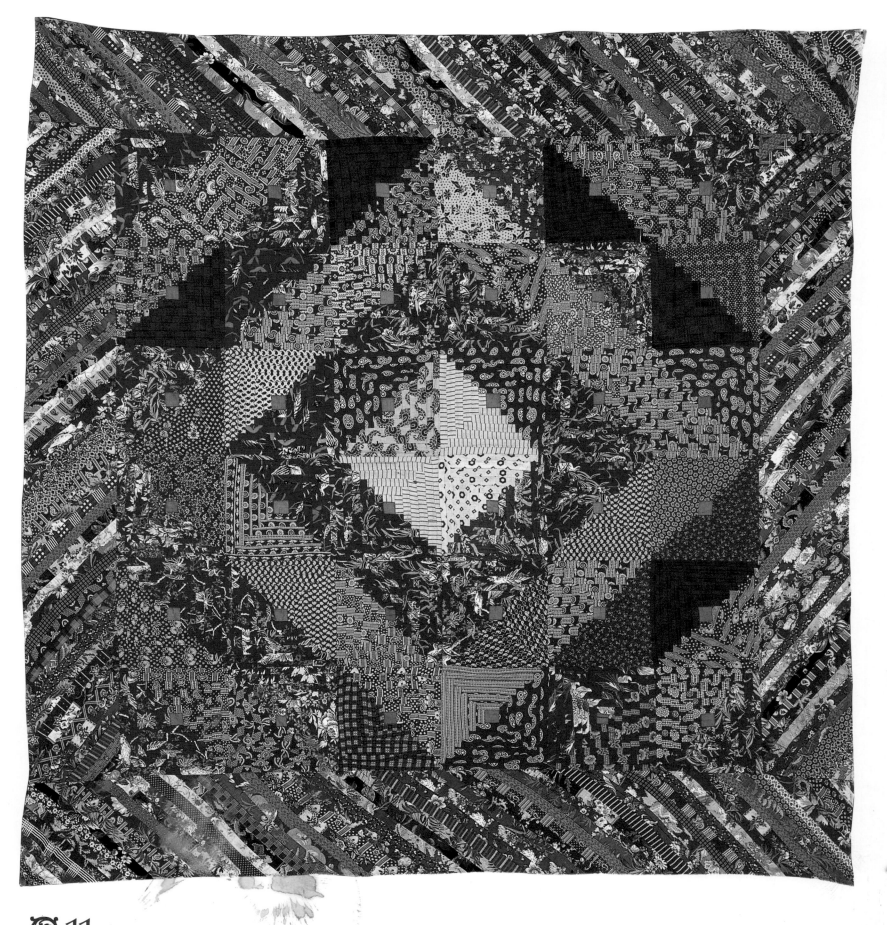

🔖 11

Log Cabin Pieced Quilt. c. 1870. Origin unknown. Cotton, 75×72". Private collection.
Photograph courtesy Martha Jackson.

The deployment of the hand-dyed cottons here is a credit to the maker's understanding of color and its interaction through placement. Compare this antique treasure with some of today's contemporary designs.

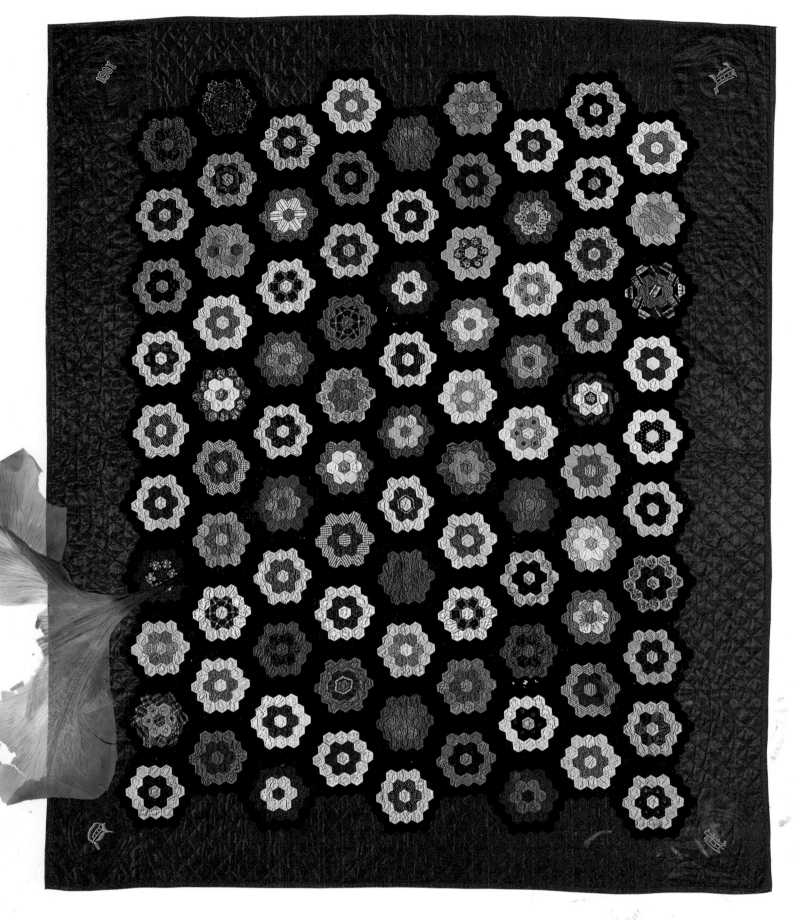

🌀 12

Hanson Penn Diltz, Carrie Diltz Elgin, and Elizabeth Diltz Cushman. *Grandmother's Flower Garden or Flower Garden Pieced Quilt*. c. 1863–1907. Cynthiana, Kentucky. Silk, 56 × 46¾".
Collection The Kentucky Historical Society, Frankfort, Kentucky. Photograph by Nathan Prichard.

Hanson was a nine-year-old boy who started making this quilt at the time of the Civil War. He cut the hexagons from a pattern made of tin, and although it has been said that the pattern "was the size of a dime," the hexagons actually measure seven-eighth of an inch in diameter; therefore it is unclear whether the size of the coin he used was larger than the usual ten-cent piece, or if the statement was a slight family exaggeration. He did all the piecing for the top, while his sisters, Carrie Diltz Elgin and Elizabeth Diltz Cushman, started the quilting. Apparently the quilt remained unfinished and was put away for many years, as one can infer by the date in one of the corners. It was completed by Hanson's sisters in 1907.

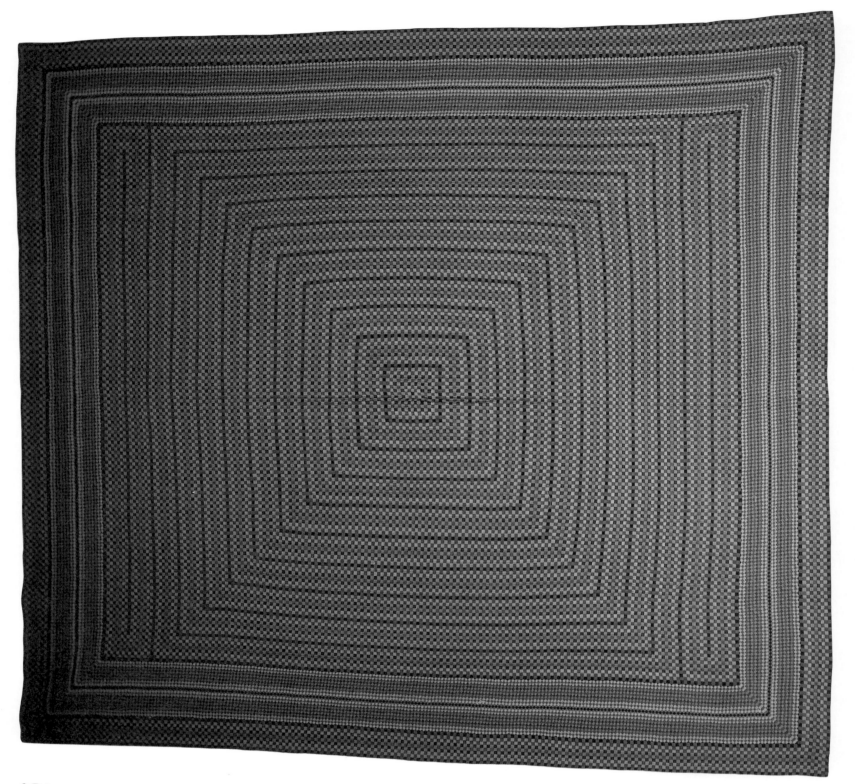

🔯 13

George W. Yarrall. *Spectrum*. 1935. Kentucky. Pieced percale, 78½ × 90¾".
The Kentucky Museum, Western Kentucky University, Bowling Green, Kentucky. Photograph by John Perkins.

This quilt is similar to other pieced-quilt patterns that employ a large number of small pieces, known variously as Around the World, Trip Around the World, and Postage Stamp.

This example was made by George W. Yarrall, an engraver for a jewelry company in Bowling Green. It is thought that he began quilting to keep his hands flexible after reading a newspaper account of a dynamite expert who quilted to keep his hands limber. Yarrall kept excellent records about this quilt: he began it on July 2, 1933, and finished on December 30, 1935. The quilt contains ten colors of percale fabric, and the squares measure three-eighths inch or one-quarter inch. A total of 66,153 pieces were used: 27,160 squares in the diagonal border, 5,152 in the panels, 25,921 in the center, and 7,920 in the outer edge.

The amount of time and patience required to complete this quilt is considerable; most quilts of this type do not contain so many pieces. Also, the arrangement of colors serves to create a vivid optical illusion. As one looks into the center the colors seem to vibrate and move.

This quilt is unusual because it was made by a man. There are very few documented examples of quilts made by men at that time; in America sewing has been an almost exclusively female pursuit. Most known cases of early quilts made by men seem to indicate that the makers were either invalids or older men who quilted as recreation or therapy.

14

Nine-Patch Postage Stamp Miniature Pieced Quilt. c. 1870. Kentucky.
Cotton, 69×59″. Collection Shelly Zegart's Quilts, Louisville, Kentucky. Photograph by Steve Mitchell.

The designation ''miniature'' does not apply to the size of this quilt but to the size of the pieces of fabric of which it is composed. The tiny squares and the sets of borders here transform a very ordinary pattern into an extraordinary quilt.

🌀 15

Eight-Pointed Star Pieced and Appliquéd Trundle Quilt. c. 1880.
Pennsylvania. Cotton, 43 × 44″. Collection Phyllis Haders.

Note that in this quilt the scallops in the center design actually touch each
point of the star. This combination of pattern elements is quite original.

⦿ 16

Mrs. Sarah Henderson. *Rose Wreath with Tulips and Kentucky Flowerpot Corners Appliqué and Pieced Quilt with Trapunto Stitching*. Late 1800s. Mt. Carmel, Kentucky. Cotton, 100 × 101½″. Collection The Kentucky Historical Society, Frankfort, Kentucky. Photograph by Nathan Prichard.

Here is a beautifully worked quilt with extraordinary details. The quilting is very fine, with rows of stitches only one-quarter inch apart. There is a different trapunto design in each of the white blocks, including wheat, bird, and flower motifs. The roses in the wreaths are appliquéd in pink and red with yellow centers. The same yellow and red are repeated in the border flowers. The flowerpots in the corners are pieced and then appliquéd. Of special interest is the treatment of the edging: a row of red piping on the top and on the back with a row of green piping sandwiched between.

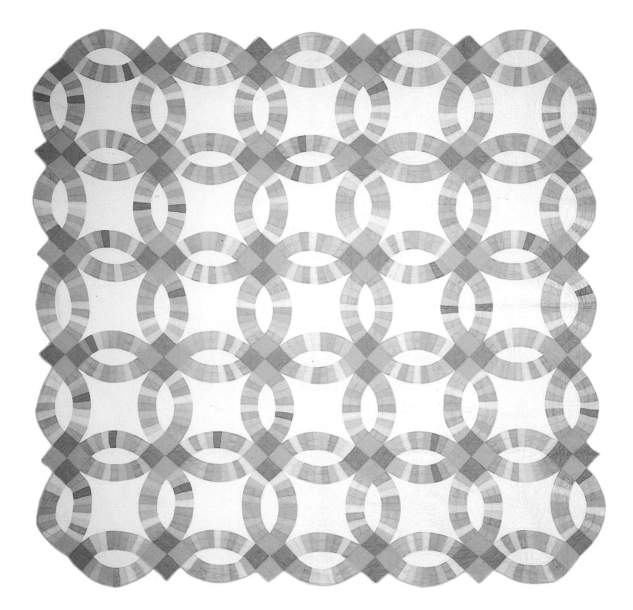

17

Double Wedding Ring Pieced Quilt. c. 1945–55. Indiana. Cotton, 80×83″. Collection Dr. Robert Bishop.

Note the rounded edges on this typically pastel version of a favorite pattern. Also note that all of the background spaces are white; in such quilts a Four-Patch is formed when the rings meet.

18

Pieced and Appliqué Quilt. c. 1910. New Jersey. Cotton, 85×85″. Collection America Hurrah Antiques, New York City. Photograph by Schechter Lee.

This quilt features a concentric kaleidoscope-like design with abstract butterfly arabesques at the corners. The time expended in planning, cutting, and positioning hundreds of pieces in diminishing sizes to create this stunning overall concept staggers the imagination. The effect here is a skillful optical illusion.

✽ 19

Ellen Smith Tooke Vanzant. *Star or Lone Star Variation Pieced Quilt*. 1890–1900. Trigg County, Kentucky. Cotton, 80×76". Collection Sammie K. Morris. Photograph courtesy The Kentucky Quilt Project, Inc.

This no-nonsense utilitarian quilt was made extra thick for warmth. The rather crude quilting in an overall diamond grid may not be as fancy as some, but it is certainly more practical, since the more quilting, the less effective the quilt is as an insulator. The technique used in making this example is known as string quilting in Kentucky and offers a good way to use up all scraps. The dark blue ground was probably intended to represent the heavens.

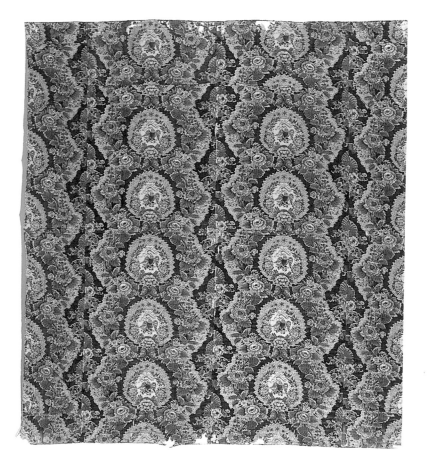

20

Pieced Whole-Cloth Quilt. c. 1862. Origin unknown. Printed cotton, 84×81". The White House Collection, Washington, D.C. Gift of Mrs. Lucy B. Mitchell.

This is considered a whole-cloth quilt because each strip is the width of the fabric and was stitched together. The width of the actual fabric was determined by the width of the loom, and in this instance it was probably 31 or 33 inches wide. The material has a brown background with green and orange floral garlands outlining medallions containing the American eagle, shield, and the ribbon inscribed *E Pluribus Unum.* Such specially printed patriotic fabrics were popular not only for use in quilts but also for such home furnishings as draperies and bed coverings. Fabrics of this type were often purchased specifically for important quilts.

21

Framed Center Design of a "John Hewson" Appliquéd Quilt. c. 1780–1800. Cotton, 106¼×103¼". The Henry Francis du Pont Museum, Winterthur, Delaware.

The fabric here is a block-print by John Hewson, and the graceful urn and flowers (center section) with butterflies and birds exemplifies his typical style. In quilts made from Hewson fabrics, the designs were usually carefully cut out and appliquéd to a plain background. Hewson was English, and he was encouraged to settle here by his friend, Benjamin Franklin. During the Revolutionary War he enlisted in the Philadelphia County militia, was captured by the British, but escaped. A master printer, he worked illegally, with a bounty on his head, because he defied the restrictions that England imposed limiting competitive textile development in the Colonies. It is said that Martha Washington ordered some of his fabrics for her wardrobe and also commissioned him to print commemorative handkerchiefs depicting her husband on horseback. Only a few documented examples of his work are extant and are very prized. The present example is a treasure.

🌀 22

Crystal Palace. c. 1850. Providence, Rhode Island. Whole-cloth pieced cotton, 81×78″.
The Shelburne Museum, Shelburne, Vermont. Gift of Mrs. Erickson, Providence, Rhode Island.
Photograph courtesy The Shelburne Museum.

This example is composed of glazed cotton with cotton ground and raw, combed cotton fill. The quilting outlines
each of the figures and the repeated images of the Crystal Palace, imparting a three-dimensional effect. The
Crystal Palace was the largest glass and cast-iron building in the world. Designed by Joseph Paxton, it housed the
displays of the 1851 Great Exhibition in London, marking the triumph of the Industrial Revolution.

🌀 23

Shoo Fly Pieced Quilt. c. 1890. Maine. Cotton, 83 × 80". Collection Kyoristu Women's College, Japan.
Photograph courtesy Bunka Publishing Bureau, Tokyo.

This represents a wonderful treatment of this pattern, worked entirely in prints, and including many
early brown textiles. It offers a first-rate sampler of the calicos in use at the time, and it also
exemplifies a very sophisticated manipulation of color.

24

Shoo Fly Pieced Quilt (detail of 23).

🎨 25

Commemorative Pieced Quilt. c. 1845. Pennsylvania. Cotton, 96 × 106″. The White House Collection, Washington, D. C. Gift of the Shelburne Museum, Shelburne, Vermont.

This pieced quilt is composed of James Knox Polk's presidential campaign flags and handkerchiefs on a blue cotton background. Polk was elected in 1844, and his likeness at the center is made up of a specially printed fabric, as are the flags surrounding it. The other names are of his vice-presidential running mate, George M. Dallas, and the governor of Pennsylvania at the time, Francis R. Shunk (which would indicate that this fabric was printed in Pennsylvania). There are 26 stars in each flag, which represent the 26 states of the union at the time (by the time of the inauguration there were 27: Florida was admitted). Texas, which was to become the twenty-eighth state, is thought to be symbolized by the Lone Star to the right of Polk's face; Polk was active in support of the annexation of Texas. Note the quilting in the light blue sections and the sawtooth borders.

26

G. Knappenberger. *Pieced and Appliquéd Centennial Quilt.* c. 1876. Pennsylvania. Cotton, 71½ × 83½".
The Museum of American Folk Art, New York. Gift of Rhea Goodman.

This is one of many quilts made to commemorate the U.S. Centennial. It is especially interesting because of the variety of patterns worked into the overall design: hearts, baskets, tulips, lilies, birds on branches and in baskets, stars and feathered stars, and more. All these elements make this quilt exceptionally joyful. The border of stylized leaves and flowers on two sides provides an original touch.

🌀 **27**

Cows: Pieced Pictorial Patchwork. c. 1920. Arkansas.
Cotton appliquéd onto feed sacks, 68 × 63″.
Collection Shelly Zegart's Quilts, Louisville, Kentucky.
Photograph by Steve Mitchell.

This quilt has a very sophisticated design concept, especially when one considers the subject matter and the materials. The viewer has to look twice to see the shapes of the cows; notice the udders delineated within a rectangular strip of blue. Were these motifs intended to be humorous? Was it made for a child? Both ideas are likely, but it is very unlikely that the quilt was made by a child. Although they do not show clearly, brand names printed on some of the feed sacks can be seen upon close examination.

🌀 **28**

Tobacco Sacks Pieced Quilt. c. 1900–20. Kentucky.
Cotton and burlap tobacco sacks, 65 × 83½″.
Collection Shelly Zegart's Quilts, Louisville, Kentucky.
Photograph by Steve Mitchell.

Karey Bresenan, president of the Quilt Market and Festival in Houston, Texas, writes:

> *Most tobacco-sack quilts were made after the turn of the century, between 1910 and 1935. They were all hand-dyed, sometimes in pastels but more commonly in deep reds, blues, and browns. For the lighter colors it was necessary to bleach the bags first. Therefore, steps included ripping out the seams of the sack, washing, bleaching, dying, piecing, and tying or quilting.*
>
> *Most of the quilts were pieced in some variation of the traditional Brickwork pattern to make the most efficient use of the shape of the sacks.*
>
> *Because the fabric is plain, embroidery is often used to decorate it, (there is a quilt from West Texas that is embroidered with the brands of the region's ranches).*

It has been suggested that this particular quilt was used to advertise tobacco sacks for sale—a patchwork billboard, so to speak.

🌀 29

Broderie Perse Pieced and Appliquéd Quilt. c. 1830.
Origin unknown. Cotton and linen, 112 × 112″.
Collection Phyllis Haders.

This embroidered, pieced, and appliquéd quilt is made
from block-printed cotton and Indian chintzes. It has a
somewhat light-hearted air; the bird at the top of the tree
with a butterfly in its beak is oversized. Other appliqué
motifs include single butterflies as well as one little rabbit.

🌀 30

Pieced and Embroidered Crazy Quilt. c. 1880.
Origin unknown. Silk, satin, and velvet, 75 × 76″.
The Museum of American Folk Art, New York.
Gift of Margaret Cavigga.

In this variation of the crazy quilt, the patterns were
worked in individual blocks and then pieced together;
each block is a separate little composition. Included are
some embroidered Kate Greenaway patterns of children,
which were popular designs to work in outline stitching
and which include girls in bonnets or on sleds, children
carrying umbrellas, watering cans, fans, sprays of flowers,
and pet lambs and other animals. Such designs could be
purchased via mail-order and were incorporated in a
number of late nineteenth-century quilts.

🌀 31

Pieced and Trapunto Quilt
(detail of 33).

🌀 32

Pieced and Trapunto Quilt
(detail of 33).

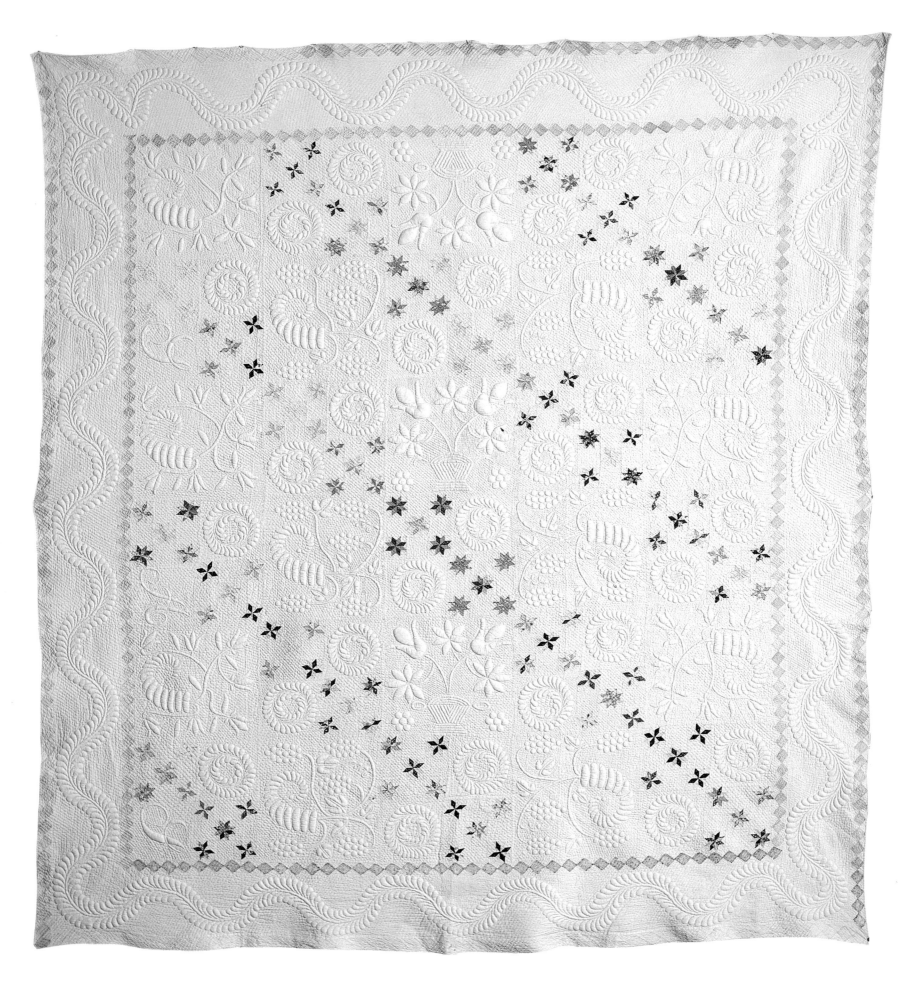

🌀 33

Pieced and Trapunto Quilt. c. 1840. Missouri. Cotton with homespun backing, 96×87".
Collection Phyllis Haders. Photograph by Leonard Nones.

This extraordinarily beautiful quilt combines pieced, eight-pointed Lemon Stars drifting diagonally across the top and two border rows of pink pieced diamonds with very detailed and defined sculptural stuffed work. The whitework includes baskets of tulips and daisies, wreaths, scrolls, cornucopias with either flowers or grapes and tendrils. The border has a running feather vine with the initials "G A" on one side; tiny white quilting stitches on the white background create the stippled effect. This quilt probably required years for an experienced needleworker to complete.

34

Baskets of Flowers Pieced and Appliqué Quilt. c.1900. Maryland. Cotton, 85 × 88″. Private collection.

Sixteen skillfully sewn squares depicting stylized rose trees, wreaths, and baskets of roses in red, yellows, and pinks evidence the special attention paid to the importance of the quilting within the framework of the piece.

35

Pieced and Appliqué Friendship Flag Quilt. 1899. Nebraska. Cotton, 76 × 84″. Collection of Philip Morris Companies, Inc.

This quilt bears the inscription "Beatrice, Nebraska, August 18, 1899," which appears on the beige field above the 45 appliqué stars. Flag quilts were often made by churchwomen as gifts for important people in their community; this piece includes 440 signatures, an unusually large number, which indicates that it probably was signed by all the people in the town. All signatures seem to have been embroidered by one individual.

36

Central Medallion Constitution *Appliqué Quilt.* c. 1860–80. Origin unknown. Cotton, 73 × 66″.
Collection America Hurrah Antiques, New York City. Photograph by Schecter Lee.

There are exceptional pictorial blocks in this quilt; many are religious and political subjects, but some are more familiar: a flower, a butterfly, a basket, and heart-in-hand motifs. It is worth taking some time to study the individual blocks, since no two are alike. The ship depicted here is the *Constitution*; the man seated at a desk to the right of the center (the seventh block from the top) has a pompadour hairdo and resembles pictures of the *Constitution's* captain. The bearded man in the oval above the center is thought to be President Garfield, and the one in the military uniform at the bottom, Ulysses S. Grant. There are a bride and groom in another block, and the man standing next to the groom is thought to be Abraham Lincoln at his son's wedding. To the left of that block is the sacrifice of Isaac. There is also Noah's Ark in the bottom row, David with his harp in the first row on the left center, Adam and Eve above Garfield, and to the right of them, Cain and Abel. Notice, too, the unusual border designed with bird motifs. This is an extremely important historical quilt.

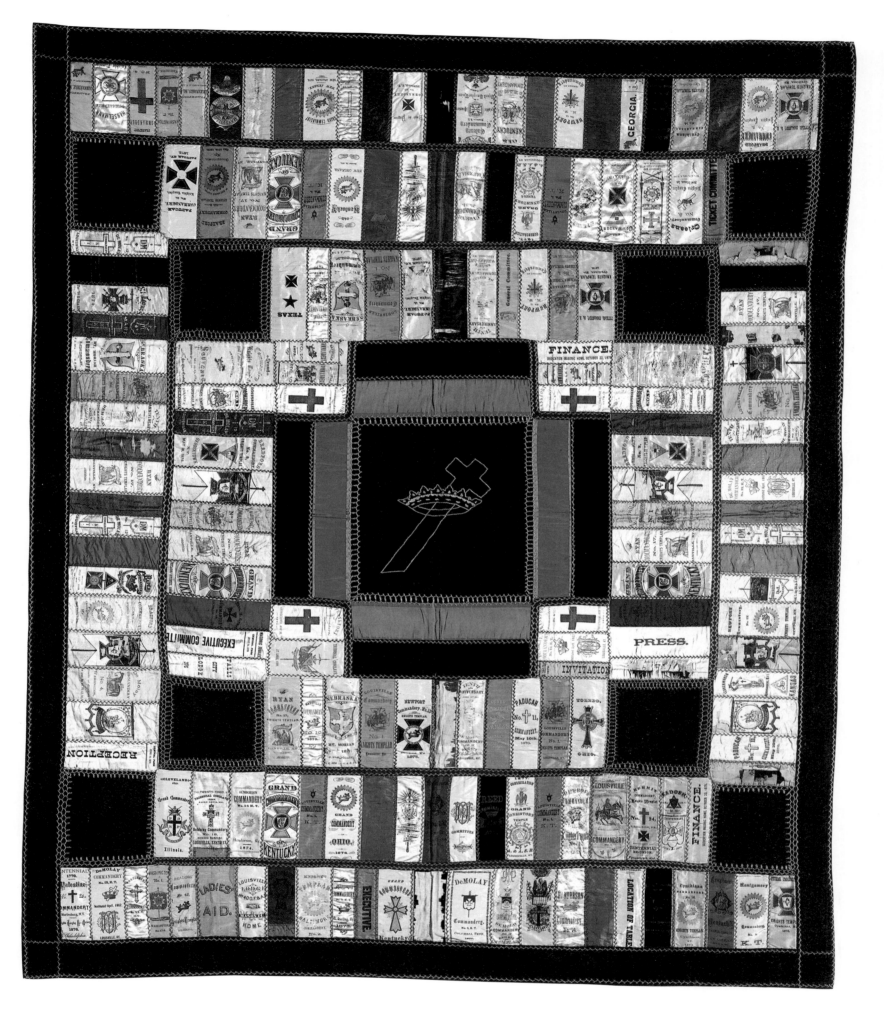

🌀 37

Masonic Ribbon Pieced and Embroidered Quilt. c. 1890. Kentucky. Silk and velvet, 66½ × 56½".
Collection The Kentucky Historical Society, Frankfort, Kentucky. Photograph by Nathan Prichard.

This quilt is typical of those made from souvenir, political, or prize ribbons. It is an especially fine
example, since it incorporates so many different ribbons that are placed around a center cross
and crown and bordered with skillful embroidery.

🌀 38

Masonic Ribbon Pieced and Embroidered Quilt (detail of 37).

39

Baltimore Album Appliqué Quilt. 1850. Baltimore, Maryland. Cotton, 107 × 104" Private collection.
Courtesy Thos. K. Woodard American Antiques & Quilts, New York. Photograph by Schecter Lee.

Bearing such insciptions as "Baltimore, The Album, E Pluribus Unum," this quilt was given to Mary E.
Updegraph of Hagerstown, Maryland, and it is signed by her family and friends. This is a rarity among Baltimore
Album quilts, because of the style of the central medallion and the inner and outer feather borders in reverse
appliqué. The layers of appliqué and the abundance of brilliant color combine to create a textile masterpiece.

🌀 40

Hannah Foote. *Baltimore Album Appliqué Quilt*. 1850. Baltimore. Cotton, 104 × 104".
Collection America Hurrah Antiques, New York City. Photograph by Schecter Lee.

This rare album quilt is signed "Hannah Foote Baltimore 1850." The pictorial blocks include such motifs as houses, people, and animals. The scenes depict various subjects, including a cow and a milkmaid and a girl feeding ducks in front of a house.

41

Ida W. Beck. *Rainbow Monogram and Initial Appliquéd and Embroidered Quilt.* 1952–54. New England.
Cotton, 94 × 90". The Shelburne Museum, Shelburne, Vermont. Gift of Ida W. Beck.

The maker remarked: "It is quite original and I was several years in planning and making it. I am over 70 years
old, a shut-in since childhood, so have always done needlework, and monogramming was my specialty for
many years." The quilt represents a true labor of love and was executed with special attention to detail.

42

Michael James. *Rhythm/Color: Spanish Dance*. 1985. Somerset Village, Massachusetts.
Pieced cotton and silk, 100×100″. The Newark Museum, Newark, New Jersey. Photograph by David Caras.

Perhaps one can see in this quilt the excitement of a folk dance; however, the artist intended it to represent a *Carmen*-like atmosphere.

QUILTS:
AMERICA'S
FOLKLORE

QUILTS: AMERICA'S FOLKLORE

Deborah Harding

Patchwork quilts have been a part of everyday life in many part of this country until well into this century. Most families owned at least one that was passed from generation to generation. Bedrooms were furnished with summer and winter quilts as well as "best quilts"—usually appliqué —which were brought out only for company. (For that reason "best quilts" have survived in good condition and make up the majority of antique quilts in many collections.) Quilts were commonplace at church bazaars, state and county fairs, and special fundraising events, or they were merely draped over the porch railing at the house next door. Only during the last twenty-five years have quilts been valued by museums as works of art and by collectors as major investments.

As Mary Washington Clarke says in *Kentucky Quilts and Their Makers*:

To a tradition-oriented person, as so many native Kentuckians are, sleeping under a "right pretty quilt" made by a member of his family or a neighbor, especially if it is in one of the old familiar patterns, conveys a subtle warmth involved with appreciation of continuity of his cultural heritage.

Quilts, their traditions and transitions, reflect the history of the country; they are the windows through which we see our ancestors. Quiltmaking is a living tradition that has flourished for centuries and grows in popularity every year. Most of this needlework is unsigned, the anonymous women who created quilts have left an indelible imprint on our society.

States such as Kentucky are fortunate in having a wide range of quilts and quilt makers. There are extraordinary examples of antique quilts, museum-quality masterpieces—such as the famous

---

PRECEDING PAGE: *Willow Oak Appliqué Quilt* (detail). c. 1840s. Boston, Massachusetts. Cotton. The Shelburne Museum, Shelburne, Vermont. Gift of Electra Havemeyer Webb. Photograph courtesy The Shelburne Museum.

Virginia Ivey quilts and the unique Graveyard quilt—and quilts produced by contemporary artists and cottage industries.

Quiltmaking has always thrived in the central states. Even when many Americans had begun ordering their bedcovers from the Sears, Roebuck catalog, people in Appalachia still took pride in making their own quilts. It is likely that, rather than snuggling under four or five quilts on a blustery winter night, many people used one or two quilts spread on top of a store-bought blanket; nevertheless, loyalty to the use of quilts never diminished.

Ruth Finley, in *Old Patchwork Quilts and the Women Who Made Them*, states that in the eighteenth century quilts were one of the few household items over which women had full control and which they actually owned. Everything else in the home, from the candlesticks, glassware, and rugs to the furniture and even the yardage for clothing, was made or purchased by men. However, women with little or no knowledge of mathematics were capable of planning and piecing the most intricate geometric designs, transforming scraps of fabric into breathtaking harmonies of color and design to add beauty to their surroundings.

Children were taught to sew when very young. Little girls made doll quilts as their first needlework projects, and this explains why one often finds large, irregular stitches on small quilts. In the cities, young girls from prosperous families were sent to school to learn needlework or were taught at home by private tutors; the basics included cross-stitch samplers and pieced quilts. In rural areas, women taught their daughters and granddaughters how to stitch, and patterns were exchanged with neighbors rather than purchased from mail-order publications such as *Godey's Lady's Book*.

Traditionally, girls had to complete twelve quilt tops by the time they became engaged. A grand party was held to announce a girl's wedding, and the tops would be quilted by friends and family. There are several superstitions relating to the thirteenth, or Bridal, quilt. One is that if a girl began working on it before she became officially engaged, she would never marry. Some sources state that the Bridal quilt had to be made only by family members and friends and that the bride to be was not allowed to put a stitch on it herself. Many agree that it was certainly bad luck for her to stitch, draw, or even accidentally touch the heart motifs included in a Bridal quilt. In fact, hearts incorporated in the quilting or in the patterns of any other quilt were often considered to bring bad luck. Other such superstitions include the following:

- *If a girl shakes a new quilt out the front door, the first man who enters will be her husband.*
- *If an unmarried girl puts in the last stitch of the quilting, she will be an old maid.*
- *If the thread breaks, it will bring bad fortune.*
- *Lone Star quilts can be bad luck in certain circumstances (although so many are extant that it is hard to believe that many people took these precautions seriously). A person who starts a Lone Star quilt will never live to finish it; if a single girl makes one, she will never marry.*
- *"Shaking the Cat" meant that a cat would be placed on a finished quilt and several girls (usually four) would grasp the edges and shake it; when the cat jumped out, the girl closest to it would be the next to marry.*
- *Never begin a quilt on a Friday.*
- *Never quilt at all on Sundays.*

- *Tulips in patterns symbolize love; pineapples indicate hospitality; a pomegranate symbolizes abundance; and rings and hearts also indicate love.*
- *Quilts should incorporate a deliberate flaw, such as mismatched colors or a pattern that is askew, as a reminder that only God can make a perfect object.*
- *If a child, especially a boy, sleeps beneath a quilt displaying a pattern called Wandering Foot, he will leave home never to return. (Later the name of the pattern was changed to Turkey Tracks.)*
- *Sleep under a new quilt and your dreams will come true!*

There were (and still are) quilters who preferred to complete quilts by themselves from start to finish. Most frequently, however, the highlight of quiltmaking was the quilting bee.

Quilting bees were social events that were anticipated with pleasure. Friends and family would be invited to assemble early in the day. Each would bring a special dish: casseroles, baked hams and turkeys, homegrown vegetables, and homemade pickles, preserves, cakes, and pies (there was an entire table of desserts alone). The women would work on the quilting in shifts while others helped in the kitchen. There would be a break for lunch in the middle of the day, but the real feast took place in the evening, when the men would return and join the festivities. Frequently, the party would culminate in a square dance. These get-togethers provided time away from life's responsibilities and offered an opportunity to relax with friends. Though quilting bees were usually held in private homes, quilters also worked at churches and in schools and libraries. Sometimes quilts from the same region and date will contain patches of matching fabric even though they were made by different people; this is because friends collected scrap bags of materials that they traded with one another, or because they all apparently shopped at the same general store.

Early quilting bees often were held to celebrate important stages of life. An engagement or wedding always called for at least one quilting bee. The coming of spring encouraged quilting the tops that had been pieced during the confinement of cold winter months. A freedom quilt was made for a young man when he turned twenty-one. (One story relates that all eligible young women in his circle each contributed a scrap of her dress fabric to the quilt.) Subjects for the design might include military or patriotic themes, which were deemed suitable for a man. Other quilts with patriotic themes were made to commemorate significant political or national events. Such quilts incorporated patriotic or political symbols: flags, eagles, specific dates, names of candidates, and specially printed commemorative handkerchiefs, campaign ribbons, and similar fabrics. (Although not quilted, flags were one of the earliest forms of patchwork.)

A number of quilts were made by groups or at least received contributions from a number of individuals. For example, there were Hand quilts, on which rows of hands were outlined and embroidered, representing family members, an organization, community leaders, or an engaged couple. (Sometimes names were embroidered on each hand.)

Other group-made examples include presentation, friendship, and album quilts, which can sometimes overlap in terms of definition. A presentation or album quilt was often presented to a minister moving to a parish in another community; members of his congregation would each contribute a block that was signed and dated. A bee would convene at the minister's home or church. The conversation at such gatherings probably took on a more serious tone than the usual gossip at other bees, and Bible verses might be embroidered on the blocks.

Friendship quilts also bore autographs or signatures that were composed into designs. Such quilts were made to raise money for a church or hospital in two ways. Individuals might pay to have their names included; thus, the more the names, the more successful the project, and the completed quilt might be auctioned or raffled.

Another type of signature quilt was the Red Cross quilt made during World War I by women raising money for the American Red Cross. Magazines published fundraising ideas, the image of the Red Cross nurse was seen everywhere, and the nation sang George M. Cohan's patriotic songs. One slogan of the time was "Make Quilts—Save the Blankets for Our Boys Over There." Red Cross quilts were made by groups to be auctioned, and the monies were then sent to the Red Cross. Nancy J. Rowley writes of a school class that raised enough money from auctioning a quilt to "adopt" three war orphans, which meant sending the sum of $36 for each child thus sponsored. In another instance, a quilt brought only $32, which was $4 short, so the money went for rehabilitation work.

There were also Friendship Medley quilts made at parties. Friends gathered to make a quilt for someone who was recently engaged or was moving away. Actually, such an event justified two parties. At the first, each individual would supply the fabric for one block from his or her own wardrobe and stitch it into a block. The recipient of the finished quilt hosted the second party, during which the blocks were joined together and quilted.

Keepsake quilts were made to memorialize significant events in an individual's life. On somber occasions, memory-keepsake quilts were made by relatives of a deceased family member, and such examples were made of her or his clothing. A happy occasion was celebrated by making a child a keepsake quilt composed of remnants of his or her baby garments. A keepsake quilt could also be made for a bride; this would include remnants of her wedding dress and veil and the dresses of her attendants and the cravat or vest of the bridegroom, as well as the mementoes from the parents, such as the mother's handkerchief and the father's necktie or his silk scarf.

Sampler, or legacy, quilts contain as many patterns as possible and provide an excellent record of the popularity of designs during a specific era. They might be a type of presentation quilt, where many people participated in the making, or they might be made by a single quilter to display her expertise. A sampler quilt and a presentation quilt might appear to be similar, but presentation quilts and other varieties of friendship quilts usually have names incorporated into the design.

The social significance of quilting bees has been recorded in various ways. Harriet Beecher Stowe wrote of a quilting bee in *The Minister's Wooing*, which first appeared in 1859 as a series in the *Atlantic Monthly*. Susan B. Anthony made her first speech for women's suffrage at a church quilting in Cleveland, and Stephen Foster's "The Quilting Party" is a perennial favorite:

> *In the sky the bright stars glittered.*
> *On the banks the pale moon shone,*
> *And 'twas from Aunt Dinah's quilting party*
> *I was seeing Nellie home.*

Quilters getting together is not a thing of the past. Women meet today all over America to work on their quilts, encouraging one another in their projects and usually planning fundraising events. This is not limited to rural areas; for example, in New York the Manhattan Quilters' Guild meets every other week. The dozen members range in age from twenty-five to fifty-five and include professional quilters who display and sell their work, a college professor, a day care worker, a teacher, a school librarian, and a corporate executive. The members work on individual quilts and at times accept group commissions, such as a quilt for the hundredth anniversary of the New York Library Club.

Conversation at these contemporary gatherings includes topics ranging from quilt patterns to current events as well as an exchange of information on antique quilt preservation and collecting, new quilt books, products, quilt shows, and quilt competitions.

Some of the earliest quilt competitions were held at county fairs. The first such fair in the United States (no quilts, however, were exhibited) was in Pittsfield, Massachusetts, in 1807, sponsored by the Berkshire Agricultural Society. One of its major purposes was to introduce the new merino breed of sheep. Some women accompanied their husbands to this fair. Concerned that there wouldn't be anything to occupy their wives, the farmers formed a committee to plan areas of competition and display that would interest women. In 1809, the fair opened with a parade led by sixty-nine yoke of cattle drawing a plow on which rode the two oldest people in the county. This was followed by a marching band and a large ox-drawn platform car holding a spinning jenny and a broadcloth loom in full operation.

The clergy were reluctant to participate in so novel an event, and some women were too shy to attend. To arouse the interest of the ladies, the society offered prizes for the best entries in categories such as cooking and needlework. These exhibits were shown in a tavern, and the winning prizes were awarded at church services. Nonetheless, many women were reluctant to claim their premiums in a church because they feared the censure of the clergy. Elkaneh Watson, the founder of the society, appealed to his wife to write to the women of the community, stating that she would personally receive them at the next fair; after that, the women flocked in. By 1811, the clergy were convinced of the innocence of the festivities, and they too began to patronize the fair.

In 1818, an expert weaver named Mrs. Perkins required a sworn affidavit signed by her husband to certify that in one year she had woven 438 yards of full-cloth wool, 171¼ yards of flannel, 53 yards of carpeting from rags, and 142¾ yards of linen tabling in her own house with only the help of her four daughters.

In Kentucky, the earliest statewide fairs were organized by private individuals; the first one was held in 1816 at Sandersville, north of Lexington. Like the Pittsfield fair, it was organized to introduce the merino sheep. Sally Turnham was the only woman to exhibit at this fair, and she entered not a quilt but a prize sow. By 1817 records show interest in entries other than livestock, including cheese, whiskey, and homemade linens (a category including quilts).

In 1902, the state legislature passed a bill to provide funds for an annual Kentucky state fair. The first was held at Churchill Downs, and attendance for five days was 75,000. There were three thousand entries in the domestic and fine-arts categories alone. "All forms of housewifery" were represented, "from cakes to counterpanes, pickles to patchwork, daintiest embroidery to rag rugs."

Surprisingly, although prices for quilts have escalated considerably, the prize money for individual categories has not. In 1934 the first place award for a cotton quilt was $6, second place was $4, and third place was $2. Silk quilts won $4 prizes for first place, and children's quilts $3. By 1970 the first place award had risen to $20. By 1986, 193 quilts were entered at the fair and a number of new categories were added: Traditional Designs, broken down into pieced, appliqué, mixed, and kit; Original Designs, which encompassed pieced, appliqué, traditional variation, and quilted article of clothing; quilted wall hangings; and Novelty Quilts, which included yo-yos, tied or puffed, Cathedral Window, embroidery, cross-stitch, candlewick, painted, machine appliqué, and machine-quilted. First prize awards, however, are only $25.

A primitive device called the "iron seamstress" was first shown at fairs in the 1800s. By midcentury it had evolved into the sewing machine as we know it. This revolutionary product quickly filtered into all levels of society. Housewives, eager to look fashionable, urged their husbands to buy "the machine that sews so fast." Edward B. Clark of the Singer firm introduced the first installment plan in 1846. His hire-purchase plan consisted of a $5 down payment, with subsequent payments of $3 a month. Over 250,000 machines were sold in 1876 alone.

Families gratefully put this time-saving device to work, turning out clothing, draperies, bedding, and other household furnishings. For the most part, however, purists preferred to stitch quilts by hand. Machine stitching was good for pieced tops and possibly for sashing and binding, but the straight rows of quilting could not compare to the artistry of handwork. Perhaps the whir of a sewing machine could not equal the soothing effect of sitting in a comfortable chair and watching a sunset while plying a needle into soft pieces of cloth.

There are almost as many quilt patterns and pattern names as there are quilts. They are passed down in families like recipes. In the hands of a dozen women the same pattern can produce a dozen different results. A change in the number of patches, the angle at which they are placed, the combination of elements, or even the arc of a curve creates a new design. Every experienced quilter delights in changing and improving traditional designs, personalizing them to suit her own idiosyncrasies. A single design may also have many different names, depending on the year or the region in which it was made. The only person who really knows the proper and indisputable name for a quilt is the one who makes it. Like snowflakes, no two quilts are ever exactly alike, even if they are made by the same quilter. It is impossible to list the thousands of recorded names of quilt patterns, but we can explore some of the chief categories and consider the definition of some of the frequently used names.

Pioneer Americans in Colonial times depended, often, for their physical and moral survival on religion, work, nature, literature, household utensils, and political and patriotic institutions that are recalled in literal, lyrical, and sometimes whimsical quilt patterns.

Every home had a Bible, and for most people religion was all-important. The Sabbath not only offered an opportunity to nourish the soul; it also provided essential social interaction. The church was usually the first building erected in a community, and it was a center of activity. Thus it is not surprising that a number of quilt patterns were inspired by the Bible, including Jacob's Ladder, Joseph's Coat, Star of Bethlehem, Crown of Thorns, Cross and Crown, Star and Cross, Crowned Cross, Cross upon Cross, King David's Crown, Job's Tears, World without End, Wonder of the World, Ecclesiastes, David and Goliath, Coronation and Hosanna, and the Rose of Sharon. (Scripture quilts were block quilts with white backgrounds and Bible verses embroidered in red.)

Quilt names relating to trades include the Ship's Wheel, Saw Tooth, Barrister's Block, Carpenter's Wheel, Carpenter's Square, Double Monkey Wrench, Churn Dash, Mariner's Compass, Water Mill, Chimney Sweep, Chips and Whetstones, Dusty Miller, the Anvil, the Reel, and the Spinner.

Patterns derived from nature include flowers, birds, and elements found in the garden. Some of these are Spider Web, Snake's Trail, Flying Geese, Goose Tracks, Brown Goose, Gray Goose, Swallows' Flight, Autumn Leaf, Flower Garden, Sun Dial, Weathervane, Rolling Stone,

Flying Bats, Dove in the Window, Turkey Tracks, Hen and Chicks, Puss in the Corner, Hovering Hawks, Birds in the Air, Rising Sun, Setting Sun, and Indian Summer. There are hundreds of flower patterns alone, featuring roses, peonies, lilies, and tulips, as well as many leaf and tree designs.

The pattern called Duck's Foot in the Mud in Long Island may be called Bear's Paw in Ohio or Kentucky and Hand of Friendship in Philadelphia. The pattern called the Ship's Wheel in localities near the ocean may be known as Harvest Sun inland, and a patch called Rock Glen in the mountains of Kentucky and Tennessee is known as Lost Ship on the coast.

Building-related names include Doors and Windows, Log Cabin, Barn Raising, Courthouse Steps, Church Steps, White House Steps, Country Farm, Schoolhouse, Cathedral Window, and Windmill.

Love and courtship are memorialized in Steps to the Altar, Young Man's Fancy, Single and Double Wedding Ring, Friendship Knot, Lovers' Knot, Bridal Stairway, Old Maid's Ramble, Widow's Troubles, and Cupid's Arrowpoint.

From square dance calls came Virginia Reel, Swing in the Corner, and Hands All Around, while games and puzzles inspired Leapfrog, Follow the Leader, Merry-Go-Round, Yankee Puzzle, Tic-Tac-Toe, Domino, and Hopscotch.

Household utensils are represented by Cakestand, Broken Dishes, Dresden Plate, Flat Iron, and Flower Pot.

The Lady of the Lake pattern was named after Sir Walter Scott's poem, while Delectable Mountains derives from an episode in Bunyan's *Pilgrim's Progress*.

Politics and politicians contributed names as well, including Whig Rose or Democrat Rose (depending on the political point of view), Whig's Defeat, Harrison Rose, the Little Giant (named after Stephen A. Douglas), Clay's Choice, Union Quilt, President's Wreath, Garfield's Monument, Free Trade Patch, Tippecanoe and Tyler Too, and Fifty-Four Forty or Fight. After the symbolic eagle was incorporated into the Great Seal of the United States in 1782, eagle motifs remained in fashion until the 1840s. A few quilt patterns were named after women of political importance, such as Martha Washington's Wreath, Mrs. Cleveland's Choice, and the Dolley Madison Star.

The pioneer ethic stressed the use of every scrap of fabric, no matter how small. Purchasing new yardage for a quilt top was a last resort; true ingenuity was a matter of recycling fabrics. In addition to cast-off clothing received from family members or garnered from thrift shops, feed sacks, sugar sacks, and tobacco and flour sacks were all saved, cut, bleached, and dyed for use in quilts. Sometimes the quilter deliberately planned a design so that the printing on the fabric would show on the top; in other instances labels were turned over or were used on the backing. For quilters lucky enough to live near factories, salvage was a wonderful source of supply. In Kentucky, for instance, there was a drapery factory near Louisville, a clothing factory in Morgantown, upholstery manufacturers, and the Union Underwear Company, Inc. (known locally as the Derby Underwear and Sleepwear) factory at Bowling Green. Salvage scraps would be collected in bundles and given to employees, sold by the pound, or taken to (and subsequently retrieved from) the city dump. Savvy quilters could recognize and identify—and even date—print fabrics from the various sources. The Derby factory remains a favorite supplier, and in 1986 the Kentucky Museum featured an exhibition of quilts made from Derby fabrics from the 1940s to the 1980s.

Another example of this waste-not–want-not philosophy is evidenced by a crazy quilt at the Kentucky Museum. It seems that members of a family in Muhlenberg County gathered in 1886 to celebrate Christmas. During the holiday there was a heavy blizzard, and they were snowed in for several days. Not wanting to sit idle, four ladies in the family decided to whip up a crazy quilt. It contains wonderfully unusual design elements including reindeers and snowflakes. "Christmas 1886" and the initials of the four quilters are embroidered on it. Perhaps running short of available fabric, they cut the linings out of men's hats and incorporated them in the quilt; some of these linings display the trademarks of the hat companies.

As recently as 1974, in interviews conducted for the Western Kentucky University Folklore and Folklife Archives, some quilters said that they still planted, ginned, and carded cotton for quilts. Such cases represent an exception, but they are not merely isolated incidents.

One method employed for making everyday quilts in and around Kentucky is string quilting. The name is derived from the use of "strings" of leftover fabric that are too narrow or small to be useful individually. The technique involves cutting a paper template and sewing the small sections of fabric onto it one piece at a time. (This is somewhat similar to log cabin construction, except that the backing is paper and the pieces are random irregular shapes rather than precise logstrips.) Any leftover piece will do, and a contrast of alternating light and dark colors is considered desirable. The paper simply serves as a temporary foundation on which to hold these small remnants together. After the sewing is completed, the paper is torn out and the edges trimmed. Occasionally a large section of string quilting will be assembled and then cut into smaller pattern pieces to fit a specific design.

The use of many tiny pieces in a quilt top is a sign not only of frugality but also of patience and pride; the maker usually remembered the number of pieces employed and told friends about it as evidence of her accomplishment. Postage Stamp quilts belong to this category since the patches are sometimes as small as actual postage stamps. Quilts composed of slightly larger pieces still bear the name. Other names for this type of quilt are Chipyard, Around the World, and Trip Around the World. The patches may be squares or rectangles or may be angled to form diamonds. The method entails beginning with a small square at the center (or several squares arranged to form a rectangle) and then adding rows of patches radiating from the center to the edge of the quilt. This design is sometimes seen in blocks of postage-stamp-size patches.

There are other one-patch patterns (made from patches all the same size), which include Hit and Miss; though the pieces were all the same size, no attempt was made to arrange colors or form a pattern. Roman Stripe, as the name suggests, employed strips separating light and dark colors. Brick Wall or Brickyard alternated rectangles by shading and arranging the patches in the same manner as brick on a wall. This pattern is found in many feed-sack quilts.

Hexagons in one-patch quilts formed Grandmother's Flower Garden or Mosaic; triangles were used for Thousand Pyramids and Birds in The Air; and diamonds were employed for Star of Bethlehem, Lone Star, Tumbling Blocks, and Baby Blocks.

Four-Patch and Nine-Patch are two fundamental block constructions; the terms refer to the division of a block into sections. The block consists of one basic shape (a square) in multiples. In the Four-Patch the block is divided into four squares, and in the Nine-Patch it is divided into nine. The patterns are developed by placing the patches to create a design; for example, alternating light and dark colors or solids and prints.

The method for making the patches for a Four-Patch is to fold a square of fabric in half and then in half again, crease, and cut into four equal squares. Repeat this procedure quite a few times with an assortment of at least two different fabrics and then reassemble the smaller squares into larger ones, mixing colors and prints. For the Nine-Patch, fold the square of fabric into thirds and then into thirds again, resulting in nine smaller squares.

Variations occur when the patches are cut again: in half-squares or in thirds to make rectangles, or on the diagonal to form triangles. Diamonds can be cut out as complete shapes or can be formed of two joined triangles. Frequently, Four-Patch or Nine-Patch blocks in a quilt top alternate with solid blocks.

All pieced straight-edge quilt patterns are made from combinations of these elements changed only in regard to the dimensions, proportion, and placement. For example, a Windmill pattern is a Four-Patch subdivided into triangles, as is a Yankee Puzzle; Shoo Fly is a Nine-Patch with the corner squares cut into triangles.

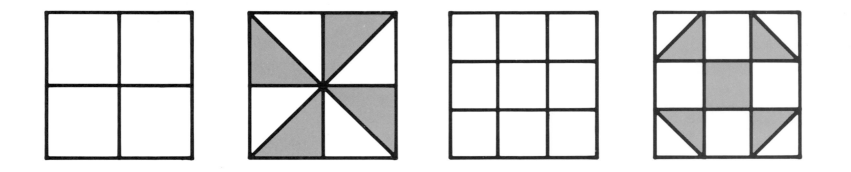

Triangles appear in Baskets, Pine Trees, and Ocean Waves as well as in Flying Geese, in which the rows of triangles are thought to represent the feet of birds flying overhead.

Many women kept and traded templates for each of their favorite designs. This meant a template for each size of each shape. These patterns for each component were traced. Some were metal, but most were made of cardboard. The template was laid on the back of the fabric and outlined, and then seam allowance was added before the material was cut, usually a quarter-inch on all sides. The Kentucky Museum has a file of templates with the pieces needed for each quilt pattern kept and labeled in separate envelopes. Some women believed that they could remember the patterns and the relation of the pieces, but more practical souls made sampler blocks whenever a new pattern caught their fancy. Unquilted blocks that turn up from time to time probably were made as samplers and were never intended to be used in a finished quilt top.

Of all the geometric patterns, stars and their variations remain the most abundant and most admired. The LeMoyne (or Lemon) Star, which is composed of diamonds, is the foundation for many of these designs. The pattern is named after the LeMoyne brothers, who settled in Louisiana in 1699 and founded New Orleans in 1718.

There are five-, six-, and eight-pointed stars. Central-star patterns such as the Lone Star and the Star of Bethlehem fill an entire quilt top, while combinations and multiples of other star designs may be sprinkled all over a quilt. A few names include Star, Ohio Star, Broken Star, Texas Star, Feathered Star (outlined with small triangles), Eastern Star, Christmas Star, Morning Star, Evening Star, Radiant Star, Blazing Star, Friendship Star, and Star of the Bluegrass. Names of similar patterns often vary from region to region or state to state. For instance, the Texas Star is a Star of Bethlehem in Pennsylvania and a Star of the East in Missouri.

Log Cabin pieced quilts are as popular in the Kentucky area as they are in other parts of the country, but some of the names vary. Sunshine and Shadow and Barn Raising are known in Kentucky as Sunshine and Shade, and Light and Dark Paths.

Pieced patterns with curved shapes are also fascinating. Rounded edges are trickier to sew but result in patterns everyone can recognize. Some of the most familiar are Double Wedding Ring (in Kentucky it is called Wedding Rings), Snake's Trail, Dresden Plate (Friendship Ring), and Fans. All of these patterns are also practical for using up small scraps of fabric. Curiously, they are stitched mainly in pastel colors, although there is no particular reason for this.

Drunkard's Path (also known as Rocky Road to Dublin and Solomon's Puzzle), Orange Peel, Millwheel, Snowball, Steeplechase, Melon Patch, and Robbing Peter to Pay Paul are all constructed of positive-negative cutouts requiring only two fabric colors. The quilter cuts an arc from the corner of a light-colored square and another from a dark-colored square and then exchanges the cut pieces. Drunkard's Path is one of the dozens of optical-illusion patterns achieved by arranging the resulting sections. The name Robbing Peter to Pay Paul derives from the practice of borrowing from one color to lend to another in alternating and overlapping designs.

Traditional appliqué lends itself to pictorial subjects. Because these designs are representational, they are easier to identify and do not require much explanation. Flowers, particularly those of the Rose of Sharon family, lead the list, but almost any flower, leaf, or figural design can be interpreted in fabric. Such types include Whig Rose, North Carolina Lily, Kentucky Flower Pot, Rose and Coxcomb, Rose Wreath, and Princess Feather.

Baltimore Album quilts are the epitome of appliqué. Made in or near Baltimore in the mid-nineteenth century, they contain incredibly complex and distinctive motifs. Elaborate floral sprays, baskets of flowers, Baltimore monuments, sailing ships, trains, and hunting and harbor scenes are characteristic subjects for these block quilts. The colors include reds, blues, greens, and other bright primary hues on white backgrounds. So intricate and similar are the designs that some believe that the blocks were designed by only a few women and sold to others to be stitched.

Every pattern mentioned here has the potential for developing into a splendid quilt, but a particular example must be cited: a spectacular Kentucky quilt, reproduced in this book for the first time, called the Virginia Ivey quilt. Virginia Mason Ivey lived in Logan County, Kentucky, in the 1800s. Her father was Captain David Ivey, who fought with Andrew Jackson at the Battle of New Orleans in 1812. He was attached to the Tennessee regiment but moved to Logan County after the war. Virginia was the family's second daughter and, as was traditional at the time, was named after her father's home state. There were also two brothers. One became a minister in New Orleans, and the other moved to Illinois. Virginia never married and spent most of her life with her father or visiting relatives. Although not formally trained, she was skilled at all forms of needlework, and her quilts always won silver cups and blue ribbons at county and state fairs. Her most famous quilt was an all-white stuffed-work quilt in the collection of the Smithsonian Institution entitled "A Representation of the Fairground Near Russellville, Kentucky, 1856," words which are stitched in quilting. Its center depicts a judging ring and an exhibition tent. Surrounding this is a parade of fairgoers including horseback riders, horses pulling carriages, people on foot, and all varieties of livestock, such as cows, sheep, and pigs, in relief, all bordered by graceful trees. The detailing is so fine that one can see the spokes in the wheels and the harnesses and saddles on the horses. It has been estimated to contain over 1,200,000 stitches.

Family correspondence indicates that two other quilts were made by this talented woman. In

1985 one of them surfaced and was identified in New York by the quilt expert and dealer Joel Kopp. Purchased by private donations, it was returned to Kentucky, where it may be seen at the J. B. Speed Museum in Louisville. The quilt includes a rendering of a statue of Henry Clay, Andrew Jackson on horseback, and a wide variety of superbly executed animals. It has the same type of whitework background as the Smithsonian example, some appliqué, and even two embroidered cardinals.

For the most part, however, quilts represent the everyday craft of everyday people. The evocative power of these quilts is aptly described in Eliza Calvert Hall's classic novel *Aunt Jane of Kentucky*:

> *You see, some folk has albums to put folks' pictures in to remember them by, and some folks has a book and writes down the things that happen every day so they won't forget but, honey, these quilts is my albums and diaries, and whenever the weather's bad and I can't get out to see folks, I just spread out my quilts and look at them and study over them, and it's like going back fifty or sixty years and living my life over again . . . there ain't nothing like a piece of calico for bringing back old times.*

The Kentucky Quilt Project was the first systematically organized group in this country to institute a method of preserving this unique American heritage for posterity. The project was the legacy of the late Louisville quilt dealer Bruce Mann, who stated, "As time passes, quilts deteriorate, are lost through negligence or catastrophe, or merely leave the state, depriving us of the privilege of their company."

Mann proposed a three-part project: Important early Kentucky quilts would be located and documented; the best of these would be collected for a major museum exhibition; and a book would be written about the quilts. Unfortunately, Mann died before the project could be launched. Two of his friends, the philanthropist and media expert Eleanor Bingham Miller and the dealer Shelly Zegart, decided to carry out his plans. They were joined by Eunice Sears, a specialist in public relations; Dorothy West, whose business background prepared her to act as coordinator; and Katy Christopherson, a quilter and a consultant representing the Kentucky Heritage Quilt Society.

They began by planning and announcing a series of Quilt Days throughout the state, and they would visit various areas and ask people to bring their quilts to this event. People came with family quilts and family histories, and at each event a $100 prize was awarded for the best nineteenth-century quilt. The quilts were identified, photographed, and recorded. There were various programs that included talks on the history and care of quilts and a film about quilting.

Even though Mrs. Zegart is a dealer, the participants were urged to keep their quilts in the family or donate them to an appropriate museum where they would be cared for properly. The slogan was clearly "Preserve Kentucky's Heritage." Over a thousand quilts were seen, and this resulted in the publication of *Kentucky Quilts 1800–1900*, and in an exhibition at Louisville's Museum of History and Science that subsequently traveled throughout the country and abroad for two years.

The success of the program inspired other states to follow suit. In Tennessee, Merikay Walkvogel of Knoxville and Bets Ramsey of Chattanooga turned up 1,400 quilts in a two-year search of twenty-five cities. These have been reproduced in *The Quilts of Tennessee*, and an exhibition including many of them will begin touring soon and will continue through 1988. Merikay Walkvogel related an interesting anecdote about one example they found:

One Quilt Day we saw a quilt which had been cut in the center and used as a poncho by a Confederate soldier. After the war, the quilt was repaired and the hole was closed up with cloth that is less faded than the original, but you can see where the seamstress matched the other flowers.

In Ohio a similar project is still under way, and Ricky Clark of Oberlin reports:

We have seen enough to know that various religious groups in Ohio have been making quilts since the mid-nineteenth century, and that those quilts are very different from each other. Amish quilts, of course, are well-known. We are also seeing marvelous quilts made by Zoarites, Quakers, Methodists, and the Apostolic Church.

Americans are proud of our quilts; they are historic and cultural documents, and we respect the efforts that are being expended, and work being done, to catalog and conserve them. We wish to share with our descendants the quilts of yesterday and today and the stories they tell.

🐦 43

Elizabeth Roseberry Mitchell. *Graveyard, Pieced, Appliquéd, and Embroidered Quilt*. 1839. Lewis County, Kentucky. Cotton, 85 × 81″. Collection The Kentucky Historical Society, Frankfort, Kentucky.

This is probably the best known of all mourning quilts. Unique, fascinating, and slightly bizarre, it is a document of social history reflecting an early nineteenth-century attitude toward death. The background is composed of alternating blocks of LeMoyne Stars. At the center is the fenced graveyard with four coffins, each bearing the name of a deceased family member. Quilting in this area outlines spaces for thirteen coffins. Twenty-one additional coffins are outlined or appliquéd around the quilt's border.

Each coffin has a paper tag bearing the name of a family member. The quilter's design was to move the coffin of a family member to the center when that person died; only two coffins were actually moved (bottom row). According to family history, Mrs. Mitchell made this quilt to assuage her grief over the death of her two young sons. The boys were buried in Ohio, where she had lived prior to moving to Kentucky. In 1838 she visited her mother near her old home and burial plots, and on her return to Kentucky she began working on this quilt to create a memorial closer to home.

There are three borders of picket fences: one around the outside of the entire quilt; a second surrounding the graveyard; and the third leading from one fence to the other along the path to the graveyard. In contrast to the quilt's somber tone, vines and flowers with pink blossoms are embroidered along the bottom, up the path, and at the entrance gate of the graveyard itself. Many experts consider this quilt a prime example of American folk art.

🪶 44

Holly Berry Appliqué Quilt. c. 1880. Michigan. Cotton, 78×78″. Collection Phyllis Haders.

Thirteen squares compose this quilt, and oddly enough (or superstitiously enough), the thirteenth is not in a green design, but is obviously blue. The quilter's deliberate imperfection is in keeping with the belief that "only God can make a perfect thing" and, therefore, she purposely included this flaw. Notice, however, the exquisite quilting.

⚘ 45

E. J. Hart(?). *Coxcomb with Rose Border Pieced and Appliqué Quilt.* c. 1860. Clark County, Kentucky.
Cotton, 97 × 90". Collection Sarah Scobee Hammet. Photograph courtesy The Kentucky Quilt Project, Inc.

Most of the quilting here is a grid, although some of it follows the contours of the leaves and flowers, which is a practice common in appliqué quilts. The central crosses are pieced, and the flowers appliquéd. Note that all the crosses are the same hue, but the flowers change color: some are pink and red, others red and white. Although the design elements appear to be random, the overall effect is delicately balanced.

🐦 46

Bias Pomegranates Appliqué Quilt. c. 1840s. Origin unknown. Cotton, 83×82".
The Shelburne Museum, Shelburne, Vermont. Gift of Electra Havemeyer Webb.

While pomegranates and trailing vines were often-used motifs in mid-nineteenth-century appliqué quilts, rarely were they incorporated in so bold an overall design as in these broad bias strips. The quilt stitches are exceptionally fine and outline the appliqué to highlight the pattern. Other motifs, including curled feathers, eight-pointed stars, and hearts, are randomly quilted on the ground.

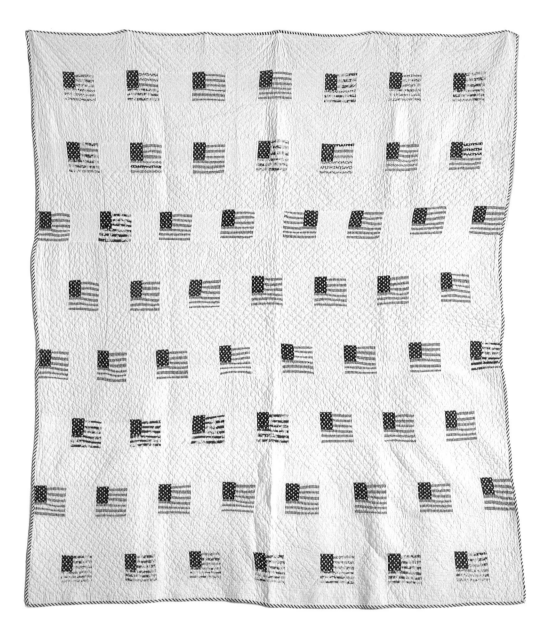

47

Flags Pieced Quilt. c. 1930. Ohio. Cotton on feed sacks, 82×70". Collection Shelly Zegart's Quilts, Louisville, Kentucky. Photograph by Steve Mitchell.

Note that in this quilt each flag's stripes are individually pieced. The entire quilt is framed by a whimsical candy-stripe border.

48

Eagle Pieced and Appliquéd Quilt. c. 1880. Pennsylvania. Cotton, 87×86". Collection Phyllis Haders.

Notable here are the wonderfully stylized birds. Note the contrast of inner sawtooth border with the generous outer border composed of vines and tulips.

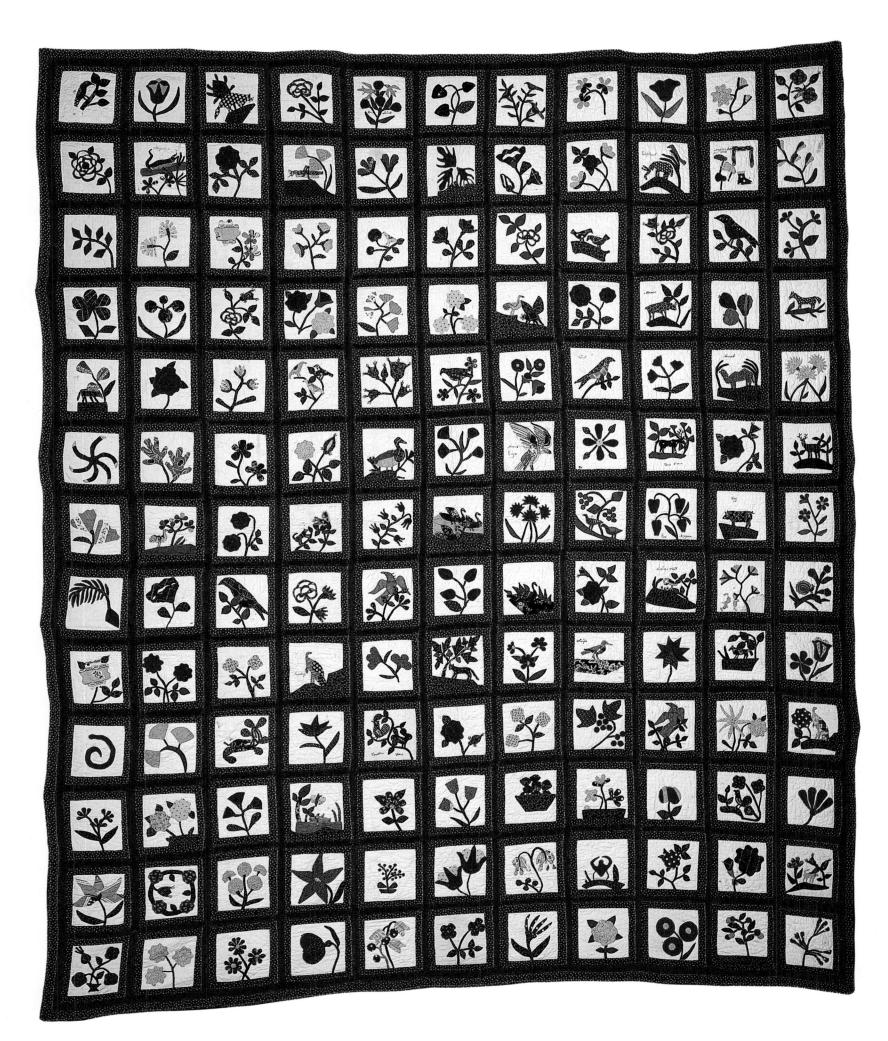

49

Album Pieced and Appliqué Quilt. c. 1850. New York State. Cotton, 96 × 93″. Private collection.
Courtesy Thos. K. Woodard American Antiques & Quilts, New York. Photograph by Schecter Lee.

This unique example contains 132 images derived from the fields of biology and zoology. Close viewing reveals the hand-stitched script as captions for some of the subjects.

🦢 50

Mrs. J. P. Williams. *Pieced, Embroidered, and Tie-Quilted. Friendship Quilt.* 1926. Harrodsburg, Kentucky. Cotton, 74½ × 58½". Collection The Kentucky Historical Society, Frankfort, Kentucky. Photograph by Nathan Prichard.

Mrs. Williams made this quilt with the collaboration of the women's group of St. Phillip's Episcopal Church in Harrodsburg. The money realized from this project was donated to A. D. Price Memorial Hospital. The quilt is executed in light blue cotton with white muslin, and tied with white embroidery floss. The names are all embroidered in blue floss. One of the wheels, or suns, contains the names of the hospital's medical staff, nursing staff, and board of directors. Another contains the names of the vestry, the rector, the organist, and the bishop of the local diocese. Other names are those of particular families or of individuals who were staying at the Hotel Harrod at the time.

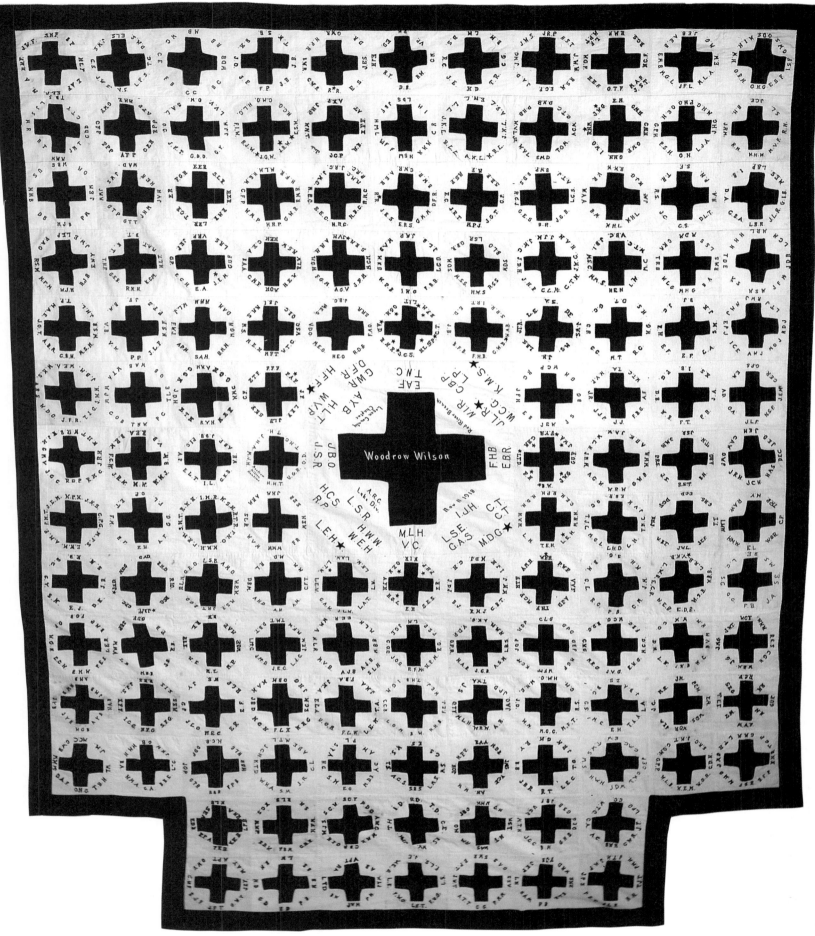

51

Jessie Bailey Orndorff and Drucilla Orndorff. *Pieced, Appliquéd, and Embroidered Red Cross Quilt.*
1918. Adairville, Kentucky. Cotton, approx. 72 × 68". Collection Cindy Watson Shields. Photograph by John Perkins.

This quilt was made during the last year of World War I as a fundraiser for the American Red Cross. Ladies of the
Red River branch of that organization embroidered the initials of their neighbors, charging ten cents per
monogram. The center red cross bears an inscription reading ''Woodrow Wilson'' and was done for a $1.00
contribution. Jessie Bailey Orndorff and her mother-in-law, Drucilla Orndorff, then pieced and quilted the
quilt. When completed (the date embroidered on the quilt is ''November 11, 1918,'' when the Armistice was
declared), the quilt was auctioned and Jessie Orndorff persisted in the bidding until she was able to buy it back.
It is now in the possession of Mrs. Orndorff's granddaughter.

 52

Friendship/Sampler Pieced Quilt. c. 1940. Mt. Vernon, Ohio. Cotton, 74×67".
Collection Shelly Zegart's Quilts, Louisville, Kentucky. Photograph by Steve Mitchell.

Each block of this quilt is in a different pattern. Each block is also signed and dated in
embroidery and incorporates embroidered Bible verses.

🐎 53

Pieced and Appliquéd Legacy or Sampler Quilt. 1908. Pennsylvania. Cotton, 84 × 82".
Collection Phyllis Haders. Photograph by Mary Anne Stets.

At first glance, this appears to be a well-executed sampler quilt incorporating many patterns. Not all the blocks are on the same scale, but especially unusual here are the motifs in the quilting, which appear on the reverse of the quilt and have a certain sense of whimsy. For example, a key is quilted in the door of the house, and the orange-and-green tree has a ladder quilted on its trunk. Both the front and the back include utilitarian tools not usually seen on quilts: on the front a saw and an ax are appliquéd, and on the back are scissors and shears. Other quilting motifs include a horse, horseshoes, four horses' heads, a lady's riding shoe, stars (on the blue field of the flag), a large basket, butterflies, four kittens, ears of corn, eyeglasses, two eagles, four bonneted women, and a handsome full-front depiction of a turkey.

54

Appliquéd Bible Quilt. c. 1860–90. Origin unknown.
Velvet and wool, 76×71″. Collection America Hurrah
Antiques, New York City. Photograph by Schecter Lee.

There is an amazing amount of detail in this quilt, and the
quality of the needlework is exceptionally fine. Some of
the noteworthy motifs include the Noah's Ark (center),
the Crucifixion (top center), the Garden of Eden (top left),
and Moses with the Tables of the Law (lower right).

The background is pale blue wool, and the appliqués
are cut from silk velvet. There are minute embroidered
touches throughout, especially on the houses and on
many of the figures as well. Notice, too, the wonderful
scalloped design around the edge, with a bird or animal
placed within each scallop. Such a quilt could easily have
taken years to make, owing to the exacting attention that
must have been lavished on every square inch and on
every detail.

55

Jane Neale Sears. *Rose of Sharon Appliquéd Quilt*.
c. 1870. Warren County, Kentucky. Cotton, 95×80″.
The Kentucky Museum, Western Kentucky University,
Bowling Green, Kentucky. Photograph by John Perkins.

The Rose of Sharon is one of the most popular nineteenth-
century appliqué patterns. Some variations are called
Whig Rose, Kentucky Rose, and Ohio Rose. The basic
design usually includes red and/or pink flowers attached
to green stems, with leaves and vines arranged in squares,
crisscrosses, or natural branch patterns. It was not unusual
to combine prints and solid fabrics in such quilts; in the
example shown here the green appliqués are worked in a
print fabric. A variety of borders may be also seen in such
quilts, and in the present one the white spaces between
the rose groupings are often filled with intricate stuffed
quilting. Note the yellow centers in the flowers and the
fine green piping of the binding around the edge.

🐦 56

Joseph's Coat Mennonite Pieced Quilt. c. 1890. Pennsylvania.
Cotton, 80×78". Collection America Hurrah Antiques, New York City. Photograph by Schecter Lee.

One of the special characteristics that distinguishes this quilt is the diagonal rainbow-striped border. Like Joseph's coat in the Bible, this is indeed "of many colors."

57

Mary Sutherlin, Nannie Elizabeth Pryor, and Cora. *Ship's Wheel or Prairie Star Pieced Quilt*. c. 1865. Grave County, Kentucky. Cotton, 84×66″. Collection Katherine Burton. Photograph courtesy The Kentucky Quilt Project, Inc.

Mary Sutherlin and Nannie Elizabeth Pryor were sisters, and Cora was their sister-in-law. The fabrics used here were probably dress materials. This popular pattern has many names, and here it is seen in a variation, with six- rather than eight-pointed stars: the family called it Kentucky Star. Star images were among the earliest and remained the most popular of quilt designs.

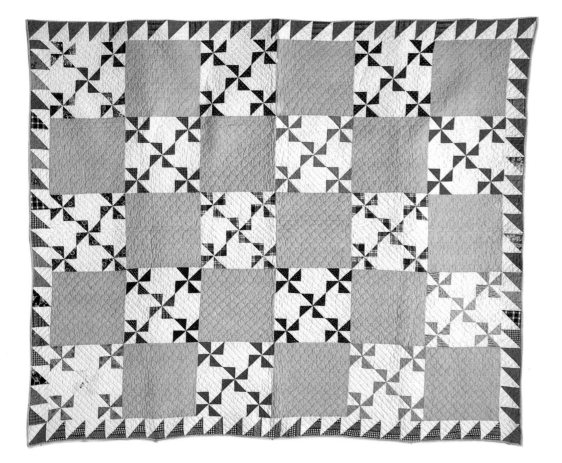

58

Pinwheels with Sawtooth Border Pieced Quilt. c. 1870. New England. Cotton, 70×82″. Collection Shelly Zegart's Quilts, Louisville, Kentucky. Photograph by Steve Mitchell.

Many calico and solid cottons are incorporated in this quilt, which is interesting because the blocks of pinwheels alternate with solid pink blocks. The color placement of the pinwheels in the blocks is somewhat unbalanced, inasmuch as there are two at top right that are predominantly blue, while most others are darker and one at bottom right is very pale.

 59

Mariner's Compass Pieced and Appliquéd Quilt. c. 1890.
Maryland. Cotton, 90 × 90″. Private collection. Photograph by Garrison Studio.

The cottons used here probably came from dress fabrics. Of special interest is the fancy border of oak leaves.

 60

Schoolhouse Pieced and Appliquéd Quilt. c. 1880. Ohio. Cotton, 76×78". Private collection. Photograph courtesy Phyllis Haders.

Here is a typical example of this pattern, stitched in a combination of calico print fabrics with a sawtooth border.

61

Houses and Weeping Willows Pieced and Appliquéd Quilt. c. 1880. New York State. Cotton, 82×94". Courtesy Thos. K. Woodard American Antiques & Quilts, New York. Photograph by Schecter Lee.

Because of the subject matter and the use of fabric, this is a rare quilt. The viewer cannot fail to appreciate the inventive deployment of plaids composing bricks for the houses, chimneys, and rooftops.

🐦 62

Broken Star or Carpenter's Wheel Pieced Quilt. c. 1880. Illinois. Cotton, 80 × 80".
General Foods Corporate Collection. Photograph courtesy Phyllis Haders.

The combination of shapes and colors in this quilt endow it with an almost three-dimensional quality.

🐦 63

Sue Cheatham Smith Montgomery (?). *Grandmother's Flower Garden Pieced and Embroidered Quilt.* c. 1875. Kentucky. Silk, 60 × 60¼″. Collection The Kentucky Historical Society, Frankfort, Kentucky. Photograph by Nathan Prichard.

This quilt is known to have been owned by Sue Cheatham Smith Montgomery (1846–1910), who lived in Kentucky, and it is possible that it was made by her.

What makes this quilt unique is the amount of embroidery contained within much of the salmon-colored background against which the hexagons are placed. Most quilts of this variety are composed entirely of multicolor hexagons, and may have embroidered borders. The present work, although having a beautifully embroidered border, also includes both pieced and embroidered sections. Some of the embroidery is done with variegated threads. Note that in some of the pieced areas print fabrics were deployed in innovative ways to create a pattern within a pattern: e.g., top row, fifth and six from left; second row from top, first and fourth from left; first in the fourth and sixth rows, and many more. Also worthy of special attention is the salmon-colored silk piping around the edge.

🐦 64

Margaret O'Sullivan Langford. *Spider's Web, Pieced Quilt.* c. 1880. Spencer County, Kentucky. Cotton, 76 × 64½″. Collection The Kentucky Historical Society, Frankfort, Kentucky. Photograph by Nathan Prichard.

The pattern here is one that is seen infrequently; it requires considerable skill to cut and fit so many sections of escalating sizes together. There is also very intricate stitching in the white spaces. The interesting pattern can be seen two ways: by concentrating on the hexagon web or by considering the white triangles around the web as points of a star with the web as a center. (Note that there is only one piece of green in the entire top.)

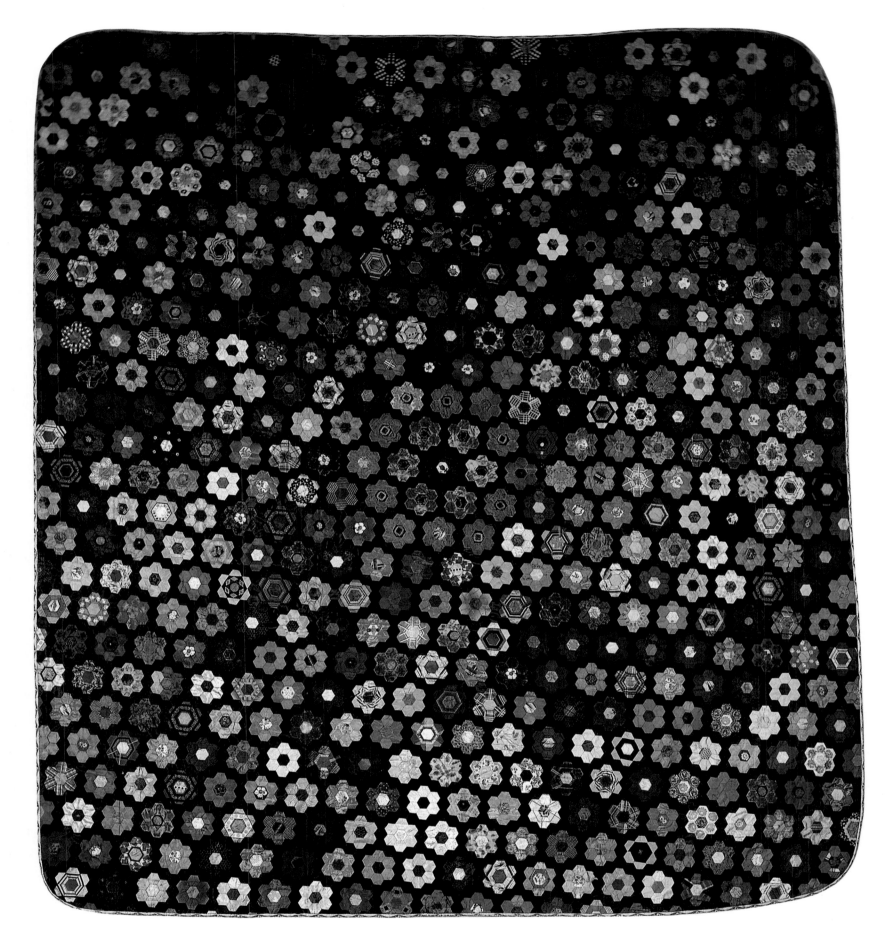

❧ 65

Bette McCarney Mitchell. *Flower Garden Pieced Quilt*. c. 1865. Bourbon County, Kentucky.
Silk with cotton backing, 83 × 74". The Kentucky Museum, Western Kentucky University, Bowling Green, Kentucky.
Photograph by John Perkins.

This quilt was made from very fine fabrics. Great care was taken in cutting and sewing the hexagons so that
stripes composed of printed fabrics would match exactly at the seams, and the floral designs are carefully
centered. Pieces are sewn together in the English style of whip-stitching, with folded edges together, rather than
in the usual style, with running stitches.

 66

Bear's Paw, Pieced Quilt. c. 1900.
Kentucky. Cotton, 72×62".
Collection Shelly Zegart's Quilts,
Louisville, Kentucky.
Photograph by Steve Mitchell.

Here is a charming example of a strong
pattern. The background and the blue
blocks, which are composed of shirting
fabric, add to the attraction of this
quilt.

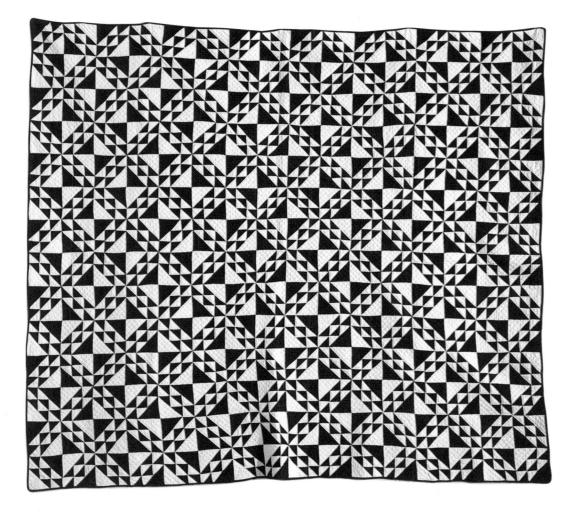

67

Lady of the Lake Pieced Quilt. 1900.
Kentucky. Cotton, 73×82".
Collection Shelly Zegart's Quilts,
Louisville, Kentucky.
Photograph by Steve Mitchell.

The Lady of the Lake pattern was
originally inspired by Sir Walter Scott's
poem. The present quilt, a very
complex and interesting geometric
design, is enhanced by outline,
windowpane, and diagonal quilting.

68

Jewell Willoughby. *Trip Around the World Pieced Quilt*. c. 1930. Kentucky. Cotton, 85×70".
Collection Deborah Harding, New York. Photograph by Rene Velez.

This quilt top is a typical example of a pattern variously known as Chipyard, Around the World, and Postage Stamp. Each of the more than 2,000 individual squares here measures one-and-one-eighth inch, and they are set at an angle to form diamonds. Such quilts are traditionally assembled from carefully hoarded remnants, and are known as "scrap quilts." By examining some of the individual rows, such as the yellow calico or the black-and-white check, you will see that the fabrics don't match exactly; thus, it must have taken considerable care and planning to save enough similar fabrics to use together. A group of patches is joined at the center to form a rectangle, and concentric rows radiate to the edges of the quilt.

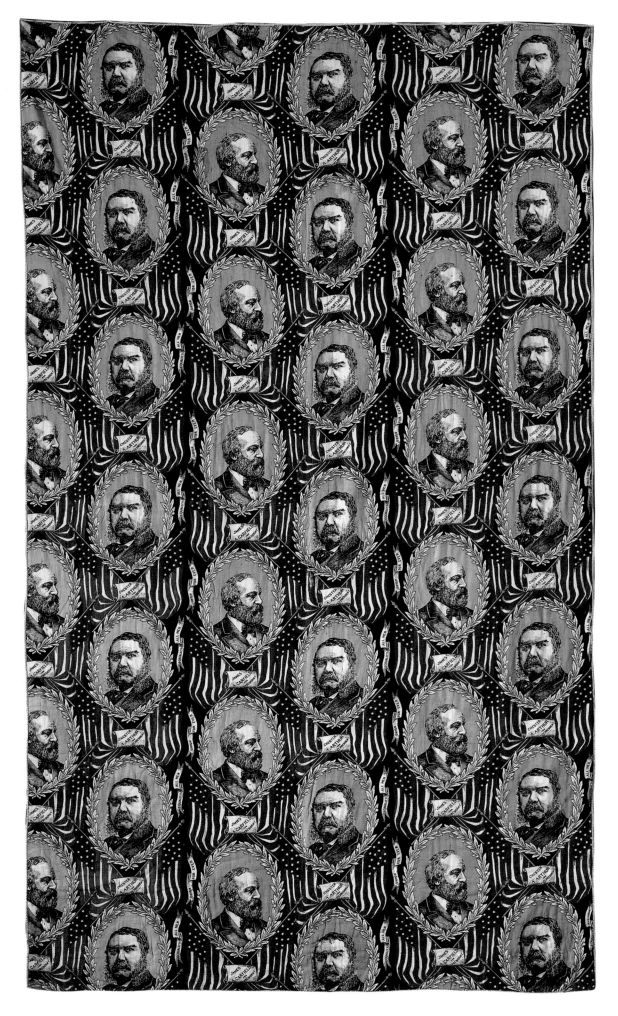

🎗 69

Garfield and Arthur Campaign Pieced Quilt. c. 1881. New Hampshire. Cotton, 102×64″.
The Shelburne Museum, Shelburne, Vermont. Gift of Mrs. Roger Preston, Holderness, New Hampshire.

In the late nineteenth century, political campaigns served as the artistic inspiration for yard goods as
well as for commemorative handkerchiefs. The maker of this quilt purchased fabric made by
Cocheco Print Works, Dover, New Hampshire, Style #6391 (dated October 17, 1881) for the backing.

🦃 70

Tippecanoe Pieced Quilt. c. 1890s. Origin unknown. Cotton, 79 × 79″. The Shelburne Museum, Shelburne, Vermont. Gift of Miss Anna Colman, Boston, Massachusetts.

Since the late eighteenth century, commemorative textiles have been incorporated in quilts. The present example, made with handkerchiefs from Benjamin Harrison and Levi P. Morton's campaign for the presidency and vice-presidency, is especially colorful.

🐢 71

Sophronia Ann Bruce. *Honeycomb or Mosaic Pieced and Appliqué Quilt*. c. 1880. Henry County, Kentucky. Cotton, wool, and silk, 107 × 92″. Collection Mrs. Ronda G. Taylor. Photograph courtesy The Kentucky Quilt Project, Inc.

Sophronia Ann Bruce was a farm wife who tended a large garden and raised turkeys. Her quilt incorporates some interesting elements as well as three different techniques: piecing, appliqué, and stuffed-work. The swag border is a type usually added to an appliqué top, but here it has been added to a pieced quilt. In addition, the mixture of fabrics is not often seen. It is also rare to find padded work in such generous border sections. Finally, an unusual feature is that all the hexagons join together to form one overall ten-pointed star.

🐢 72

Crossed-T's Pieced Quilt. c. 1850. Logan County, Kentucky. Cotton, 80½ × 156″. Kentucky Museum, Western Kentucky University, Bowling Green, Kentucky. Photograph by John Perkins.

The Crossed-T is but one of a whole family of pieced patterns employing the T form, including the T-Quartet, Four-T's, Mixed T's, Boxed T, and the T-Quilt. All are minor variants that mostly differ in the placement of the T. In the Crossed-T, the four T-shapes all face the center of the square. With the exception of the small square corner pieces, this quilt is composed entirely of triangular and diamond-shaped patches. The Crossed-T is an optical illusion pattern, and the T's can easily be lost among the combination of rectangles and triangles. With this quilt, one is best able to identify the T's by focusing on the blue pattern, thinking of the white as negative space.

This quilt was made in Logan County, Kentucky, in the Southeastern part of the state. Recent research conducted by the Kentucky Heritage Quilt Society and the Kentucky Museum has identified Logan County as an area with a particularly rich quilting heritage. From the early part of the nineteenth century to the present day, the women of this rural part of the state have continued to produce a wide variety of quilts of outstanding craftsmanship. The present quilt originally belonged to the Pearce family of Logan County.

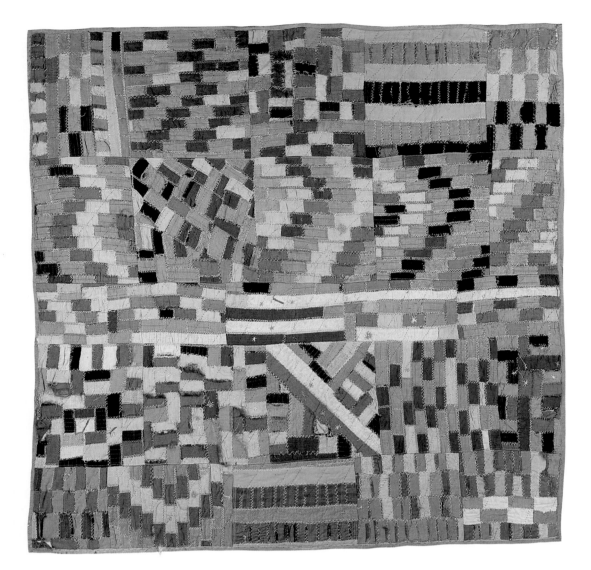

73

Annie Burnett Anderson. *Brick or Brickyard Pieced One-Patch Quilt.* c. 1900. Knoxville, Knox County, Tennessee. Wool, 69½ × 68¾". Collection Terry Irwin. Courtesy Quilts of Tennessee Project. Photograph by David Luttrell.

This is an absolutely classic example of the pattern that incorporates the colors and placement of patches to simulate a brick wall. What makes the quilt memorable is that it includes several variations of brick-wall designs. It is also representative of Brick quilts composed of men's suiting fabrics. The batting is a handwoven wool blanket, the edge has been turned back to front, and the quilting is in diagonal rows three inches apart extending over the entire surface of the quilt. Special surface techniques include embroidery over the seams.

74

Triangles or Thousand Pyramids Pieced Quilt. c. 1880. Origin unknown. Cotton, 78 × 78". Collection Phyllis Haders. Photograph by Mary Anne Stets.

The unique interpretation of the pattern makes this an unusually graphic quilt. It is an excellent example of what can be accomplished from a single shape: in this case, a triangle.

🐚 75

Puss in the Corner Amish Pieced Quilt. c. 1920. Pennsylvania. Wool and crepe, 79 × 80".
The Esprit Collection, San Francisco.

This beautifully balanced version of the Nine-Patch is executed in luminous purple- and
coral-colored fabrics. It is composed of many scraps but includes the same coral color in the
center of each block. Oval rose wreaths are quilted onto the outer border.

76

Four-Patch Amish Pieced Crib Quilt. c. 1925. Holmes County, Ohio. Cotton, 39 × 30". The Esprit Collection, San Francisco.

In this example, the Four-Patch is set diagonally to create a type of Jacob's Ladder. The color, including the Lightning Streak, is enhanced by the use of black, a combination common in Holmes County quilts.

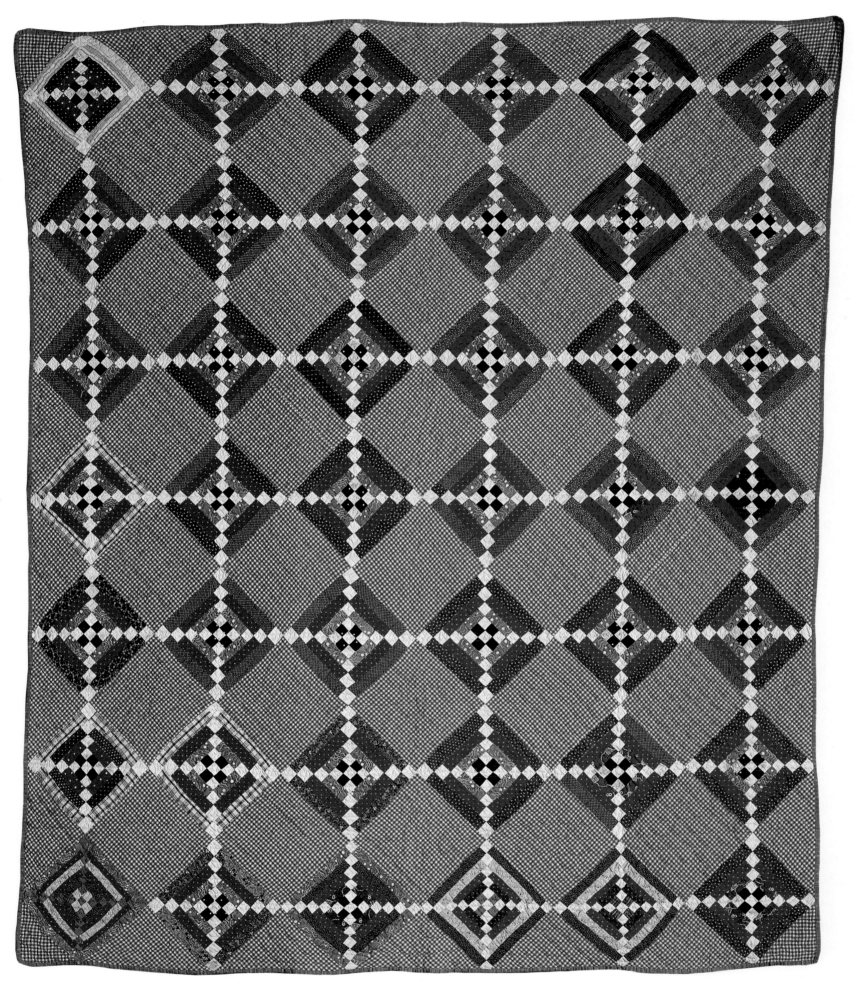

🐦 77

Martha Ann Brown Hambrick. *Nine-Patch Variation Pieced Quilt*. c. 1860. Nicholasville, Kentucky.
Cotton, 81 × 69". Collection The Kentucky Historical Society, Frankfort, Kentucky. Photograph by Nathan Prichard.

Martha Ann Brown Hambrick lived from 1823 to 1912, and it is said that she wore only black and white, and that therefore the blacks on this quilt came from scraps of her own clothing; her daughter preferred to wear dark blues and white, so the dark blue are scraps from her wardrobe. All the fabrics in other colors came from Mrs. Hambrick's grandchildren's clothes.

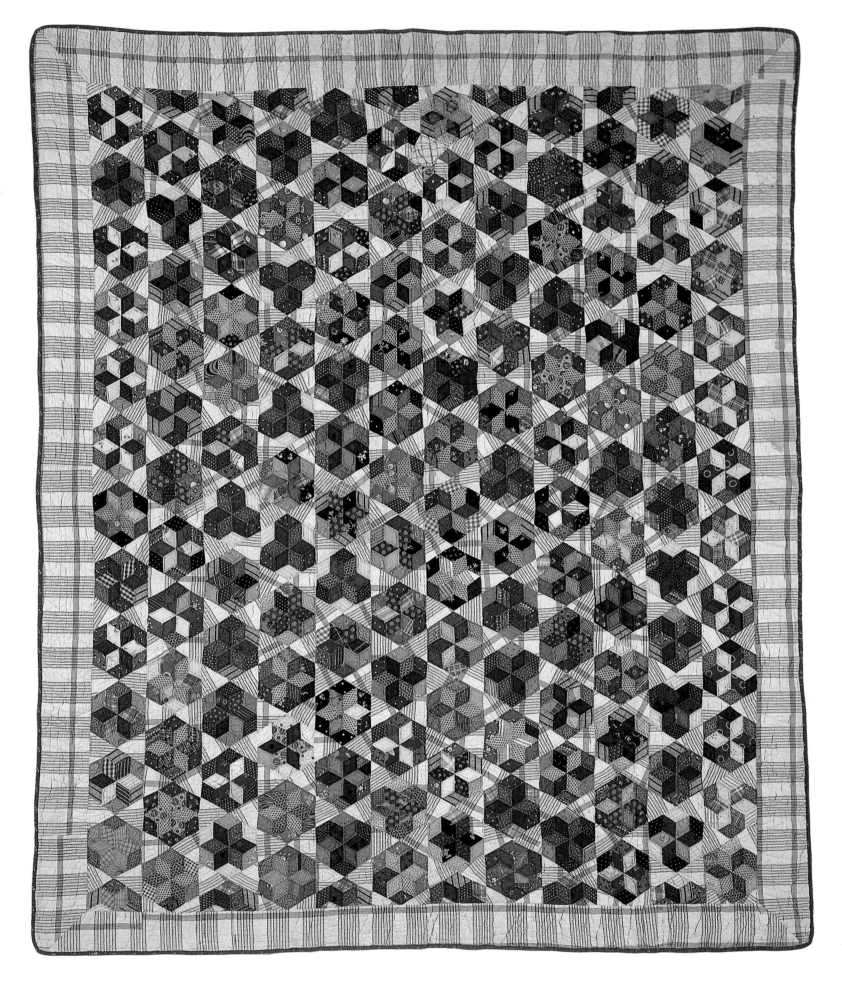

 78

Mary Alexander. *Pieced Hexagonal Star Quilt*. c. 1880. Cumberland County, Kentucky. Cotton, 91×76½".
Collection Julia Neal. Photograph courtesy The Kentucky Quilt Project, Inc.

The cotton fabrics in this pieced quilt were salvaged from no-longer-wearable shirts and wash-dresses. The design is cleverly constructed of diamonds arranged in light and dark colors. The eye can perceive the design in at least two ways: as a flat star, or as clusters of tumbling blocks. The hexagon enclosing each star also becomes the center of a large six-pointed star, the arms composed of the light-colored triangles that fill the spaces between the hexagons. This quilt is a masterful accomplishment.

79

Margaret Shanks. *Le Moyne Star, or Lemon Star, Pieced Quilt*. 1840. Lincoln County, Kentucky. Cotton, 77 × 72″. Collection The Kentucky Historical Society, Frankfort, Kentucky. Photograph by Nathan Prichard.

Margaret Shanks was a great-niece of Governor William Owsley. Her quilt displays eight-pointed stars alternating with blocks of solid yellow. The unusual shade of butternut yellow and the sad fact that many of the browns are starting to deteriorate suggest that the fabrics were colored with homemade dyes.

80

Robbing Peter to Pay Paul Pieced Quilt. c. 1890. Kentucky. Satin, 68 × 61″. Collection Shelly Zegart's Quilts, Louisville, Kentucky. Photograph by Steve Mitchell.

It is rare to find this traditional folk pattern worked in satin, and the combination of style and material seems a contradiction. Nevertheless, the shimmer of the satin helps strengthen the optical illusion offered by the pattern.

81

Kentucky Pinwheel Pieced and Appliquéd Quilt.
c. 1880. Kentucky.
Cotton, 84 × 72″. Private collection.
Photograph courtesy Bettie Mintz.

The red sections appliquéd onto a splendid whitework background are rendered in designs that seem to draw the viewers' attention to the central red star with its solid white center. Note also the feathered border.

82

Fannie Sales Trabue. *Pieced Star Quilt with Appliqué Bouquets*. c. 1860. Todd County, Kentucky.
Silk and velvet, 70×70″. Collection Sara Lee Trabue Lacy. Photograph courtesy The Kentucky Quilt Project, Inc.

Here is an especially handsome Star quilt. The outer border is formed of diamonds, which contrast with the curved style of the flower appliqués.

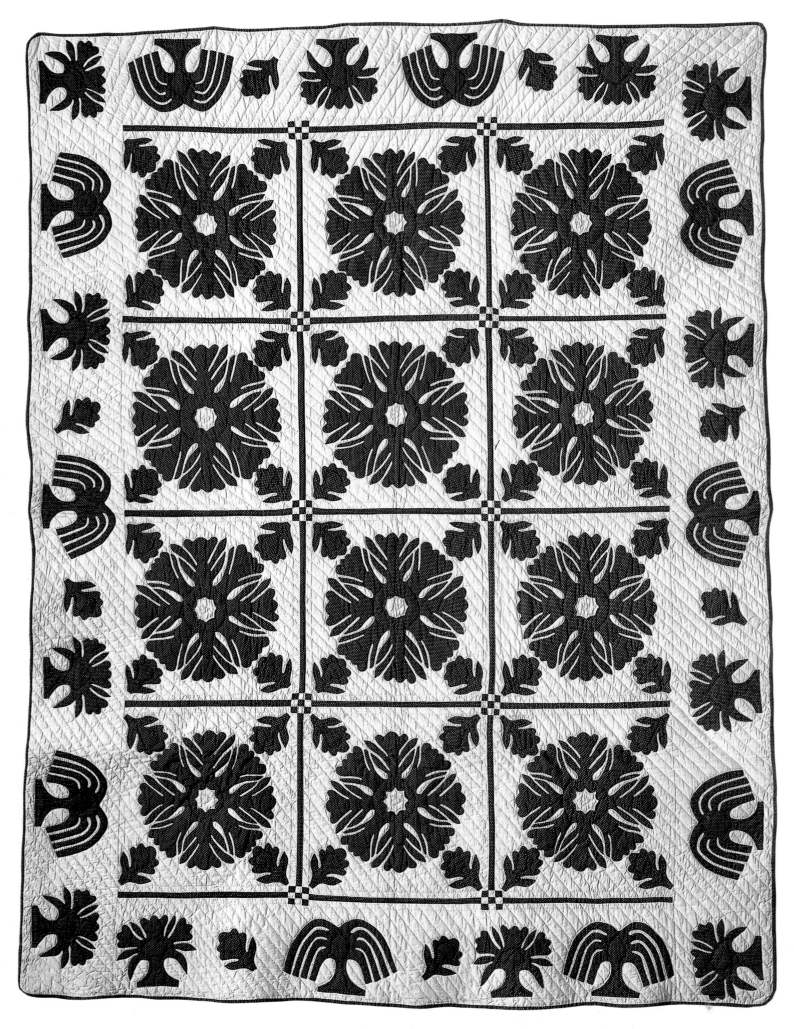

🪡 83

Willow Oak Appliqué Quilt. c. 1840s. Boston, Massachusetts. Cotton, 92×72". The Shelburne Museum, Shelburne, Vermont. Gift of Electra Havemeyer Webb. Photograph courtesy The Shelburne Museum.

The abstract snowflake pattern of this quilt is strongly reminiscent of the bold medallion pattern used on jacquard woven coverlets of the same period. The previous owner stated: "[the quilt] was made in Boston on Beacon Street . . . [and was found] wrapped in a handwoven sheet and a newspaper dated 1861 . . . packed away in a chest."

84

Pieced and Appliqué Sampler Quilt. c. 1850. Sheffield, Massachusetts.
Cotton, 92 × 88″. Collection America Hurrah Antiques, New York City. Photograph by Schecter Lee.

The compass blocks here are surrounded by sampler patches. Many motifs have been incorporated in this quilt, including rows of triangles for Flying Geese, Four-Patch, Broken Dishes, Pinwheels, Star variations, and two vertical rows of mosaic Grandmother's Flower Garden. The outside border contains appliqué flowers. An exceptional detail in the needlework is the triple-bias insert binding in red, green, and gold. The quilt radiates an air of joyfulness.

85

Basket of Flowers with Floral Vine Border Pieced Quilt. c. 1930. Pennsylvania. Cotton sateen, 86 × 78″.
Private collection. Courtesy Thos. K. Woodard American Antiques & Quilts, New York. Photograph by Schecter Lee.

Made of cotton sateen, a fabric used for fancy quilts during this period, this work features an unusual latticework woven basket and fine quilting.

86

Virginia Mason Ivey. *The Virginia Ivey Appliqué and Figural Stuffed-Work Quilt.* c. 1850. Logan County, Kentucky. Cotton, 92×78". The J.B. Speed Museum, Louisville, Kentucky. Photograph courtesy America Hurrah Antiques, New York City.

Virginia Ivey also made Kentucky's most publicized quilt, the whitework example entitled *A Representation of the Fair Ground Near Russellville, Kentucky, 1856* in the collection of the Smithsonian Institution. The extremely important quilt shown here was only identified and returned to Kentucky in 1985. It is thought that a third Virginia Ivey quilt in black silk exists, but it has yet to be found. The Speed Museum's quilt includes a central floral bouquet with cherry and other flowering trees, two crewel-embroidered cardinals, and grapevine border. The figures quilted in the white stuffed-work include a rendering of a statue of Henry Clay (his name sewn in quilting below the statue) and the figure of a man on horseback thought to be Andrew Jackson. The field of quilting also includes many horses, cows, dogs, birds, ducks, pigs, and floral motifs. Under one cow is quilted the phrase "Young Cow," which is either the bovine's name or a description. The details of relief work here have seldom been equalled.

There is reverse appliqué throughout, with tiny cross-stitching holding it down, and there are twenty-four quilting stitches per inch. The quilt still has its original crocheted and knotted fringe around the edge.

This superb quilt is an absolute masterpiece.

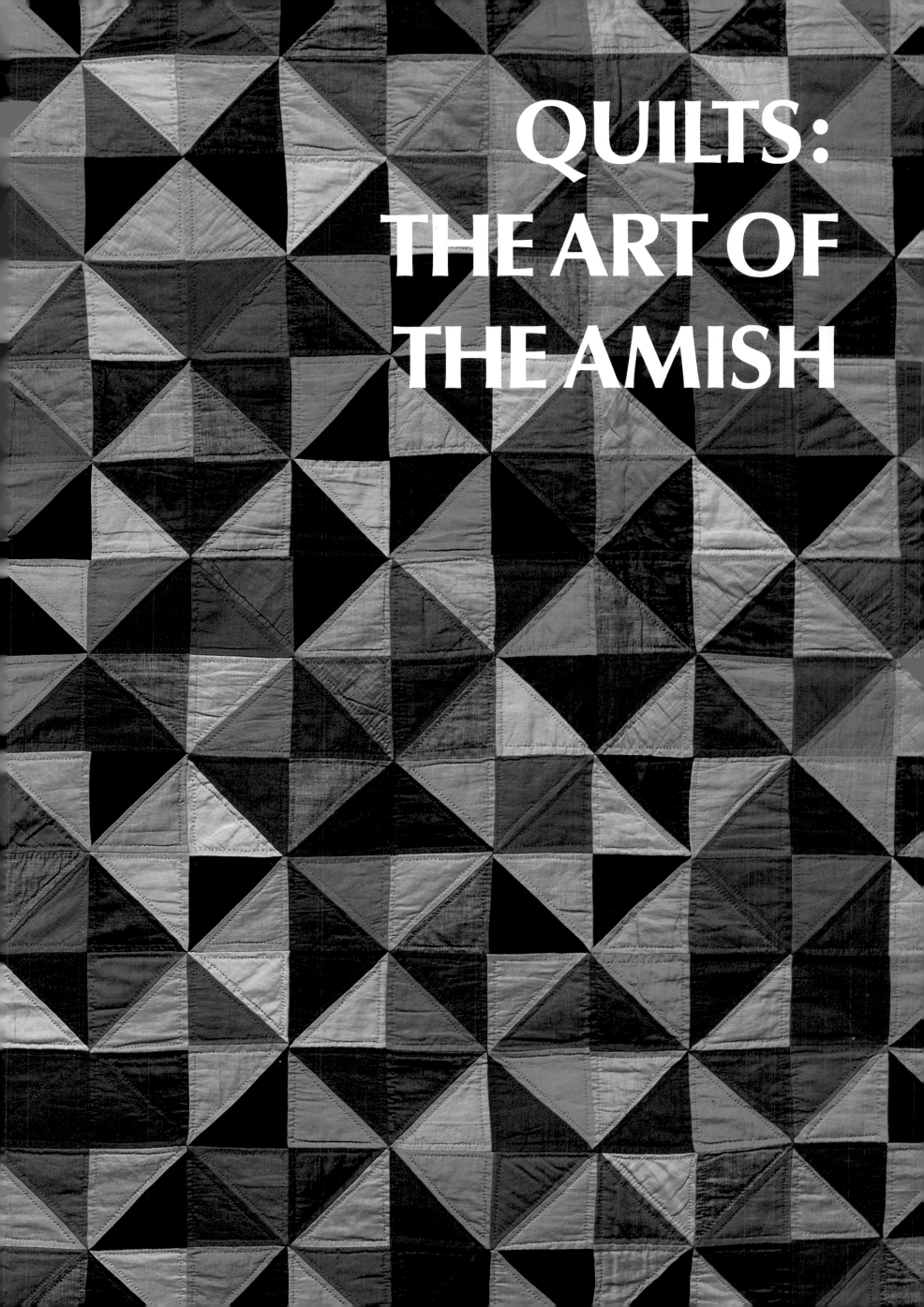

QUILTS: THE ART OF THE AMISH

QUILTS: THE ART OF THE AMISH

Phyllis Haders

hen I was a child living in Indiana and Ohio, quilts were a familiar sight; my mother's quilts were on all the beds, with extras locked away for cold weather or company. On rainy days my grandmother's fabric scrap bag was a source of wonder and delight, and I would play at placing pieces of fabric together like a jigsaw puzzle to form patterns. In the summers I visited my Aunt Helen in Howe, Indiana, who would tell me about the craft of quilt-making and teach me how to learn the names of some of the patterns.

It was only natural that I would grow up with an appreciation of fine quilts and begin collecting them, along with other American folk art. When my husband, Richard, and I were first married and living in the Northeast, we attended country auctions and house sales on weekends. At this time collecting was only a hobby, but my zest for it became a profession and later a full-time business.

The quilts I first bought were mostly appliqué and pieced examples, similar to those I remembered from my Midwestern childhood. I found one quilt when Aunt Helen and I visited a neighbor's home; it was an appliqué. When the family's grandmother heard that I was interested in quilts, she said they had one they had placed between the mattress and springs on one of the beds since they didn't consider it good enough to display. She said that one day her sister "went out in the yard and picked up a leaf that had fallen from a tree and simply traced around it to make a pattern." Unearthed from the bedding, the quilt turned out to be a charming 1872 appliqué with leaves at the corners and wonderful stitching in the center.

By the 1960s, Richard and I were traveling regularly to Pennsylvania, where I bought my first Amish quilt. One weekend we attended a Mennonite relief sale in Morgantown with another

PRECEDING PAGE: *Broken Dishes Amish Pieced Quilt* (detail). c. 1930. Midwest. Cotton. The Esprit Collection, San Francisco.

couple. It poured that day, and as it grew late our husbands became restless and wanted to go home. As we drove away, we saw a little house that had a sign in front reading "Quilts for Sale." Naturally, I insisted that we turn back to investigate. As we were looking at a display in the garage, we heard a voice from the kitchen, and a young man came from the house carrying four Amish quilts. His father bought tobacco from the Amish, and they had sold him a few of what they considered "old, dark quilts." As he unfolded them, I was immediately struck by their visual impact—an extraordinary juxtaposition of glowing colors and a powerful simplicity of design that parallels abstract art at its best.

I bought three of the quilts: two cost $70 each, and the third was $80. I didn't buy the fourth because there seemed to be something sad about it, and I later learned it had been made by a woman with several sick children. I took the quilts home, where I displayed them framed on the wall as works of art. Years later one of the $70 quilts was sold to a major museum; it is currently valued at over $10,000.

As my fascination with Amish quilts grew, I would often return to Pennsylvania and buy quilts at Amish auctions where they were listed with livestock, farm equipment, buggies, sleds, dishes, and kitchenware. I've discovered excellent quilts casually tossed over bales of hay, in the backs of trucks, or airing on clotheslines.

When I was only nine, my Aunt Helen took me to an Amish community in Indiana. My first feeling was one of awe accompanied by fear of the unknown. Who were these people? Why did they all dress alike and wear so much black? What was the "foreign" language they spoke? Why couldn't they own cars, have electricity, or send their children to public schools? However, I loved the sturdy gray and black buggies drawn by graceful and spirited horses and admired the beautifully kept farms with their freshly painted buildings.

Visiting the Amish as an adult and getting to know some of them, I developed a profound respect for these gentle people and their ordered life-style.

History and Customs

In 1693, the Swiss bishop Jacob Ammann split the Mennonite movement in two because he believed that the prevailing practice of "shunning" those who would not follow strict Anabaptist practice was insufficiently severe and that many believers were becoming too "worldly." At that time the custom of shunning consisted of merely expelling a member from the communion table, but Ammann insisted that the strictures should be extended to include social and domestic matters. His followers formed a new sect and eventually became known as the Amish. The Amish represented the strictest and most reactionary sect among the Mennonites, whose other sects accept modern technology and favor higher education.

The Amish migrated to that portion of the Palatinate along the Rhine that is now Alsace-Lorraine. Harshly persecuted for their religious beliefs, they began to migrate to the New World in 1727. The first Amish in America settled in Pennsylvania, especially in the Lancaster and Berks County areas; today Lancaster County is considered the capital of the Amish world. In America more divisions would occur, the major one being between the Old Order, or House Amish, and the Mennonite Amish. The latter group worships in church, while the members of the Old Order adhere to worshiping in members' homes instead of church buildings, to the prohibition of missionary work, and to the ceremony of foot washing, at which each member washes another's feet according to John 13:14: "If I then, your Lord and Master, have washed your feet; ye also ought to wash one another's feet."

Today there are over 80,000 Amish in Pennsylvania, Ohio, Indiana, Illinois, Missouri, and Iowa.

One of the major principles of the Amish is to remain separate from the world; they live in it but are not of it. Those outside their community are called "the English," and their life-style is avoided. Religious services are held every other Sunday in the homes of the members of a congregation. A "community" or "district" is determined by how far a horse and buggy can travel on a Sunday morning and return home in time for the animals to be fed by nightfall, or by how many can sit for worship services in one family's home. Church officials are chosen by lot and serve for life. A list of eligible candidates is compiled (any male member can serve), and after a regular worship service on an announced date a group of Bibles is assembled—the same number of Bibles as candidates—and a piece of paper with a verse from the Scriptures is placed in one of the Bibles. Each candidate selects a Bible, and the Bibles are opened one at a time until one candidate finds the slip of paper; that candidate is then chosen to serve.

Officials include deacons, ministers, and bishops. The bishop is the chief authority and leader of the congregation and has the final word on matters of conduct. He performs marriage ceremonies, announces punishments for violations of moral or church laws, administers communion and baptism (there is no infant baptism—new members are baptized when they are between fifteen and eighteen years of age), and presides over the community.

The Old Order Amish are a world apart, a community of very conservative Christians who believe that simple living, hard work, self-sufficiency, humility, and strict adherence to the Bible give meaning to life and provide hope for salvation after death. They pay income and real-estate taxes but do not accept Social Security or any other government benefit. Children are educated in one-room schoolhouses and do not attend high school.

There is a prescribed order of dress and hairstyle. Women must never cut their hair and must keep their heads covered with white prayer caps at all times (if they disobey, their hair may be shorn). Their dresses follow the same pattern handed down for generations. The only slight variation allowed is color, but it must be a solid, usually black, blue, green, tan, dark purple, or burgundy. Scarlet, orange, and yellow are prohibited, as are prints, stripes, checks, and dots. However, rich magenta, mauve, and turquoise blue often are seen in men's shirts and women's dresses. An apron is worn over the dress. Married women wear either black aprons or aprons that are the same color as their dress; unmarried women wear white aprons.

A married man must wear a beard, but a mustache is forbidden. Men dress in black or midnight-blue suits with "frontfall" pants held up by suspenders. Neckties are proscribed, but in their place a narrow black ribbon is sometimes worn to worship services and on special occasions. The suit jacket has no lapels or outside pockets, and hooks and eyes are substituted for buttons as a symbol of rejection of the military and of violence (according to some sources, the original function of buttons on overcoats or suit coats was to hold back the garment so that a sword could be easily unsheathed). Hats are worn year-round: in winter, a flat-crowned, broad-brimmed black felt hat; in summer, the same style made of natural-color straw with a black or navy-blue band.

Also proscribed are musical instruments, electricity, insurance, movies, dancing, jewelry (even wedding rings), cosmetics, automobiles, private telephones, radios, television, doorbells, curtains, and wallpaper. Lightning rods are also forbidden, but if a barn burns down, hundreds of neighbors gather to raise a new one. The use of alcohol and tobacco is also forbidden, even though tobacco is a major Amish crop.

Photographs are usually frowned on as signs of vanity. Dolls are faceless for the same reason. There is no divorce. Women do all their own cooking and baking, which often means three large meals a day and twenty to thirty pies a week. They make most of the family's clothes, keep their homes spotlessly clean, tend the vegetable gardens, put up preserves, milk the cows, and share in the care of the animals and in some of the other farm work. The flower gardens are beautifully tended and offer a rare opportunity for Amish women to work freely with color.

Since everything must be functional, interiors are severely and sparsely furnished, lacking ornate furniture and other worldly appointments. There are dark-blue or green shades at the windows, and except for a few pieces of decorated china, tea towels, a calendar on the wall, and the flowers in the window boxes, the only source of color may be found in the quilts covering the daybeds and regular beds. A treasure trove of similar textiles is most likely put away for use on special occasions such as weddings, visits by the bishop, large family gatherings, and worship services.

Quilting has played an important role in the lives of Amish women for more than a century. It affords them a creative outlet, a chance to experiment with brilliant colors and to socialize with other women at quilting bees. Quiltmaking is permitted because a quilt is utilitarian, and its construction is considered a natural extension of other matronly duties. However, quilting offers an escape from the daily routine of rural life and provides an opportunity to make something beautiful without being considered prideful or sinful. Perhaps it is the blend of such intrinsic values and the absence of worldly sophistication that has produced the unique style and genius of the great Amish quilts. They differ from other quilts because of the simplicity of design, the instinctive approach to mixing vivid colors, the nonrepresentational patterns, and the exceedingly intricate stitching—all achieved by individuals uninhibited by the limitations imposed by the study of art history and the rules governing form. Thus, Amish quilts dating from 1860 to 1940 have become prized and desirable collectibles.

The quilts illustrated in this chapter were all made before 1940. The Amish are still making quilts, but the look is drastically different even when the same patterns are reproduced. Synthetic fabrics lack the hand and richness of color, and synthetic battings make it difficult to duplicate the very fine stitching; therefore, the overall effect is simply not the same. It is truly a lost art; the outward form can be reproduced, but the inner spirit has changed.

Patterns

All Pennsylvania Amish quilts are composed of straight-edged geometric shapes—rectangles, squares, triangles, and diamonds. However, the combinations, placement, and scale of these basic shapes are endless. Large rectangles line up to create Bars and Split Bars, smaller ones are worked into Straight Furrows, and very narrow ones link up in Log Cabins. Triangles are transformed in Flying Geese, Sawtooth, Pinwheel, Basket, and Bow Tie quilts. A square set at an angle becomes a diamond, and smaller diamonds joined together can make a star.

For the most part, Pennsylvania Amish quilts are composed of large sections of fabric, and one can therefore assume that such fabric was specifically purchased for quiltmaking. In some districts the bishops forbade Amish women to construct quilts with too many pieces, as this could be considered a source of pride; two notable exceptions are Sunshine and Shadow and the Double Nine-Patch, both of which were developed after 1900.

Midwestern Amish quilts reveal a greater variety of patterns, with smaller designs and repetitive motifs. Some believe that these geometric shapes were inspired by nature and the landscape: ploughed furrows, bales of hay, rows of corn, green pastures, windmill blades, doors windows, and barn rafters. Even the fans in the quilts of this region suggest the spokes of buggy wheels.

Another view is that such designs were inspired by the bindings on Ausbands, the Amish hymnals found in every home. According to *A Gallery of Amish Quilts, Design Diversity from a Plain People* (1969), by Robert Bishop and Elizabeth Safands: "The Ausbands printed in the 17th, 18th and 19th centuries were bound in leather with brass ornamentations to protect the book from excessive wear . . . the shape and placement of the brass bosses resembles the basic design of a pieced Amish quilt." Some bindings are decorated with brass center squares and diamonds and squares and diamonds at each corner. Some of the most recognizable quilt patterns in this style include the Center Square, Square within a Diamond, Diamond in a Square, and Bars. All are usually outlined and framed by at least one border. Rectangular borders may contain corner blocks or can be edged with rows of small triangles forming a sawtooth border.

Multiple-patch patterns composed of small squares can be arranged as One-Patch, Four-Patch, Nine-Patch, and Double Nine-Patch. Sunshine and Shadow is a dramatic way of contrasting light and dark colors to create an optical illusion. In the Midwest there are also Fan quilts, Ocean Waves, Basket of Chips, Shoo Fly, and Streak O' Lightning patterns. Here, too, one can find more adaptations of traditional American patterns, since Amish communities in this part of the country were not as concentrated and therefore were open to more exposure from outside influences.

"Plain" quilts or oblong quilts are essentially one overall color framed with one or two simple colored borders.

Colors

Amish quilts—particularly those made before 1940 in Old Order settlements—can be considered unique in several respects, chiefly in their especially vivid colors and color combinations.

As stated in *The World of Amish Quilts* (1984), by Rachel and Kenneth Pellman:

Amish quiltmakers, because of their limited access to color and fashion trends, work in a nearly uninhibited color world. Most children in the larger society begin early in their lives to subconsciously develop a color sense. Their socks match their pants; their pants match their shirt; their sweaters are coordinated. All this takes place in homes where carpets, draperies and walls are synchronized with accessories and furnishings.

In an Amish setting, one style of clothing is worn and only part of its color changes from day to day. One never need worry about whether one's pink dress matches one's black stockings and black shoes. Most Amish homes do not contain upholstered furniture, their walls are generally painted a solid blue or green, and carpets, where found, are often handwoven rag rugs [or plain patterned linoleum]. This lack of color consciousness among the Amish leaves them completely open to the possible use of fabrics from their scrap bag.

Amish women were not told that color hues vary depending on their reference point. But they could see and feel it happening.

Amish quilts employ only solid-color fabrics, except in backings, where prints may be used. The Pennsylvania quilts are made mainly from very lightweight wool and contain woolen batting. The early wools were homespun, and since wool is extremely receptive to color, it absorbed the natural dyes made from barks, berries, walnuts, and weeds with lustrous results and maximum intensity. Commercially woven and dyed wools, including stroud cloth, challis, and "bertha" cloth, became available at the end of the nineteenth century. However, the colors chosen for quilts were usually the same hues as those found in the home-dyed fabrics. Whatever the fabric or dyeing method, the predominant colors include red, plum, purple, mauve, navy blue, soldier blue, indigo, turquoise, magenta, mustard, gold, green, brown, tan, black, and gray. Curiously, the religious restrictions regarding color in dress did not seem to apply to quilts, and yellows, scarlet, and orange were often used.

Midwestern quilts are usually composed of cotton materials including sateen, twill, and even flannel with cotton batting. Black was a popular choice for backgrounds, and it is not unusual to see several shades of black in a quilt top resulting from the use of different types of cotton or from a single fabric's nap arranged in varying directions. White is also found in some Midwest Amish quilts although not in Pennsylvania examples. It is interesting that the outer border or binding on Amish quilts is frequently executed in a color not used in the main design. (It is often possible to ascertain the age of a quilt by studying its binding. On an old quilt the crease will be firmly established and will probably show some wear. To establish how long the crease has existed, bend the binding between the fingers.)

Stitching

Amish quilt tops are pieced rather than appliquéd. After the 1860s, the piecing was accomplished with a foot-operated treadle sewing machine. The machine stitching on a quilt top is not seen after the quilt is assembled. However, a guide to the quality of the sewing is provided by the machine stitching along the binding, which remains visible. A good deal of accuracy was required to line up all the edges evenly and to cut and distribute the tension of the fabric (on the bias) so that it would lie flat and not pucker.

The quilting stitches themselves are all done by hand and are extremely intricate, demonstrating the superior craftsmanship; Amish quilts often contain twenty stitches per inch. Early Pennsylvania quilts may be stitched entirely in black thread.

Piecing was done either by one woman or by several generations in one family. Most of the quilting, however, took place at quilting bees or frolics, which were held mainly in winter when there was less farm work. A bee was an all-day event that began after the children were sent to school. Frequently the quilt top had already been taken to a woman in the community who was especially skilled in placing the patterns, and thus they were marked on the top and ready for stitching. The quilt was then stretched on the frame, and as many as eight to twelve women sat around it. Children too young to attend school were permitted to play around or under the frame and often helped by threading the needles. The bee was an important social occasion, a time for participants to catch up on local news and events, with genealogy, weddings, and babies providing favored subjects. A hearty noonday meal was served that included numerous baked goods and several courses. After they had eaten, the women returned to quilting. Some stayed the entire day, while others came and went.

The quilting patterns contrast with the geometric pieced patterns, as they are often flowing and flowery, rounded and spiraled. Chief among the quilting patterns are feathers, scrolls, roses, tulips alone or in combination, wreaths, single stars and stars within stars, clusters of grapes, leaves and tendrils, primroses, baskets (mostly used in borders), hearts (for Bridal quilts), an occasional bird, and cables and grids of diamonds. The large sections of solid-color fabric in the tops provide the perfect background for the multiples of quilting patterns. For example, in a Center Diamond there may be one series of quilting designs within the diamond itself (often concentric stars or a star within a wreath), another design in each border (such as pumpkin seed in the narrow borders and feathers in the wider ones), and yet other quilt patterns in the triangles and corner blocks. In a Bars quilt, the entire top may be quilted in a single pattern, such as an overall grid, or each stripe may contain a different quilting design.

In keeping with the strict religious traditions, Pennsylvania Amish quilts are rarely signed or dated, but the corners of some Midwest quilts bear the maker's initials and the date, either quilted or embroidered.

There are few crib quilts from Pennsylvania, but more from the Midwest. Only the scale differs in these smaller quilts; the patterns remain the same, and there is no representational subject matter.

Once completed, a quilt is used in utilitarian ways: as a cover for beds, cradles, trundle beds, and sometimes for the daybeds that served as couches. Every Old Order Amish family opens its home for church services at least once a year, and a particularly fine display of quilts may be put out at this time. Not all quilts are used once they have been made; some are put away for a daughter's dowry or as gifts. Family heirlooms that have gained the respectability of age are also brought out for special worship services, for weddings, and for funerals.

Within only a few generations this unique form of expression has peaked and faded away. For those of us who cannot directly share the Amish experience, these quilts remain unique works of art, symbolizing a lost era of creative skill and aesthetic sensitivity.

◆ 87

Church Amish Women Quilting. Photograph by Blair Seitz.

This depicts a monthly quilting bee held in the basement of the Weavertown Church near Intercourse, Pennsylvania, in Lancaster County. The Lone Star quilt being worked on was later auctioned to benefit a retirement home.

◆ 88

Amish Quilt-Seller, Lancaster County, Pennsylvania. Photograph courtesy Robert Clark Jr./Profile.

An Amish quilt-seller stands in a field holding a quilt executed in one of the most famous of all the Amish patterns—the Bars; this particular quilt dates from the turn of the century. Noted for his ability to find the very best antique Amish quilts, this man enjoys sharing his peoples' history as well as his love for one of their most notable art forms.

◆ 89

A Woman and Her Quilts, Lancaster County, Pennsylvania. Photograph courtesy Robert Clark Jr./Profile.

A quilter stands in a room in her house displaying her quilts. Many of the Amish and Mennonite in Lancaster County sell their quilts from their homes.

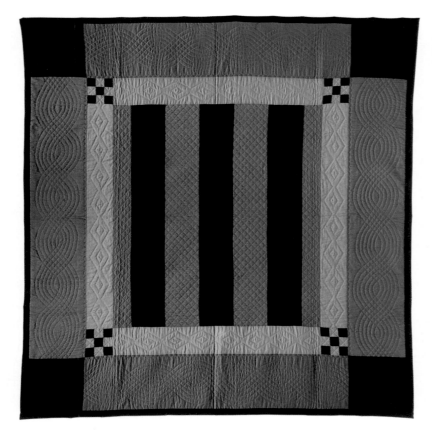

◆ 90

Bars with Nine-Patch Corners Amish Pieced Quilt. c. 1910.
Lancaster County, Pennsylvania. Wool, 80×82".
Collection America Hurrah Antiques, New York City.
Photograph by Schecter Lee.

The color combination used here—turquoise, brown,
and black—is very sophisticated. The Nine-Patch corners
in a Bars design are also extremely unusual.

◆ 91

Mahala Yoder. *Amish Pieced Oblong or Rectangle Quilt.* 1909.
Indiana. Cotton sateen, 86×63". Collection Phyllis Haders.

This is one of the earliest forms of Amish quilt, embodying
the essence of simplicity. The quilt is signed "Mahala
Yoder 1909." The extraordinary quilting features stylized
tulips, urns, feathers, and birds. The stitching is easily
discernible on the sheen of the sateen.

◆ 92

Broken Bars Amish Pieced Quilt. c. 1900–10. Lancaster
County, Pennsylvania. Wool, 74×62". Collection America
Hurrah Antiques, New York City. Photograph by Schecter Lee.

The pattern of this early twentieth-century quilt offers an
unusual variation for a Lancaster Amish piece. It is amazingly
contemporary in feeling and even suggestive of a work by
Paul Klee.

◆ 93

Amish Pieced Quilt. c. 1900. Ohio. Cotton, 79 × 64".
Collection Mr. and Mrs. Joseph Carter, III. Photograph courtesy Phyllis Haders.

The combination of electric blues, mauves, and purples (especially the violet) makes
this an unusual and beautiful piece.

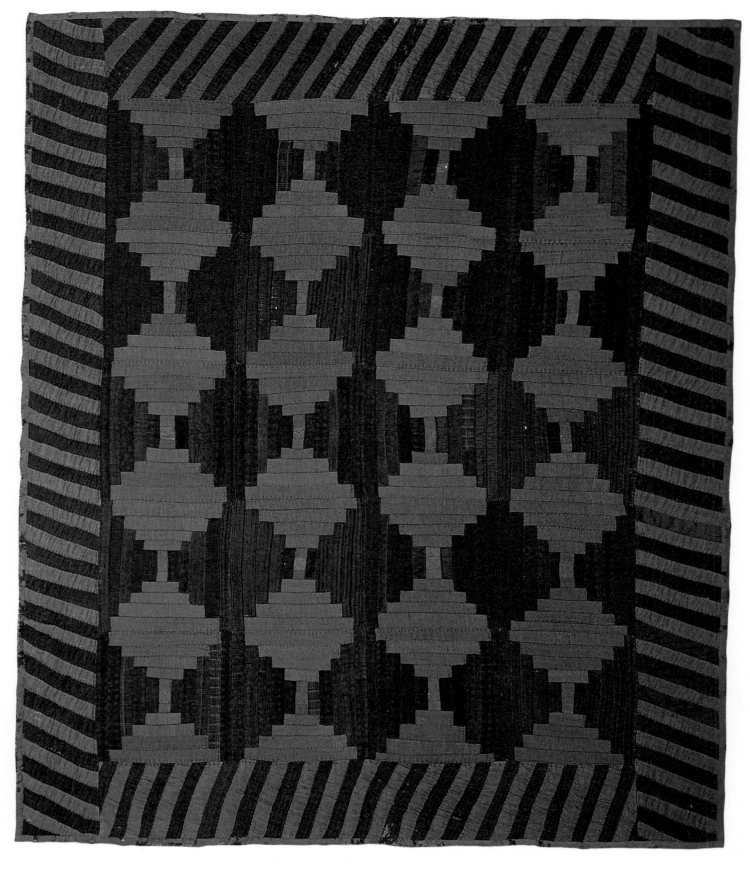

◆ 94

Log Cabin Amish Pieced Cradle Quilt. c. 1860. Lancaster County, Pennsylvania.
Wool, 43×36″. Private collection. Photograph courtesy Phyllis Haders.

A cradle quilt is easily indentifiable because of its size; the dimensions are often half those of a regular bed covering. The quilt is, of course, lighter in weight, as well. With the Amish, such differences are accentuated, particularly as they appear in the Log Cabin motif. Although this design element did not originate with the Amish, they made it one of their own. In this example the Log Cabin design is rendered in a simple, almost nonrepresentational form; each pink square represents a chimney, and each strip represents a log. Bordering the "cabins" are slightly angled bars that suggest plowed fields. The many shades of black, brown, and green, from olive to deep blue, both light and dark, blend to create the Log Cabin form. These elements are punctuated in Amish style by the addition of vivid shocking pink accents; the same pink appears in the outer binding. As with many quilts of the Log Cabin variety, the top and back are joined with simple stitches outlining the rectangular strips. There is no filler or batting between the top and the backing.

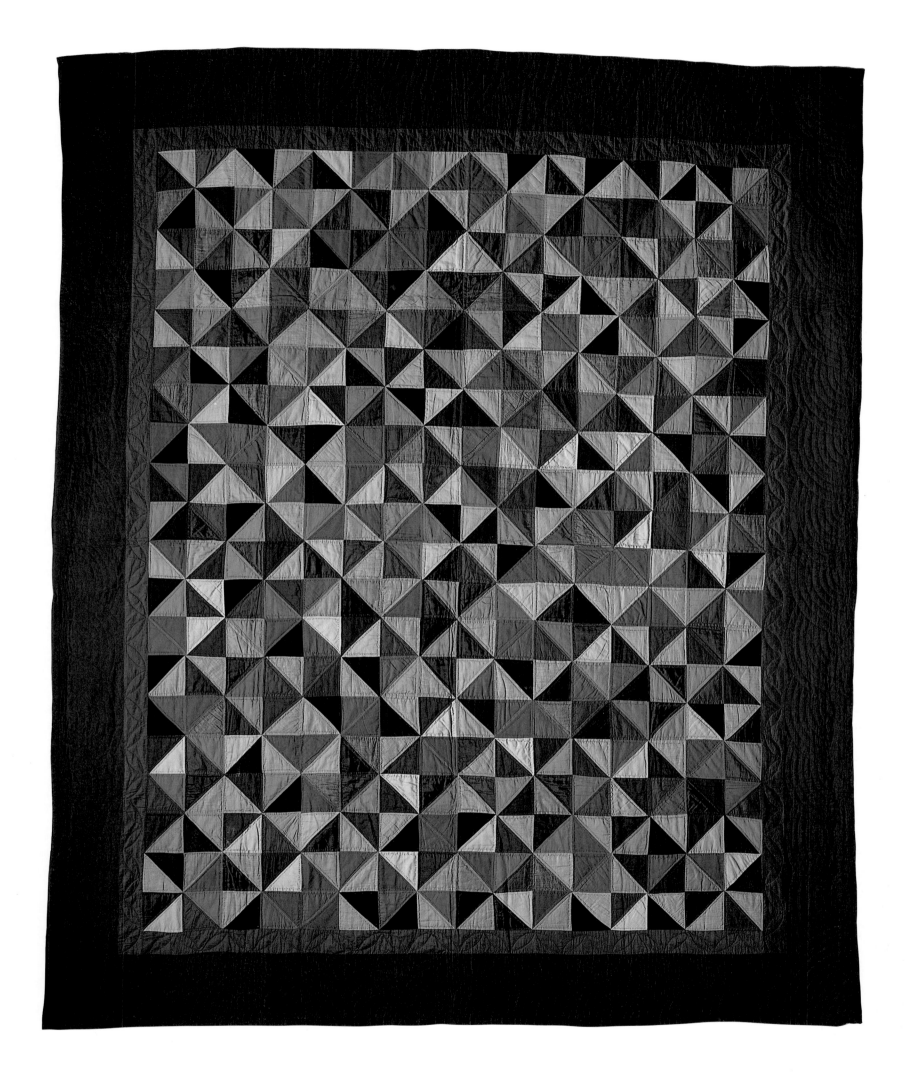

 95

Broken Dishes Amish Pieced Quilt. c. 1930. Midwest. Cotton, 81½ × 69". The Esprit Collection, San Francisco.

This quilt offers a variation of the Pinwheel design, with the "shards" held within the wide outer and narrow inner borders that are typical of Midwestern Amish quilts. The color placement creates an extraordinary impression of movement.

◆ **96**

Prairie Star Pieced and Appliquéd Mennonite Quilt. c. 1870. Upstate New York. Wool, 78×78″. Collection Laura Fisher Quilts and Americana, New York.

The pattern of this Mennonite quilt is also known as Harvest Star, Harvest Sun, and Ship's Wheel. The example combines patterns, materials, and techniques in a unique fashion. The lavender motif appliquéd in the corners of each block is sometimes called Double Hearts or Oak Leaf, and, in this case, is worked in heavy wool, which is unusual for so intricate a design. There is elaborate piecing in the sashing, which joins the star blocks with diamond forms, echoing the construction of the main pattern. The attention to fine detail even extends to the border, which is appliquéd with an inward-facing sawtooth edge framing the entire composition. It's an anomaly to find such fine detailing in combination with such rugged fabrics.

◆ **97**

Double Nine-Patch Amish Pieced Quilt. c. 1920. Lancaster County, Pennsylvania. Wool, 78×80″. The Esprit Collection, San Francisco.

This example is distinguished by the unusual split-bars inner border, and by the way the colors are placed to form a large X through the quilt's center.

 98

Cobweb and Stars Amish Pieced Quilt. c. 1910–20. Iowa. Wool, 63×32″.
Collection America Hurrah Antiques, New York City. Photograph by Schecter Lee.

Because of its dimensions, this size quilt is sometimes called a Hired Man's, as it
would fit the narrow beds intended for itinerant farm workers. However, it seems
unlikely that this particular quilt was used for that purpose. Here, too, the colors
and forms remind one of abstract paintings, especially the work of the French
artist Robert Delaunay.

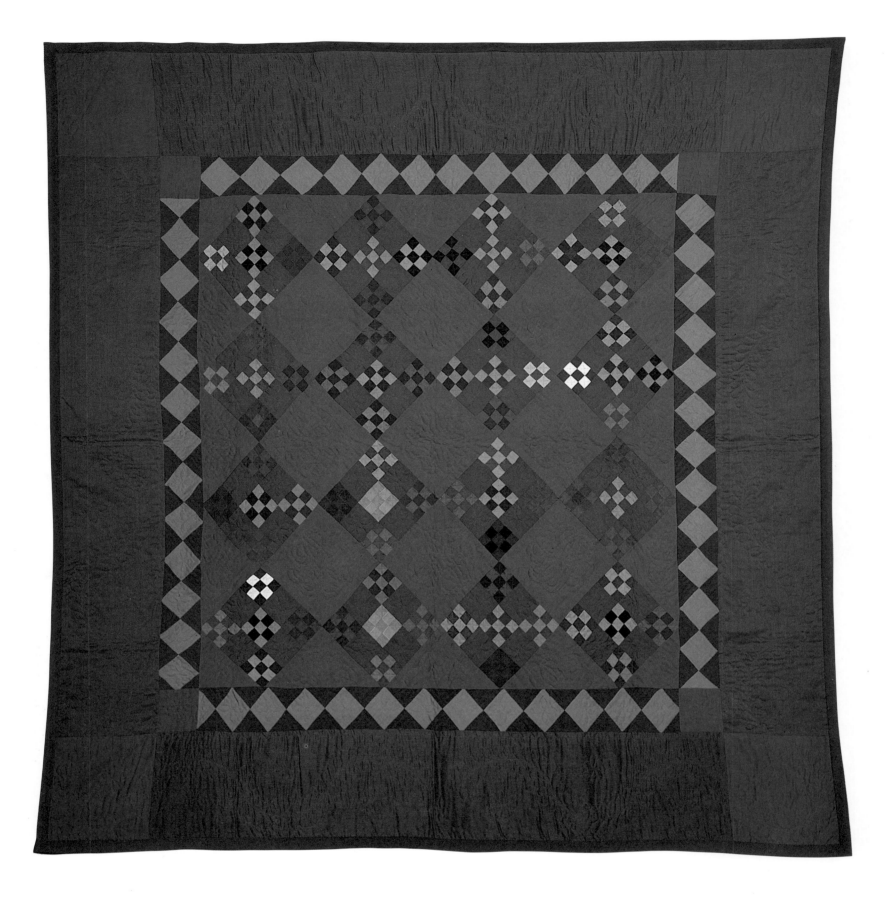

◆ 99

Double Nine-Patch Amish Pieced Quilt. c. 1930. Lancaster County, Pennsylvania. Wool, 82×83".
Collection Phyllis Haders.

The Nine-Patch design is not unique with the Amish, and nine equal squares or diamonds forming a block is found in other American work of the nineteenth century. When five of such blocks are broken up to form nine equal squares or diamonds the design is called a Double Nine-Patch. The handling of color here is unusual: purples, greens, and pinks are of an intensity rarely encountered elsewhere, and they interact stunningly with the blues and reds to define the shapes. The plain blue diamonds hold color and design in place, and the vibrant green diamonds surrounding the center field suggest a fence around a flower garden. The quilting here is limited to the four-petal flowers within the small solid diamonds and in the green diamonds in the border; this is interspersed with the flowing feather stitches of the outer purple border. An unknown quilting pattern was employed in the blue diamonds.

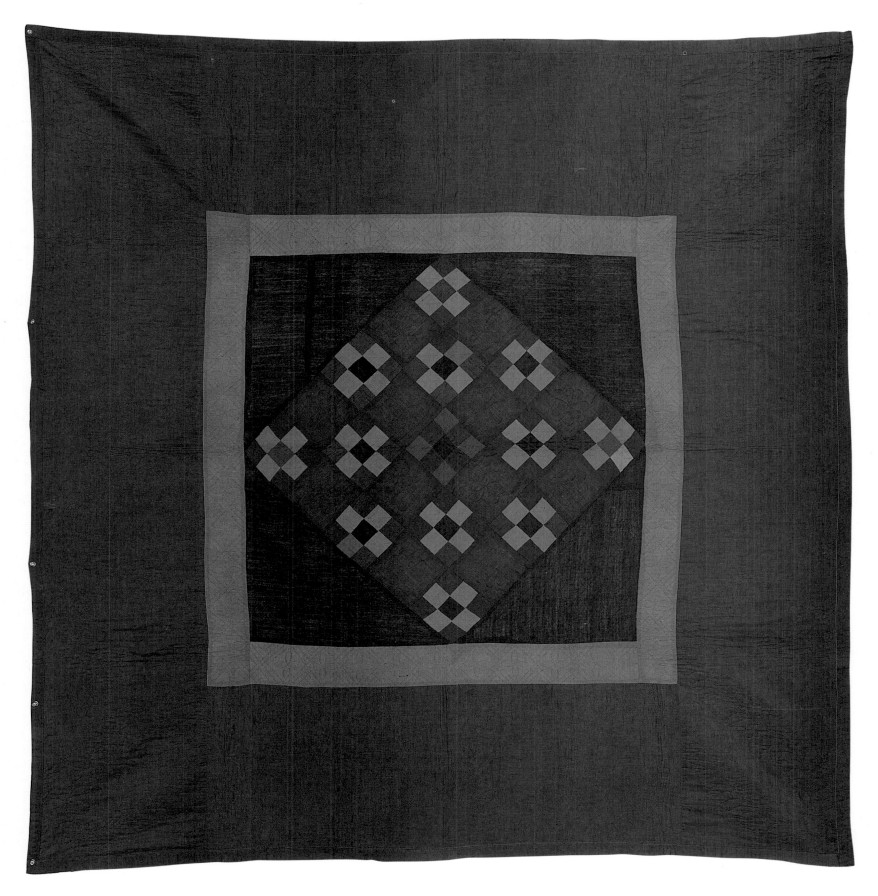

◆ 100

Nine-Patch Diamond in the Square Pieced Quilt. c. 1900. Lancaster County,
Pennsylvania. Wool, 60×62″. Collection Bettie Mintz. Photograph courtesy Bettie Mintz:
All of Us Americans' Folk Art, Bethesda, Maryland.

The design on this quilt is especially rare. Of special note is the central Nine-Patch variation
and the bright scarlet border.

◆ 101

Diamond Amish Pieced Quilt. c. 1900. Lancaster County, Pennsylvania. Wool, 80×80″. Collection Phyllis Haders.

This version of the Diamond is sometimes called Floating Diamond because of the omission of corner blocks. The combination of colors here offers a breathtaking example of the instinctive Amish skill in combining contrasting and complementary hues.

◆ 102

Triple Bars Amish Pieced Quilt. c. 1885. Lancaster County, Pennsylvania. Wool, 80×80″. Collection America Hurrah Antiques, New York City. Photograph by Schecter Lee.

This quilt is exceptionally beautiful because of its subtle colors and the exquisite quilting: especially notable are the eight-pointed star and the wreaths contained in the octagon at center, the baskets in the wide border, and the clusters of grapes and leaves within the narrower border.

◆ 103

Bars Pieced Quilt. c. 1910. Lancaster County, Pennsylvania. Wool, 80×80″. The *Good Housekeeping* Collection. Photograph courtesy Phyllis Haders.

The stitching on this Amish quilt is intricate and well-executed; it offers a good example of the contrast between the bold geometric patterns of the piecing and the graceful, finely detailed patterns of the quilting. The binding here is an exception in such quilts, as it repeats the red.

◆ 104

Diamond in a Square Amish Pieced Quilt. c. 1920. Lancaster County, Pennsylvania.
Wool, 80×80". Collection Bettie Mintz.

The quilting within the border of this quilt attracts the viewer's eye to the quilted cross
located within the scarlet center.

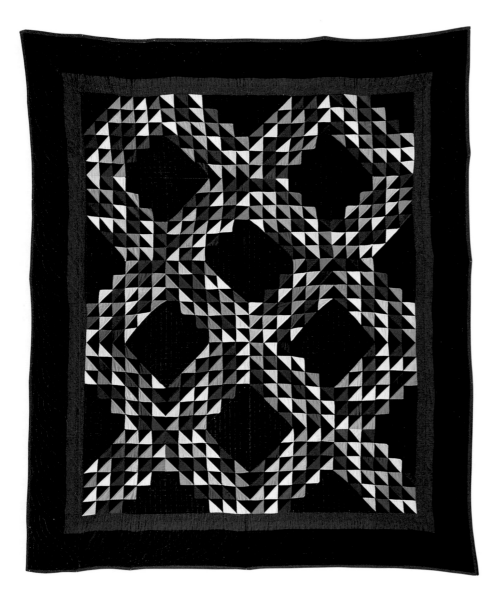

◆ 105

Ocean Waves Amish Pieced Quilt. c. 1930–40.
Holmes County, Ohio. Cotton, 76×68″.
Collection America Hurrah Antiques,
New York City. Photograph by Schecter Lee.

The color and placement of the triangles offer a
kaleidoscopic effect reminiscent of 1960s Op
Art. Note, too, the double-banded inner border.

◆ 106

Hand-Pieced Amish Quilt. c. 1935. Indiana. Cotton,
80×68″. The *Good Housekeeping* Collection.
Photograph courtesy Phyllis Haders.

Note here the only red hand motif in the center
row, third from the bottom. The name for this
pattern should not be confused with Hand quilts,
the designs of which were rendered by tracing
the contour of actual hands.

◆ 107

Solomon's Puzzle Amish Pieced Quilt. c. 1940. Ohio. Wool, 53½ × 38¼".
Collection Deborah Harding, New York. Photograph by Rene Velez.

The colors in this crib quilt—especially the celadon gray-green—are subdued and very sophisticated for a Midwest Amish quilt of the period. This pattern, known elsewhere as Drunkard's Path, is accomplished by cutting arcs out of squares and then arranging the pieces in a positive-negative relation. There is outline-quilting around the sections in the center of the piece, a rope-pattern is in the black border, and interlocking diamonds and ovals are in the outer green border.

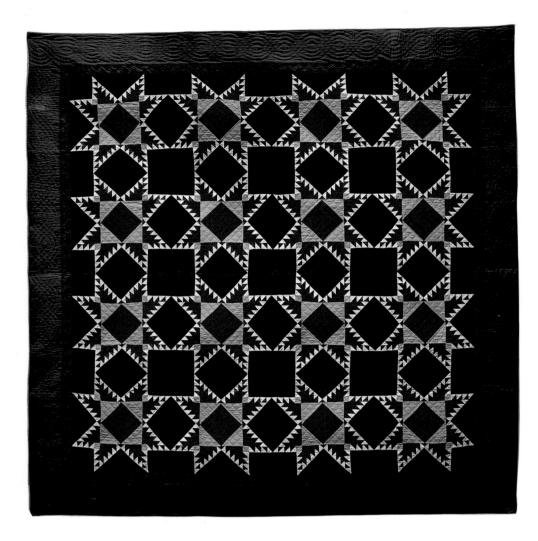

◆ **108**

Feathered Star with Streak O' Lightning Border Mennonite Quilt. c. 1890. Pennsylvania. Cotton, 80×80″. Private collection. Photograph by Schecter Lee, courtesy America Hurrah Antiques, New York City.

The use of the pattern here is interesting because the stars are touching and the white sawtooth "feathers" offer a dramatic highlight framing the stars.

◆ **109**

Schoolhouse Amish Pieced Quilt. c. 1920. Ohio. Cotton, 77×69″. The Esprit Collection, San Francisco.

The Amish rarely employ representational designs; perhaps they take the biblical injunction literally and thus believe that they are prohibited from making "graven images." Therefore, this work represents an extremely unusual— as well as a highly successful—example of an Ohio Amish quilt. Notable, too, are the Nine-Patch blocks and the feathered wreath quilting over each house motif.

◆ 110

"Lizzie's Quilt": Fans Amish Pieced Quilt. 1899. Topeka, Indiana. Wool, cotton, and silk, 66×76".
Collection Phyllis Haders.

On May 10, 1899, sixteen-year-old Lizzie Amanda Sundheimer was invited to a quilting bee in an Amish home. An orphan since the age of eight, she lived with various relatives who provided her with the guidance and love that mark any Old Order homestead. Because Lizzie was considered to be a "sweet and sunny girl," her friends in the community decided to make her a quilt as a sign of their affection. "Forget Me Not," "Remember Me," and "Think of Me" were some of the simple sentiments embroidered in the individual squares. The quilters' names are there too, along with Lizzie's: Katie, Ida, and Sarah, among others. It is said that this quilt once included other good wishes and other names, but these were ripped out when a church deacon proclaimed that the design was a "little worldly." Indeed it is. The embroidery or decorative stitches are unusual for an Amish quilt, and the colored fan shapes are very exuberant in tonality and texture. While primarily made of wool, the fan strips also are made of fine cotton and even a few heavy silk brocades and ribbons. Such costly fabrics could be used by the Amish only if they were received as gifts and used as a measure of frugality. Cherished and rare bits of cloth show the love and devotion that went into making this quilt. As in many other Amish pieces, the quilting is executed in a subdued and graceful feather pattern. A single tulip appears at the base of each fan. All that strikes the unpracticed eye, however, are the strong bands of patterned color. When Lizzie Sundheimer first saw her friendship album, the quilting had yet to be completed, and this was accomplished in one day. It was, one witness declared, "the best bee ever sat."

HAWAIIAN QUILTS

HAWAIIAN QUILTS

Lee S. Wild

hen the Hawaiian Islands were annexed by the United States in 1898, our nation inherited the art of Hawaiian quilting. Western influences on the native culture of the Hawaiians evolved along indigenous lines into a distinctive type of needlework, the designs of which incorporate and reflect personal expressions of beauty, memories shared and recorded, and events commemorated and preserved. To appreciate the Hawaiian quilt, it is necessary to investigate the evolution of this Hawaiian craft and to understand how it was influenced by Western culture.

Long before native Hawaiians were thrust into contact with Western culture they were proficient in making *tapa*, a paperlike fabric used for clothing, bed coverings, burial wrappings, and even lamp wicks. Most tapa was made from the inner bark of the *wauke* plant (*Broussonetia papyrifera*, or paper mulberry). Tapa was usually made by women, who employed wooden mallets to pound the strips of bark together to form sheets of various sizes, textures, and thicknesses. Color and decoration were then added, making each piece unique.

Bark-clothing bedding, or *kapa moe*, was used for coverlets; most often these were made of four or five sheets of uniform-sized tapa placed over bedding that consisted of multilayered mats piled on the floor. The undecorated inner sheets of the *kapa moe* were topped by a colored or decorated cover called *kilohana*. The various layers were attached to one another by beating along one edge of the sheets of tapa, although sometimes the edges were glued together with diluted poi, a Hawaiian foodstuff made from taro root. Tapa was colored by native dyes, and the decoration consisted of freehand designs applied with single-pronged and—possibly —multipronged pens.

With the discovery of the Hawaiian Islands by Captain James Cook in 1778 and the subsequent arrival of explorers, merchants, whalers, and missionaries, new techniques and designs developed and were incorporated or creatively adapted by the native Hawaiians. These foreign elements were rapidly integrated into the traditional culture, and the indigenous craftsmen recognized that

---

PRECEDING PAGE: *Ku´u Hae Aloha (My Beloved Flag) Appliqué Quilt* (detail). Before 1918. Waimea (Big Island). Cotton. Honolulu Academy of Arts. Gift of Mrs. Richard A. Cooke, 1927.

newly introduced metal tools could easily be adapted to traditional techniques. Designs and motifs thus became increasingly detailed. Thin stampers were made from split bamboo, and delicate and refined designs were incised onto them. Such stampers were colored with dye and used to print designs on the tapa. In the eighteenth and nineteenth centuries, complex watermark designs became a hallmark of Hawaiian tapa; the eighteenth-century stamped designs are believed to have been executed in a technique unique to the islands.

Western cloth was introduced during these centuries, with calicoes, chintzes, and Chinese silks gradually becoming available via trade with the West and China. As a result, the pen-drawn or hand-printed decorations on the tapa soon began to imitate the patterns of these fabrics.

Eventually a new technique was invented to decorate the cover sheets of the *kapa moe*: Shredded red cloth was overlaid onto white *kapa*, and the two were beaten together to form a single sheet called *pa'i'ula*. Sewing the edges of *kapa moe* together replaced the methods of beating and gluing. Needles were made of wood or bone, and the thread was a strip of white tapa or a two-ply fiber.

Although these new techniques were the result of Western contact, the use to which they were put illustrates the Hawaiian characteristic of adapting to change. Indigenous Hawaiians also began imitating what they believed to be a superior culture by closely approximating fashionable Western clothing and accessories. Archibald Campbell (who came to Hawaii aboard a Russian vessel in 1809), a Scottish resident of the islands in the early nineteenth century, wrote:

> *It is astonishing how soon they [the natives] acquire the useful arts from their visitors. Many of the natives are employed as carpenters, coopers, blacksmiths, and tailors, and do their work as perfectly as Europeans.*

In 1819, Louis de Freycinet, captain of the French vessel *Uranie*, noted:

> *Some of the chiefs have adopted the European type of clothing either completely or in part. . . . The same is true of women living with whites on Wahou [Oahu].*

It is not known exactly when the appliquéd Hawaiian quilt evolved; however, the making of patchwork quilts was introduced to Hawaiians by the wives of American missionaries. The first missionaries arrived aboard the brig *Thaddeus* in 1820; they were welcomed warmly by some of the highest chiefs of the nation. Lucy Thurston, the wife of one of these missionaries, recorded in her journal that one of the Hawaiian women had on board

> *. . . a web of white cambric to have a dress made for herself in the fashion of those of our ladies, and was very particular in her wish to have it finished while sailing, before reaching the king. . . . Monday morning, April 3rd [1820], the first sewing circle was formed that the sun ever looked down upon in his Hawaiian realm. Kalakua, queen-dowager, was directress. She requested all the seven white ladies to take seats with them on mats, on the deck of the* Thaddeus. *Mrs. Holman and Mrs. Ruggles were executive officers to ply the scissors and prepare the work. . . . The four native women of distinction were furnished with calico patchwork to sew—a new employment to them.*

The missionaries' program included the teaching of domestic arts, among which was sewing. It was initially taught on an informal basis in homes and was introduced into the school curriculum in 1830. As Hawaiians' skills became more proficient, the women chiefly used rich

Chinese silks and brocades acquired through barter and made dresses for themselves similar to those worn by the newly arrived white women.

The products of these endeavors were leftover scraps of fabric that were ideal for patchwork quilting, and students of both sexes were instructed in this art. The son of one of the missionaries (who was to become a general and found Hampton Institute in Virginia), Samuel Chapman Armstrong, wrote:

> *My own earliest recollection [around 1850, when the writer was eleven] . . . of Mrs. Rice's sewing class, where we made quilts for the Oregon Indians . . . [when dismissed from the room] we would scamper out of doors—but not until our too often disapproved stitching had been examined.*

As patchwork quilting developed, Hawaiian women began to incorporate traditional and familiar tapa designs into their quilts. According to Dorothy B. Barrere,

> *most Hawaiian patchwork quilts . . . tend to follow traditional patterns, with individuality expressed by color arrangement. The traditional patterns are extensions of* kapa *designs, especially the* kapa *beater motifs. . . . The Hawaiian appliquéd quilt—*kapa lau *or* kapa 'apana*—likewise was inspired by the* kapa *patterns.*

As the Western cloth, fashions, and quilts were integrated into native ways, the making of tapa declined, and by the end of the nineteenth century it was no longer being produced. The *kapa moe* was therefore replaced by the *kapa*, or Hawaiian appliqué quilt, which was developed into a distinctive art. The most striking characteristic of what eventually became a traditional craft lies in the technique, which entailed cutting an overall design from a single piece of fabric that was then appliquéd onto a solid-color cloth, after which it was quilted.

There are different theories regarding the origin of this uniquely Hawaiian method. According to a popular story, a woman set up a sheet to dry on the grass; noticing a design cast on it, formed by the leafy shadow of a nearby tree, she was inspired to incorporate it into the quilt design. Stella Jones, a noted pioneer in the study of Hawaiian quilts, wrote:

> *To cut new materials into bits to be sewn together [for a patchwork quilt] seemed a futile waste of time. It was quite natural, therefore, that these women, accustomed each to her own design on her tapa beater and her own individual woodlocked patterns, should produce patterns of their own.*

In her study of the quilts of Polynesia, Joyce Hammond offers the following theory:

> *The Hawaiian appliqué quilt probably represents the Hawaiian modification of Western appliqué quilts. Such quilts did exist at the time the missionaries introduced the more practical piece-work quilt of everyday use. . . . There are many indications that the aura of prestige and wealth associated with the less common Western appliqué quilt may have influenced the Hawaiians in their selection of a quilt style to emulate. Although the method of cutting an overall design from a single piece of fabric is unique to Polynesia, the Hawaiians may have developed the technique after seeing small Western appliqué designs created in a similar manner.*

Perhaps we shall never know exactly how or when this distinctive art form originated.

Nevertheless, it resulted from the successful integration of styles and techniques from diverse cultures.

The techniques inherent in *kapa* making followed certain progressive steps. The material was washed to make sure of its color fastness. In early times this task was often relegated to children, who took the fabric to the shore and rinsed it in sea water. A piece of material too small to incorporate the entire design was seamed lengthwise. The fabric was then folded into eighths, the border was cut, and then the center design was cut. Some quilters preferred a quarter fold as opposed to the more traditional eighths. Some women cut the design freehand with scissors; others first cut a paper pattern.

In some cases the central design consisted of four or more separate pieces placed symmetrically around the quilt's center. Of course, the designer was not limited to such options, and there were many variations of these basic guidelines.

The cut design was then basted to the top sheet (often with the help of friends or relatives), starting at the center and working outward to the edges. The actual appliqué work was most often done only by the owner of the quilt. Batting was then inserted between the decorated top sheet and the fabric backing. Materials used for batting included soft fibers from tree fern (*pulu*), wool, cotton, and domestic animal hair. The three layers were stitched together, again starting at the center and working outward. At times quilting was a group project; at other times it was done entirely by the owner. Quilting horses (large frames onto which the quilt was rolled) were set close to the ground so that the quilters could sit on mats.

Early appliqué designs tended to be attenuated and fairly simple, with much of the background fabric remaining visible, but it was not long before the designs became progressively bolder and more complex. At first the quilting styles were those taught by the missionaries: parallel, circular, or diagonal lines. The Hawaiians eventually incorporated stitching forms inspired by their own traditional crafts, such as the woven patterns of *lauhala* mats, tapa designs, and motifs taken from nature, including shells, fish scales, and turtleshells; some of these patterns are believed to be uniquely Hawaiian. Eventually this evolved into what is now regarded as the typical Hawaiian technique of quilting: stitching that paralleled the inner and outer edges of the appliquéd designs. This type of contour quilting (also known as echo quilting) is called *kuiki lau* and imparts a three-dimensional or relief quality to the quilt, which often is described as resembling the waves of the ocean. Such wavelike rows of quilting impart life to the quilt and create a complementary motif.

The stitching used in such appliqué quilts was usually an overcast stitch, and ideally the parallel rows of stitches should be half an inch apart. However, other types of stitching were also employed to reflect the creativity—and doubtless the patience as well—of the quilter.

At first, fabric selection depended on what was available. A bright solid color was usually chosen for the appliquéd design, and white sheeting was used for the background. In the early 1800s, turkey red (named after the country, not the fowl) was the most common Western fabric available in Hawaii, and many early quilts incorporated a red-on-white color scheme. Some have suggested that the origin of this combination of colors was the red-on-white *pa'i'ula* cover sheets seen on many of the *kapa moe*. As new fabrics became available, they were incorporated into this evolving art form; chintzes, calicoes, and dotted swiss soon appeared on these quilts.

The variety of designs of the Hawaiian *kapa* was limited only by the imagination of the maker and was a matter of personal inspiration and self-expression. Early designs echoed the patterns on the tapas, but they gradually evolved in new directions, capturing the beauty of plant life and recording personal experiences, episodes of daily life, and the changing course of the Hawaiian nation. Important personal or historic incidents, symbols of the islands' beloved and trusted royalty, and images evoked by dreams were memorialized.

Designs inspired by nature were probably the first and most frequently used. The *lehua* blossom of the island of Hawaii, the *kukui* of Molokai, the *ilima* of Oahu, the *lokelani* of Maui, and the *mokihana* of Kauai were all popular subjects for quilters residing on those islands. The *ulu*, or breadfruit—a major food source for Hawaiians—was incorporated in designs by quilters throughout the islands. Today it is traditional that the first piece put on a quilt should ideally be the breadfruit design—if this motif is added first, the quilter will continue to make many additional quilts. As new plants were introduced to the islands, they found their way into the designs. The fuchsia, plumeria, hibiscus, torch ginger (*Phaeomaria magnifica*), hydrangea, morning glory, carnation, tuberose, chrysanthemum, pineapple (which, despite popular belief, is not native), tobacco, and many others began to appear. Among the most popular floral motifs were lilies, and soon there were quilts called Lily of the Valley, Kohala's Star Lily, Lily of Ireland, Lily of Nuuanu, Lilies in a Vase, Day Lily, Lily of Spain, Drooping Lily, and others.

Also inspired by nature were designs evoking the winds and rains so vital to the islanders' life: the Crackling Winds of Kohala, the Winds of Waimea, the Soft Rainfall of Manoa, the Mist of Mount Kaala, the Chilly Wind of Kipahulu, and the Rain of Haao.

Historic events and personal incidents were commemorated in the following quilts: *Manu Lawe Leka* (the Carrier Pigeon) was reputed to record the beginning of regular mail service to the island of Kauai; *Ka Hoku Hele O Ka PakiPika* celebrated the appearance of Halley's Comet; *Ehuwai O Niakala* (Mist of Niagara Falls) recorded a visit to those falls; *Ka Mokupuni Kihapai* (the Garden Island) commemorated the founding of the newspaper in 1904; and *Nani O Niumalu* (Niumalu Beauty) commemorated the new harbor at Nawiliwili on Kauai.

Symbols of royalty signified the unquestionable trust the Hawaiians placed in the guardians of their culture—their *alii* (sovereigns). Favorite subjects that appeared in many combinations were the kingdom's coat of arms, crowns, fans, *kahili* (royal standards), and the rulers' wreaths. Designs depict Queen Kaahumanu's (favorite wife of King Kamehameha I; following his death, she co-ruled the kingdom with Kamehameha II) crown and her *kahili*; Queen Emma's (wife of Kamehameha IV) vase, garden, lamp, and home; and the crowns, fans, and *kahili* of Queen Kapiolani (King Kalakaua's wife), Queen Liliuokalani (sister of Kalakana and last ruling monarch of Hawaii), and Princess Kaiulani (Liliuokalani's niece, who was designated her heir, but who died before Liliuokalani). Among the other monarchs and their symbols represented in the quilts are King Kamehameha IV, King Lunalilo, and King Kalakaua.

There are also a number of quilts depicting chandeliers in the royal residences, including those in the palace in Kona—Queen Emma's home—and those hanging in the spectacular Iolani Palace. The palace was completed in 1882 during the reign of King Kalakaua and became an inspiration for many quilters. The gaslights of the palace, the vases etched in the glass of the doors, and the torches on the grounds also were depicted in many contemporary Hawaiian quilts. The pavilion constructed for Kalakaua's coronation in 1883 also became a popular motif, as did his private residence, Haleakala, which was built on the palace grounds.

Perhaps the most beloved of all were quilts named *Kuu Hae Aloha* (My Beloved Flag), depicting the flag of the Hawaiian kingdom. The Hawaiian Flag quilt may have appeared as early as 1843 when Lord George Paulet of the British Navy claimed possession of the Sandwich Islands (named by Captain Cook) for Great Britain. Although the Union Jack flew over the Islands for only five months—after which sovereignty was returned to King Kamehameha III—the Hawaiian people realized the tenuous status of their island nation, and it is probable that the Hawaiian Flag quilt was designed during that period. There was a great resurgence in this special pattern when Queen Liliuokalani was deposed in 1893 and when the United States annexed the islands in 1898. Although Hawaiian Flag quilts and Coat of Arms quilts appear in a variety of styles, each remains a special reminder of a kingdom that no longer exists.

Naming a quilt was a highly personal matter. The inspiration for a particular design was not necessarily reflected in the name given by the quilter; as they designed, many women incorporated meanings known only to themselves. Thus, the name bears no relation to the subject matter depicted, and the interpretation is kept secret. Some quilts have a meaning expressed with Hawaiian subtlety, some are allegorical, yet others embody a completely private meaning (*kaona*).

Many quilt makers guarded their designs jealously, while others freely shared their patterns as a mark of friendship with the understanding that each quilt made from that particular pattern would bear the same name the quilter gave it. Others shared their designs with the understanding that the name of the quilt per se would be changed. Today some quilters share their patterns with the entreaty that the new owner change it to please herself and give it her own name. Jealously guarded designs were rarely copied without permission of the owner for fear of embarrassment or shame should the "theft" be discovered.

As a result of these traditions many variations of a basic design bearing a variety of names may be found today. The original design, the intent of the quilter, and the original name have been lost. In such cases a recurring theme found in the names of these pieces often gives a clue to the origin. For example, the quilt design generically known as *Ka U'i O Maui* (the Beauty of Maui) has also been named *Lei Roselani* (Heavenly Rose Lei, the rose being the flower of the island of Maui), *Noho O Pi'ilani* (Pi'ilani Ancestry, the Pi'ilani family being a royal family of Maui), *Piko O Haleakala* (the Summit of Haleakala, Haleakala being a volcano on Maui), and *Kahului Breakwater* (Kahului is located on Maui). From these examples it could be inferred that the design originated on the island of Maui. However, a few quilt makers have no particular reason to refer to Maui when giving their quilts such names; thus, a "Maui" design can also be called Helene's Lei, the Pearl of Ewa (on Oahu), and *Lihilihi Anuenue* (the Edge of the Rainbow).

In most cases the more variations on a basic design and the greater variety of names given to that particular design, the older it is believed to be. This makes students of Hawaiian quiltmaking especially curious regarding the origin of the design and the intent of its maker.

Today Hawaiian quilting is practiced with the same creativity and enthusiasm. New designs are invented to memorialize current local events, newly introduced plants, and memories worthy of preservation. Old designs are still utilized, incorporating subtle alterations that enhance the beauty of each piece, and patterns are still shared. There are many quilting classes and clubs throughout the state, and Hawaiian quilts may be seen in most local museums. The Waianae branch of the Library of Hawaii houses a collection of some four hundred quilt patterns that are available to anyone wishing to copy them, and a thriving commercial pattern industry also exists.

Although there are still individuals who prefer not to share their patterns or refuse to have their older quilts photographed (a prerogative respected by those who understand the traditions of the past), many of the old taboos surrounding this art are dying out.

 111

Appliqué Quilt. Nineteenth century. Hawaiian Islands. Cotton, 99½ × 84". Honolulu Academy of Arts. Gift of Mrs. Herman V. Von Holt, 1966.

This stunning quilt is unnamed, or at least its original name and significance have been lost. It belonged to the family of the donor.

112

Lei Mamo (Mamo Lei) Appliqué Quilt. Late nineteenth century. Hawaiian Islands. Cotton, 80 × 80″.
Honolulu Academy of Arts. Gift of Damon Giffard, 1959.

The motif is a stylization of a native blossom. The quilt was a prizewinner in the 1943 quilt competition held in conjunction with an exhibition at the Honolulu Academy, "Hawaii Farm as Home." It belonged to the grandmother of the donor, who was born a Brickwood, the family for which this quilt was made.

113

Mary Sophie Rice ("Mother Rice"). *Na Kalaunu Me Na Kahali (Crowns and Kahalis) Appliqué Quilt*. 1886. Island of Kauai. Cotton, 75×75". Honolulu Academy of Arts. Gift of Mrs. Thomas D. King, Jr., 1973.

It is thought that the creator of this stunning piece—popularly known as Mother Rice—made the quilt when she was 69; she lived another quarter-century, and died in 1911 at the age of 94.

114

Ku-U-Hae Appliqué Quilt. c. 1900. Hawaii. Cotton, 79×79". The Shelburne Museum, Shelburne, Vermont. Gift of George G. Frelinghuysen, California.

The royal Hawaiian flag has continued to remain a popular quilt motif, although the last member of the royal family abdicated almost a century ago. This appliquéd quilt incorporates the Islands' coat of arms surrounded by Hawaiian flags. Flag quilts such as this are not as typical as quilts bearing motifs inspired by nature.

115

Garden Island Appliqué Quilt. 1904, Island of Kauai. Cotton, 83½×73½". Honolulu Academy of Arts. Gift of Mrs. C.M. Cooke Estate, 1938.

This pattern commemorates the founding of *Garden Island*, the first newspaper published on the Island of Kauai in 1904. The pattern consists of floral motifs.

116

Lihilili Anuenue (The Edge of the Rainbow) Appliqué Quilt. Before 1918. Hawaiian Islands.
Cotton, 87×87". Honolulu Academy of Arts. Gift of Mrs. C. M. Cooke Estate, 1938.

This pattern was originally identified as a probable variation of *Kaui O Maui* (Maui Beauty); the present, highly poetic name was given in an article that appeared in the November 1949 issue of *Paradise of the Pacific*, when the quilt was shown at the Honolulu Academy of Arts.

117

Kaomi Malie (Press Gently) Appliqué Quilt. Before 1918. Hawaiian Islands. Cotton, 85 × 83½". Honolulu Academy of Arts. Gift of Mrs. Albert Wilcox, 1927.

This widely exhibited quilt incorporates the typical Hawaiian floral/foliate motifs.

118

Ka Na Kani Lehau (The Rain that Rustles Lehua Blossoms) Appliqué Quilt. Before 1918. Hawaiian Islands. Cotton, 82½ × 99½". Hololulu Academy of Arts. Gift of Mrs. Levi Laurence, 1956. This example contrasts with a warm glow with the quilt above and shows how the foliate motif is a point of departure for variations in the pairing of joyful colors.

🔲 119

Na Kihapi Nani Lua 'Ole O Edena A Me Elenale (The Garden of Eden and the Garden of Elenale) Appliqué Quilt. Before 1918. Hawaiian Islands. Cotton, 86 × 98" (including fringe). Honolulu Academy of Arts. Gift of Mrs. Charles M. Cooke, 1929.

Ioela Kaikahi, who sold the quilt to the foundress of the Honolulu Academy of Arts, Mrs. C. M. Cooke, recorded that it was "made by a great, great-granduncle of my husband and handed down to him by an uncle." In 1985, a highly respected and still active Hawaiian quilter, Mr. F. C. M. Kaikainahaole, reported that the oral history of his Kaikaina-haole/Puhalahua family confirms such an origin, although he did not know how the quilt passed from the possession of his grandmother, Mrs. Koolau K. Maile, who he believes owned it prior to her death in the 1920s, to Mrs. Kaihaki.

    The design depicts the biblical progenitors and a celebrated hero and heroine from Hawaiian lore, whose romance was serialized in the magazine *Ka Lei Momi* in the early 1900s: the first known work written by a Hawaiian in the Hawaiian language. There are many different versions of the romance and of the origins of Elenale, the otherworldly hero raised in a magical garden, and of Leinaala, oftentimes depicted as an earthly princess (in the quilter's imagination, and hence in this design, she strongly resembles photographs of Queen Emma). The Garden of Elenale and the Garden of Eden were popularly considered "the two most beautif ' gardens ever known."

![120]

Ku'u Hae Aloha (My Beloved Flag) Appliqué Quilt. Before 1918. Waimea (Big Island). Cotton, 85½ × 83″. Honolulu Academy of Arts. Gift of Mrs. Richard A. Cooke, 1927.

Richly colored and patterned, this quilt is yet another reflection of the Hawaiian affection for their national flag.

121

Ku'u Hae Aloha (My Beloved Flag) Appliqué Quilt. Before 1918. Hawaiian Islands. Cotton, 99½ × 82½".
Honolulu Academy of Arts. Gift of Mrs. Levi Laurence, 1956.

The present work, exemplifying the Hawaiian affection for their flag, is extremely colorful, and represents a departure from the usual two-color Hawaiian quilts. The eight flags, paired in groups, surround a central motif depicting the Islands' coat of arms.

 122

Appliquéd Hawaiian Quilt. c. 1920. Hawaii.
Cotton, 81×59". Collection Phyllis Haders.

The appliqués exemplify the typical Hawaiian technique
of pattern design, that of folding paper squares into quarters
and cutting out the design. However, it is more usual to
find one large design on a quilt top rather than four designs
with a top and bottom border as in the present example.
The stitching here is particularly fine.

123

Mrs. Montgomery. *Niumalu or Nawilili Beauty Appliqué
Quilt*. 1930. Hawaiian Islands. Cotton, 91×61". Honolulu
Academy of Arts. Gift of Dora Isenberg, 1940.

The present example was first exhibited off-island in
1938–39, when it was shown at the Folk Arts Center in
New York.

124

Mary Hussey. *Ka Uhi Wai O Kaala (Mist of Mt. Kaala)
Appliqué Quilt*. 1955. Kailua, Hawaii.
Cotton, 84×84". Bernice Pauahi Bishop Museum.

This fine example of Hawaiian quilting is one of the type
usually known to natives as *Ka Uhi Wai O Kaala* (The Mist
of Mt. Kaala, or Kaala Mist). The sensitive use of maroon
and white cottons demonstrates the maker's sincere expression of the true meaning of *Aloha*. This piece was
exhibited at the prestigious Mission Houses Museum in
Honolulu.

125

Na Kalauno (Crowns) Appliqué Quilt. Before 1918. Hawaiian Islands. Cotton, 82½ × 81½".
Honolulu Academy of Arts. Gift of Mrs. C. M. Cooke Estate, 1938.

Eight crowns surround a central leaf medallion that in turn is surrounded by palm-like fronds. The rich colors are complementary: lavender and yellow.

QUILTS—
CRAZY
MEMORIES

QUILTS— CRAZY MEMORIES

Virginia Gunn

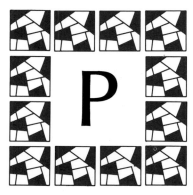

eople have speculated about the maker of the first crazy quilt. Such quilts captured public attention in the decade following the United States Centennial, a time during which Americans succumbed to a mania for the decorative arts. Crazy quilts differed greatly from the traditional variety composed of symmetrically arranged and carefully matched pieces. To make a crazy-quilt block, one began with a foundation square of calico or muslin and covered it completely with odd-shaped scraps of silk in an asymmetrical or randomly haphazard arrangement, then overlapped the irregular pieces, turned in the raw edges, and invisibly stitched the scraps in place. Finally, using embroidery silk or filoselle, the quilt maker decorated the seams with point Russe, feather, herringbone, and other fancy stitches. On the most elaborate blocks, embroidered, appliquéd, or painted designs were also added to the individual pieces. These busy, intricate blocks then were assembled to create crazy-quilt tops with "frantic" or exotic effects.

By 1884, it appeared to the editor of *Dorcas Magazine* that "of all the 'crazes' which have swept over and fairly engulfed some of us, there is none which has taken a deeper hold upon the fair women of our land than this one of crazy patchwork."

Demorest's Monthly Magazine reported that in one year, members of a quiet New York City family used crazywork on three quilts, three large pillows, several table scarfs, chair cushions, and a piano cover, and planned to do even more. Crazy quilts sold for the extraordinary sums of $75 to $100, and one featuring Oscar Wilde in Aesthete costume brought $150 at a fair. Although entrepreneurs such as the Yale Silk Works claimed in their advertisements to be "the originators

---

PRECEDING PAGE: Florence Elizabeth Marvin. *Pieced, Appliqué, and Embroidered Crazy Quilt* (detail). 1886. Brooklyn Heights, New York. Silk and velvet. Collection America Hurrah Antiques, New York City. Photograph by Schecter Lee.

of the Silk Patchwork Craze,'' crazy quilts really represent a grass-roots response to Aesthetic era influences.[1]

The earliest mention of a crazy quilt so far discovered appears in *Our Acre and Its Harvest*, the history of the Soldiers' Aid Society of Northern Ohio (a branch of the United States Sanitary Commission). Mary Brayton described an innovative fundraising idea used at the Cleveland Sanitary Fair in February 1864:

> *Above the grim surroundings of this busy corner hangs the ''crazy bedquilt,'' a grotesque piece of newspaper patchwork, which is sold by lot every day, with the express condition that the unlucky possessor is not obliged to keep it, but will be allowed to present it to the fair. A considerable sum of money and a great deal of fun are realized by this transaction which takes place every noon just as the clock strikes twelve.[2]*

Cleveland women used the word ''crazy'' to describe a design they found unusual and ''grotesque.'' They recognized the quilt's fantastic or bizarre quality, which was created by combining strange elements in an incongruous manner for eye-catching effect. This newspaper patchwork ''crazy quilt'' does not seem to have inspired the hundreds of women who saw it to make copies in fabric. After the war, city women made fewer patchwork quilts, preferring to decorate their bedrooms with commercially prepared white counterpanes and Marseilles spreads. Country women continued to make quilts in the traditional manner.

Beautiful silk Log Cabin quilts had been prominently displayed at Civil War sanitary fairs. This type became very popular in the 1870s, although rural women often made them of wool or cotton instead of silk. Agricultural fair committees even created special categories for the numerous Log Cabin quilts. In making log cabin blocks, women utilized the pressed patchwork technique. They worked on a foundation fabric block and covered it by stitching strips of fabric around a center or starter piece. They later adjusted this method to make crazy quilts.

New needlework ideas inspired interest as the influence of Japanese design—as well as the Aesthetic philosophies of England's John Ruskin and William Morris—began to reach America. In 1872 Charles Eastlake's *Hints on Household Taste* found a ready audience and inspired others to write articles urging women to use ''artistic furniture'' and create ''artistic homes.'' In democratic America it was believed that beauty should not be limited to the luxurious mansions of the wealthy but should also be found in humble homes throughout the land. Women could overcome economic handicaps with good taste and skill and could beautify even the simplest homes with their own labor and handiwork. As the Centennial year approached, many women began to believe that it was their paramount duty to make their homes as interesting and attractive as possible. Writers assured them that even the humblest attempts to beautify a home could help lead one's family to higher and nobler paths in life. Women thus added aesthetic duties to the other chores of the domestic sphere and attempted to make their homes artistic havens from an ugly outside world.

Ladies' periodicals offered helpful advice. In 1865, *Peterson's Magazine* suggested that regular patchwork could be decorated with embroidery along the same lines to create a mosaic effect. It subsequently offered ideas for ''mosaic appliqué'' and ''oriental embroidery,'' in which herringbone and buttonhole stitches ornamented the edges of appliquéd shapes. In 1874, the magazine's editor, Jane Weaver, featured a striped patchwork cushion trimmed with ''ornamental fancy work'' in colored silk thread.[3]

Inspired by an interest in art and design, women eagerly attended the Centennial Exhibition in Philadelphia. Over 9,700,000 people visited this world's fair, which stimulated interest in art education as well as the decorative arts, including areas related to the furnishing and decoration of the home. The displays from Japan and from England's Royal School of Art Needlework in particular appear to have inspired women to develop unique crazy quilts.

More than 250 Japanese exhibitors showed their wares in Philadelphia, and the Japanese section became one of the main centers of attraction. Critics often found the unusual, asymmetrical designs grotesque at first glance, but delightful and artistic upon second thought. They predicted that Japanese art would make a deep impression on the artistic mind of America. Visitors carefully inspected bronze sculpture, porcelains, lacquerware, silk fabrics, embroideries, and beautiful screens decorated with a combination of embroidery and painting on silk. A carved bedstead with a silk cover and pillow shams, priced at a thousand dollars, caught their attention. Americans found these new items curious and bizarre but appreciated the exquisite and intricate workmanship. Japanese design became very influential.[4]

No one knows whether American women copied the uneven pavement designs in a Japanese panel of needlework, the crazed background on certain Japanese ceramics, or the asymmetrical patchwork techniques found on some Japanese kimonos. However, in 1879 the editor of *Peterson's Magazine* reported seeing a "new work, which consists of scraps of all kinds being appliquéd onto serge, and ornamented with colored silks, in imitation of Eastern work. Stars, circles, and all sorts of shapes, are brought into use." Three years later, Janett Rets, of *Demorest's*, noted that "the old patchwork quilts, which usurped so large a portion of our grandmother's time, are replaced by others made in more elaborate style, which, if well done, are quite Eastern in effect. . . . These quilts are quite bewildering in their combination of colors and stuffs." *Harper's Bazaar* stated that geometric designs for quilts had been discarded so that modern quilts looked "more like the changing figures of the kaleidoscope, or the beauty and infinite variety of Oriental mosaics." To achieve an Oriental or mosaic effect women adapted the familiar log cabin technique, substituting irregular pieces of silk for the regular strips of the log cabin and arranging them in hit-or-miss fashion on a foundation fabric about 11 to 18 inches square. Adding silk embroidery and decorative appliqué to the joined blocks, they created an elaborate covering referred to as a Japanese silk or embroidered quilt.[5]

The Centennial display of the Royal School of Art Needlework also influenced the development of the new quilt style. Visitors to the school's pavilion entered a magnificent tentlike booth constructed of embroidered purple velvet hangings. Inside they found superb specimens of embroidery and needlework. Founded in 1872 in London, the school trained needy gentlewomen to embroider designs from antique sources or from those by well-known contemporary designers such as William Morris, Walter Crane, and Fairfax Wade. The women worked in ladylike and anonymous privacy to finish artistic works for the school's salesroom. This novel idea of capitalizing on women's traditional skills appealed to American women in need of employment after the Civil War and the depression of the 1870s.

Mrs. Candace Wheeler believed that a similar venture could be launched in this country. Returning to New York after visiting the exposition, she provided leadership for the socialite women who founded the New York Society of Decorative Arts in the spring of 1877. The society offered classes and opened a salesroom for consignments of artistic handiwork submitted by women across the country. A committee of experts screened the offerings to assure high artistic standards. The society's activities and displays generated favorable publicity, and fashionable periodicals began to view it as an arbiter of national taste. It soon launched its own publication, *The Art Interchange*, to spread its ideas. Other leading cities opened decorative-art societies or schools of art needlework. Women quickly responded to these new opportunities, and they also incorporated art-needlework techniques into their quiltmaking.[6]

The asymmetrical placement of irregularly shaped pieces in each Japanese-style patchwork quilt assured a degree of originality that was considered desirable in a work of art. The use of silk and the added embroidery permitted such quilts to be classified as artistic needlework. However, elite tastemakers felt that the quilts could be elevated to the highest and truly artistic level only if the pieces of plain silk were additionally enriched with the type of painted or embroidered designs espoused by decorative-art societies.

Desiring to create the highest-quality work, women made the embroidered silk quilt the pièce-de-résistance of art needlework. The asymmetrical patches formed a background to which the quilter then added every variety of fashionable decorative needlework recommended— Kensington embroidery, outline work, silk painting, arrasene embroidery, appliquéd plush- and satinwork, and ribbon and tinsel embroidery. In 1883, *Godey's Lady's Book* reported seeing quilts "embroidered so elaborately that the silk pieces were almost lost sight of." Little wonder that in October 1882 *The Art Amateur* could report that "when the present favorite style of quilt was introduced it was called the Japanese, but the national sense of humor has been too keen, and the Japanese is now generally known as the 'crazy' quilt." Certainly, these quilts contained a variety of bizarre and fantastic elements arranged in eye-catching fashion. The heavily decorated crazy quilt received recognition as a work of art from fashionable and elite tastemakers who felt that these elaborate examples were often sufficiently handsome to justify the enthusiasm and effort involved in making them.[7]

Popular women's magazines followed rather than led the crazy-quilt trend, publishing detailed directions only after the style had reached its full development; magazines did, however, feature useful embroidery designs reproduced in black-and-white contour. Leaders of the art-needlework movement encouraged women to use such patterns if they felt incapable of creating original decoration on their own.

Frequently employed motifs included nursery-rhyme and storybook characters such as Kate Greenaway children; aesthetic flowers such as sunflowers, lilies, and daisies; and Japanese motifs such as fans, cranes, and peacock feathers. Since the black-and-white reproductions did not include coloring directions, women planned to use their needles and thread artistically to fill in color. If Kensington shaded embroidery proved too difficult, a simple outline stitch or silk painting could substitute.

Women expected their artistic crazy quilts to be admired and closely inspected by friends, neighbors, and family members. Crazy quilts usually incorporate needlework details that can be fully appreciated only when examined at close range. Those quilts became parlor conversation pieces, but they also decorated beds and could be placed directly over the white spread or counterpane. Women knew that a crazy quilt served as an "ornamental affair" and they did not intend to conceal any of its beauty or craft by tucking it into beds or draping it in folds. Wide borders of velvet, plush, or satin in deep rich hues of dark garnet, crimson, navy blue, purple, green, cardinal, black, or brown could soften the brilliancy of the crazywork and set it off in much the same way that a suitable frame enhances a painting. Since these quilts would not be tucked between mattress and springs or slept under like ordinary bedclothes, the edges could be decorated with fancy fringes, braids, tassels, and laces.

China silk and silk foulard provided luxurious linings for these quilts, but recycled skirts from discarded silk dresses served as economical substitutes. Some women preferred warmer fabrics such as cashmere, wool delaine, and cotton flannel for quilt backs. Others made do with old sheets or pillow slips. Although crazy quilts often contained an inner batting of thick fleecy "wadding," they usually were not quilted in the traditional sense of the term. Batting could be inserted between the top and the lining and tied in place, as in a comforter. It could also be placed between the foundation square with the irregular pieces attached to each block. Some women made hand-quilted backings for their crazywork tops; others purchased machine-quilted satin fabric like that lining readymade coats and capes.

The completion of an artistic crazy quilt demanded a heavy commitment of time and effort. In 1884, *Harper's Bazaar* estimated that some crazy quilts took 1,500 hours of labor, or an hour a day for over four years. Little wonder that women proudly displayed such quilts at home and at fairs, charged high prices if they considered selling them, and carefully preserved them when they went out of style. Such time-consuming and artistic work seemed to have heirloom qualities.[8]

If women lacked the time, energy, money, or materials to make a bed-sized quilt, they could warm and brighten the bedroom with a crazywork scarf draped casually across the foot of the bed. Crazywork also could be incorporated into fashionable decorative accessories, including sofa cushions, chair tidies, lambrequins, table and piano covers, banner screens, curtain borders, mantle scarves, ottoman covers, and work bags. Very few homes lacked some form of crazywork, which became almost a mania in home decoration. Even fashionable young men hoped to possess a crazy quilt composed of patches, each contributed by a young lady admirer to be shown off as a sign of social prowess.

Commercial manufacturers quickly sensed potential profit in the crazywork fad. As women depleted their personal supplies of silks—odd scraps, ribbons, old clothes, hat linings, discarded flounces, babies' sashes, and gentleman's neckties—American silk companies such as the Yale Silk Works and L. G. Fowler & Co. of New Haven offered remnant packages of silks, satins, brocades, and velvets for prices ranging from twenty-five cents to a dollar. To encourage the making of crazy quilts among the hesitant or unsure, they offered pieced and embroidered sample blocks for thirty cents. Embroidery on a crazy block might require a skein or more of embroidery silk or filoselle, making an average of fifty skeins for one quilt; a truly fancy quilt might use twice as many. Silk-thread firms such as Brainerd and Armstrong Spool Silk Company offered books of crazy-stitch variations as aids and incentives for their customers.

Entrepreneurs prepared mail-order catalogs of outline designs for embroidery or painting. Original patterns and those imported from the Royal School of Art Needlework carried prestige, but since copyright protection did not exist, merchants often procured designs by copying them from published sources. By the mid-1880s, patterns of questionable artistic merit flooded the market. Many of these had to be punched or perforated before being transferred to the background fabric with stamping powder. Needlework shops provided this service when women found it too tedious. Briggs & Company manufactured patented warm-iron transfer designs that made the entire process faster and easier.

Women who wished to eliminate the time spent painting or embroidering designs could find alternative ways to convert their quilts into beautiful artistic works by purchasing hand-painted silk blocks to incorporate in their patchwork. The Kursheedt Manufacturing Company offered silk-embroidered appliqués that could be attached easily to the silk background. Enterprising merchants suggested making lace crazywork and jewel crazywork highlighted with metallic thread embroidery. Contemporary businessmen provided all sorts of "artistic" help and therefore felt that they should not be blamed for lowering taste. They shrewdly sensed that customers wanted novelty and preferred to buy it under the name of art.

As crazywork became increasingly commercialized and commonplace in homes across the nation, tastemakers in the decorative art and art-needlework movements turned their backs on it. By 1884, *Harper's Bazaar* was of the opinion that the crazy quilt represented a petty aim of "misdirected energy and perseverance." In 1887, the editor of *Godey's* found "the time, patience, stitches and mistakes the crazy quilt represents . . . too awful for words." The next year, after several crazy quilts took prizes in the 1887 Canfield Company Competition, *Godey's* recommended that this "most childish, and unsatisfactory of all work done with the needle" be omitted from future contests.[9]

Despite such disparaging remarks, women across America continued to make crazy quilts well into the twentieth century. In the 1890s, women in rural areas often substituted woolens for silks. Stereopticon slides show children sleeping under these wool crazy quilts made in sizes large enough to tuck in and finished with traditional bindings or edgings. These later crazy quilts tended to be practical, with less fancy embroidery and art-needlework decoration. Some women began to control their crazywork by placing it within traditional patchwork patterns.

Women obviously derived satisfaction and pleasure from making crazy quilts. The makers of such quilts enjoyed an artistic challenge and felt rewarded when friends and neighbors recognized their endeavors. Reporting on the county fair held in Akron, Ohio, in October 1885, the editor of the *Summit County Beacon* noted:

> *Domestic Hall is a perfect heaven especially for the ladies. There has never been a richer or finer display of goods in this hall than is the case this year. The handiwork of women appears to have been fairly outdone. There are samples of needle work that fairly dazzle one in brightness of color and bewitch the beholder with their beauty. Crazy quilts that make the heart ache in longings to possess them. If a woman can go through this hall in less than half a day she must have a strong mind to draw her eyes from the things that will there surely rivet them fast.*

Such complimentary remarks encouraged women. As a *Dorcas Magazine* editor wisely noted in 1884, "many a woman with strong artistic taste finds no other outlet for it than in work such as this."[10]

Crazy quilts also functioned as testimonials of friendship or albums commemorating happy times. Quilts made from scraps contributed by friends and neighbors became treasured repositories of memories, with each square calling to mind pleasant reminiscences of the contributors. Commemorative ribbons placed in quilts were reminders of a family's participation in such events as fairs, military reunions, and political campaigns.

The quiltmaking process had its own rewards. In making a crazy quilt, a woman could achieve a sense of simple satisfaction in using up accumulated scraps while at the same time finding relief from onerous household tasks. While working on her quilt she could dream and hope for a brighter future. If it didn't materialize, she at least had a handsome piece of work to enjoy and cherish. The finished quilt served as a visible sign of accomplishment that stood in contrast to the routine chores that had to be continually redone.

In her *Ladies' Manual of Fancy Work*, nationally known author and journalist Jane Croly, writing as Jennie June, understood "that there may be values, which they [the critics] are not capable of measuring; and that whatever has made a place for itself, and keeps it, must have merit and hold within itself its own reason for existence." A completed crazy quilt or crazy accessory symbolized a woman's concern and care for the artistic and finer qualities of life and their effects on her family and home. Jennie June assured women that if they worked with "trust, love, patience, and hope," any item they created would be "sure to possess an influence beyond the place which it occupies or the duration of its existence. In this way we can endow even fancy work with a soul—with immortality."[11]

Crazy quilts reflect creative responses to late-nineteenth-century artistic ideals and domestic life-styles. American women took inspiring ideals and reshaped them to suit their own aesthetic tastes and needs. They fashioned unique and glorified patchwork crazy quilts of an amazing richness of color and detail. These quilts still elicit a sense of wonder. Highly admired in their own day, crazy quilts now serve as fitting reminders of women's energetic involvement in American culture during the Aesthetic era.

NOTES

1. "Crazy Patchwork," *Dorcas Magazine* (October 1884), p. 263; Lisle Lester, "Crazy Patchwork," *Demorest's Monthly Magazine* (August 1884), pp. 621–22; "Crazy Work," in *Treasures of Use and Beauty*, Springfield, Mass., W.C. King and Co., 1883, p. 461.

2. Cleveland Branch of the U.S. Sanitary Commission [written by Clark Brayton and Ellen F. Terry], *Our Acre and Its Harvest: Historical Sketch of the Soldiers' Aid Society of Northern Ohio*, Cleveland: Fairbanks, Benedict & Co., 1869, p. 279. For more information on quilts at sanitary fairs, see Virginia Gunn, "Quilts for Union Soldiers in the Civil War," *Uncoverings '85*, Mill Valley, Calif., American Quilt Study Group, 1986.

3. *Peterson's Magazine* (December 1865), p. 444; (November 1867), p. 382; (March 1870), p. 240; and (August 1874), p. 143.

4. J. S. Ingram, *The Centennial Exposition*, Philadelphia, Hubbard Bros., 1876, p. 559; *Historical Register of the Centennial Exposition*, New York, Frank Leslie, 1876, p. 249; Henry J. Vernon, "The Centennial in Pen and Pencil —No. III," *Peterson's Magazine* (June 1876), p. 393.

5. "What to Do with Old Things," *Harper's Bazaar*, (June 2, 1882), p. 342; "Editor's Table—Making Table Borders," *Peterson's Magazine* (November 1879), p. 406; Janett Ruez Rets, "Finishing Touches," *Demorest's*

Monthly Magazine (November 1882), p. 27; "Patchwork," *Harper's Bazaar* (September 16, 1882), p. 583; Hetta L. H. Ward, "Home Art and Home Comfort, Bed-Spreads," *Demorest's Monthly Magazine* (April 1884), p. 362.

6. See Virginia Gunn, "Crazy Quilts and Outline Quilts: Popular Responses to the Decorative Art/Art Needlework Movement, 1876–1893," *Uncoverings '84*, Mill Valley, Calif., American Quilt Study Group, 1985, pp. 131–52.

7. "Mosaic Patchwork," *Godey's Lady's Book* (April 1883), p. 371; "Mosaic Patchwork—Continued," *Godey's Lady's Book* (May 1883), p. 463; "Crazy Quilts," *The Art Amateur* (October 1882), p. 108. For an excellent analysis of crazy-quilt motifs, see Penny McMorris, *Crazy Quilts*, New York, E.P. Dutton, 1984.

8. "Crazy Work and Sane Work," *Harper's Bazaar* (September 13, 1884), p. 578.

9. *Ibid.*; "Instead of a Crazy Quilt," *Godey's Lady's Book* (September 1887), p. 248; "The Second Competitive Exhibition of the Canfield Art Needlework," *Godey's Lady's Book* (February 1888), p. 184.

10. "Crazy Patchwork," *Dorcas Magazine* (October 1884), p. 263.

11. Jennie June, Preface to *Ladies' Manual of Fancy Work*, New York, A.L. Burt, 1884.

126

Augusta Elizabeth Duvall Bussey. *Crazy Patch Slumber Throw*. Baltimore, Maryland.
Silk, 73×73". The Smithsonian Institution, Washington, D.C.

This work reveals the love that Ms. Bussey (1843-1932), a botanist, must have felt for her profession. Fine examples of fabric flowers, embroidered holly, strawberries, and cockscomb compose the center of each crazy square.

127

Mrs. Samuel Glover Haskins. *The Haskins Quilt*. c. 1865. Rochester, Vermont. Pieced, embroidered, and appliquéd cotton, 69×82". The Shelburne Museum, Shelburne, Vermont. Gift of Electra Havemeyer Webb; purchased from a member of the Haskins family.

During the last third of the nineteenth century, the crazy quilt was by far the most popular type being made in the country. But although most crazy-quilt makers relied on brilliantly patterned fabrics and elaborate embroidered designs to embellish their creations, Mrs. Samuel Glover Haskins chose to decorate each of the 42 blocks in this piece with a variety of appliquéd motifs. These include such local wildlife as a moose, a mountain lion, a fox, and squirrels, which are interspersed with such exotic creatures as camels and giraffes. The maker made original and amusing choices of fabrics: striped cotton for the tiger's body, a wavy-patterned material for human hair, and small-patterned calicos that costume the figures of human beings.

![128] 128

Pieced and Embroidered Floral Album Crazy Quilt. c. 1880. New Jersey. Silk and silk-satin, 80×72".
Collection Laura Fisher, New York.

Each of the eighteen square blocks as well as the larger center rectangle includes at least one fine silk-embroidered flower. The embroidery is so skillful, and the likeness of each different flower is so accurate, that it is quite probable the maker was an avid gardener or knew quite a bit about botany. Refined and consistent, the quality of the needlework seems to be the work of a single individual; the borders incorporate different versions of two species of flower: compare the yellow and white blossoms at the top and bottom with the red and golden blossoms at the sides. Other motifs include a few Kate Greenaway-type figures and some interesting arrows, but it is unusual to find so heavy a concentration of floral subjects on such a quilt.

 129

Annie Hines Miller. *Chester Dare Embroidered and Appliquéd Crazy Quilt*. c. 1877. Warren County, Kentucky. Cotton, wool, and velvet, 79½ × 84½". Kentucky Museum, Western Kentucky University, Bowling Green, Kentucky. Photograph by John Perkins.

This quilt commemorates a famous Kentucky racehorse, Chester Dare, and the steed's image may be seen in the center panel. The romantic story behind this piece is related by Mary Washington Clarke in *Kentucky Quilts and Their Makers*:

> In the great heritage of Kentucky saddle horses a distinguished line of ancestors, including such horses as Washington Denmark, King William, Mollie, and Black Squirrel, produced a magnificent bay stallion in 1882, Chester Dare. He lived until 1904 and was prominent in Kentucky saddle-horse circles during most of that long life-span. In 1877 a young housewife in Warren County, Annie Hines Miller, started on an intricate parlor throw. Working with pieces of smooth durable woolens and heavy fine-textured cottons lavishly stitched with colored ornamental stitching that varied from one piece to another, she took several years to complete the quilt. She enriched the effect by embroidery on the patches, depicting themes of her rural life —flowers, birds and animals. She worked her own signature into the finished product after she had appliquéd a remarkable velvet portrait of Chester Dare as a centerpiece. According to family legend, hairs from Chester Dare's tail were carried by riverboat from New Orleans to use in shopping for a piece of velvet that would match the horse properly for the portrait.

Legend adds that Annie was much younger than her husband and that he was so jealous of her that he was overly zealous about keeping her at home. If so, he may have unwittingly contributed to the completion of her masterpiece. It is also said that he carried away her shoes when he was absent from home, and that she once decided to walk barefoot to her mother's neighboring farm in the snow, and died at the age of twenty-six from the resulting pneumonia.

🔳 130

Anna Lou Holland and Christine Holland Ross. *Pieced and Embroidered Crazy Quilt*. 1878.
Madisonville, Kentucky. Silk and velvet, 86 × 74". Collection The Kentucky Historical Society, Frankfort, Kentucky.
Photograph by Nathan Prichard.

This quilt, designed in blocks, does not contain many embroidered motifs; however, those that are incorporated
are very delicate. The pieced flag section (with embroidered stars) and the words in ink "Tilden and Hendricks"
refer to the 1876 presidential campaign, when Samuel Tilden ran for president with Thomas Hendricks as his
vice-presidential running mate. The Tilden–Hendricks ticket won the popular vote but lost in the electoral
college by one vote to Rutherford B. Hayes.

131

"Grandmother Bell." *Pieced, Embroidered, and Painted Crazy Quilt*. c. 1880. Englewood, New Jersey.
Silk, taffeta, and velvet, 72 × 61½". The Shelburne Museum, Shelburne, Vermont. Gift of Mr. Ralph Reimund
(grandson of the maker). Photograph courtesy The Shelburne Museum.

"Grandmother Bell" made this crazy quilt of fancy patterned fabrics and embroidered the randomly placed pieces with
silk and chenille yarns. Some of the 30 squares are also decorated with painted designs.

132

Cleveland–Hendricks Political Pieced and Embroidered Crazy Quilt. c. 1885. Origin unknown. Silk, satin, and velvet, 76⅜ × 76⅜". The Museum of American Folk Art, New York. Gift of Margaret Cavigga.

This quilt contains lithographed silk ribbons and other souvenirs of the 1884 presidential campaign, which culminated in the election of Grover Cleveland and his vice-presidential running mate, Thomas A. Hendricks.

One ribbon reads: "Democratic Barbecue at Ithaca, Nov. 20, 1884. Marshal." In the quilt's gold silk center square is a bright red strutting rooster, a symbol used by the Democratic Party during the 1880s and 1890s. The rooster is surrounded by four octagonal patches, at least two of which contain portraits of Cleveland and Hendricks. A bright pink patch above the rooster contains the heads of both candidates (Hendricks is to the left and slightly behind Cleveland). Other ribbons read: "March 4th, 1885" (Inauguration Day); Cleveland's slogan, "Public Office is a Public Trust;" and "Turn the Rascals Out." The large Japanese-style fans in the corners are typical of Victorian crazy quilts, as are the numerous embroidered floral sprays. (The irregular shapes of crazy-quilt patches originated because frugal quilters didn't want to waste a single scrap of fabric by trimming remnants to uniform shapes; they therefore used the entire scrap regardless of its evenness or its dimensions.)

133

Florence Elizabeth Marvin. *Pieced, Appliqué, and Embroidered Crazy Quilt*. 1886. Brooklyn Heights, New York. Silk and velvet, 80 × 76″. Collection America Hurrah Antiques, New York City. Photograph by Schecter Lee.

In addition to the beautiful needlework, the number of animals included in this quilt makes it unusual. Most of them are padded and stuffed to give them a three-dimensional effect. Another nice touch here is the gold-gloved hand holding a silk scarf.

13

...beth T...as Willis. *Pieced and Embroidered Crazy Quilt*. Late nineteenth century. Louisville, Kentucky.
...l, velvet, and other fabrics, 66×53". Collection The Kentucky Historical Society, Frankfort, Kentucky.
...ograph by Nathan Prichard.

...beth Thomas Willis "was from Cox's Creek and was a sister of Smith Thomas who was Minister of the Baptist
Church there." This quilt bears close examination to discern all the details and motifs common to many crazy quilts:
fans, butterflies, flowers, and horseshoes. Look also for unusual features: a house and trees in the center (the
maker's house?), the birdcage with canaries, acorns, roosters, cows, a horseback rider (probably a hunter with
foxhounds), a cornucopia of flowers with the initial "B," a latticed basket, a section of Grandmother's Flower Garden
pattern, strawberries, parasols, and a girl. An interesting contrast to the richly embroidered velvets are the sections
of wool, especially those across the top, which make the quilt seem homey and unsophisticated.

135

Anna Marie Steinbock. *Pieced and Embroidered Crazy Quilt.* 1890. Louisville, Kentucky.
Silk and velvet, 89×84". Collection Elizabeth Steinbock Mills. Photograph courtesy The Kentucky Quilt Project, Inc.

Anna Marie made this quilt the year of her marriage to Edmund Steinbock. The center diamond bears a beautiful bouquet of three-dimensional flowers. Around this center, like the points of a star, are the names of her family: Father, Mother, Willie, Josephine, Henry, Augusta, Annie, and George. Angels embroidered next to some of the names indicate these individuals had died. There are also fans, spiderwebs, little girls, a horseshoe, a butterfly, assorted flowers, an alphabet and numbers, and the name of her hometown (see detail). Annie's husband was a tailor, and it is known that she worked with him in his shop; thus, although sewing was a part of her life, it probably was not usually employed in a decorative manner. The needlework is extremely skillful.

136

Anna Marie Steinbock. *Pieced and Embroidered Crazy Quilt* (detail of 135).

137

Mrs. Newton (Mattie) Layman. *Pieced and Embroidered Friendship Crazy Quilt.* c. 1896. Kentucky.
Wool with cotton backing, 70½ × 78¼". Kentucky Museum, Western Kentucky University, Bowling Green, Kentucky.
Photograph by John Perkins.

The crewel-work embroidered names on this example place it in the category of a friendship quilt. Some of these quilts were made as remembrances and given to friends leaving the community, in which case they are also called presentation quilts, while others were given as wedding and engagement gifts, made by the bride's family or childhood friends.

    According to family history, this particular quilt contains the names of friends who visited the quilter while she was making it, and it may well also incorporate scraps of their clothing. One friend apparently did not live to see the finished quilt, since one patch reads "Chesley is in Heaven" (see detail).

138

Mrs. Newton Layman. *Pieced and Embroidered Friendship Crazy Quilt* (detail of 137).

139

Mary Lou Hotchkiss. *Pieced Crazy Quilt* (detail) . c. 1954. San Bernardino, California. Silk, 66½ × 88½". The Lyndon Baines Johnson Library and Museum, Austin, Texas.

This unique memory quilt took more than 33 years to assemble. Each piece is from the dress of a governor's wife, and 48 states are represented. Each section was autographed by its owner, and Ms. Hotchkiss then embroidered these signatures. The finished top is backed with green silk.

140

Pieced and Embroidered Crazy Quilt. c. 1890. Ohio. Cotton and silk, 68 × 62". Collection Bettie Mintz.

This gorgeous example seems to express a gardener's dream, although it is quite possible that it presents an accurate quilted reproduction of the maker's own treasured plot. Each of the sixteen squares features a special attention-grabbing element; a particular favorite of the present owner is the one reading "Daisies Won't Tell."

141

Jean Ray Laury. *Pieced Crazy Quilt*. 1982. Clovis, California. Cotton, 61×61".
Private collection. Photograph courtesy Jean Ray Laury.

This is a very contemporary 1980s original interpretation based on the traditional concept of a crazy quilt. It is composed of a collection of scraps and pieces left over from previous quilt projects. The pieces are joined so that colors and patterns relate and connect, with darks and lights moving across the plane of the quilt. The center is set in a wide red field that affords an open contrast to the complexity of the pieced section.

BABY, CRIB, AND DOLL QUILTS

BABY, CRIB,
AND DOLL QUILTS

Pat Long and Dennis Duke

rib and doll quilts, which were made for children and sometimes by children, are among the most appealing, as well as eminently collectible, examples of the genre. These scaled-down examples of full-size bed quilts frequently incorporated excellent workmanship and an innovative deployment of color and design. Those created by adults were frequently intended as a gift of love to a child. Children's learning pieces, with their wandering stitches and the perseverance they represent, appeal to the child in us all.

The history of crib, cradle, and doll quilts is closely linked to the history of the furniture they were made to cover. Cradles are listed in seventeenth- and eighteenth-century inventories, and early examples can be found in the collections of the Metropolitan Museum of Art, Winterthur, the Shelburne Museum, and the Henry Ford Museum, to name a few. The styles of these early cradles echo the furniture styles of the time; for example, Windsor-style cradles are similar to Windsor-style chairs. Hooded cradles were used frequently in the drafty rooms of Colonial America. Regional variants can be seen in Pennsylvania Dutch cradles with their painted motifs and heart-shaped hand holes. Some of these cradles were made by cabinetmakers; others were made at home.

Nineteenth-century cradles also echo contemporary furniture styles. There is an interesting example in the Shelburne Museum of a sleigh cradle, from around 1834, that is similar to sleigh beds of the period.

Doll cradles and doll beds were also popular in the eighteenth and nineteenth centuries. These miniature pieces of furniture were made in many shapes and sizes and ranged from the simplest homemade boxes to the most elegant examples of the cabinetmaker's art. Doll-size

---

PRECEDING PAGE: *Diagonal Stripes Mennonite Pieced Crib Quilt* (detail). c. 1875. Pennsylvania. Cotton. Collection America Hurrah Antiques, New York City. Photograph by Schecter Lee.

quilting frames and quilt racks also exist from this period. Dollhouse beds, made on a scale of one inch to one foot, also enjoyed a vogue in the nineteenth century. Beds and cradles, as well as quilts and Marseilles quilts, are listed in the inventory of an 1864 dollhouse owned by the Museum of the City of New York.

Yet another type of nineteenth-century children's bed was the trundle bed, for which accompanying quilts were made. The trundle, or truckle, bed is a low bed moved on casters and usually pushed under another bed when not in use. Lillian Baker Carlisle notes: "In medieval times the body servant slept on such a bed so that he could guard his master during the night."[1]

Just as nineteenth-century baby cradles and doll cradles echoed the furniture styles of the era, that century's crib and doll quilts reflect the general quilt-design tradition. The major nineteenth-century design themes—medallion, strip, whole-cloth, appliquéd chintz, block style (pieced and appliquéd), Log Cabin, crazy, and embroidered—may all be found in the crib and doll quilts of the period. Such quilts were smaller versions of their larger counterparts.

The fabrics used in these crib quilts were the same as those used in bed-sized quilts. Imported chintzes, English and French copperplate prints, and block-printed and roller-printed fabrics were employed in the first half of the nineteenth century. Later in that century these were succeeded by roller-printed fabrics, calicoes, checks and plaids, challis, and furnishing fabrics. There were very few prints with animals or other childhood themes used for crib quilts at that time. Rare exceptions were the crib quilts made from handkerchiefs specifically printed for children. Such squares depicted religious and holiday themes as well as popular moral or cautionary tenets such as industry, cleanliness, piety, and patriotism. Episodes from children's stories were also illustrated on handkerchiefs.

Most nineteenth-century crib and doll quilts exhibit the same techniques as those employed for full-size quilts: hand and machine piecing, hand and machine appliqué and quilting, press piecing onto a backing of fabric or paper, and embroidery. The charm of these pieces lies in the reduction of scale.

The pictorial elements used on some nineteenth-century crazy quilts were intended to enlighten or amuse children and were the first quilts to incorporate designs reflecting childhood themes. Such designs were followed closely by embroidered quilts using red outline embroidery on white muslin to depict animals, flowers, birds, children, and toys. Merle Kline of Shafferstown, Pennsylvania, recalls embroidering this type of quilt when she was a preschool child during the early years of this century. She bought designs that included a rabbit and other motifs for a penny and executed the embroidery under the watchful eye of her aunt. After she completed embroidering the squares, her mother and aunt sewed them together and quilted them for her. The next quilt she made was a Nine-Patch design, a pattern that has long been a favorite with beginning quilt makers.

An early example of a late-nineteenth-century appliquéd animal quilt is in the collection of the American Museum of Bath, England. This "Children's Menagerie Quilt" includes a variety of appliquéd animal designs executed on a block-style quilt using scrap fabric. It is a forerunner of the appliquéd animal designs of our century.

In the 1920s and 1930s, a period of great quilting activity, there was frequent use of childhood themes on crib quilts. Nursery-rhyme characters, animals, and the ubiquitous Sunbonnet Sue were among the most popular motifs. During the same decades, small-scale versions of traditional pieced and appliquéd designs were executed according to the nineteenth-century custom of crib quilts that are reduced-scale versions of adult's quilts.

The adoption of a recessive color palette in the 1930s marked the beginning of pastel colors for baby quilts. Pink for girls and blue for boys evidenced this era's predilection for light-valued colors.

In the 1980s, with quiltmaking enjoying a vital rebirth, we are witnessing a resurgence of crib quilts and small wall hangings executed in traditional small-scale designs and rendered in a varied palette of colors. Innovative contemporary designs reflect the influence of the art quilt.

To understand crib and doll quilts thoroughly, it is necessary to regard them within the social context of the periods when they were made. In the nineteenth century, sewing was an essential skill. Until the second half of the century, when the sewing machine became more common in homes, it was mandatory that a woman of any social class learn to ply her needle. Lucy Larcom, writing in 1889 about her childhood earlier in the century, expressed her feelings about the overwhelming amount of sewing expected of women in her milieu. As a small child, walking behind her father on the way to church, she looked up at him and thought, "How tall he is. And how long his coat looks. And how many thousand-thousands stitches there must be in his coat and pantaloons. And I suppose I have got to grow up and have a husband, and put all those little stitches in *his* coat and pantaloons. Oh, I never, never can do it."[2] She never married.

In the nineteenth century women of various social strata took pleasure and comfort in making quilts, especially those intended for an expected child. Working with the bright bits of cloth, the arrangement colors, and the design provided a pleasant contrast to the everyday drudgery of essential sewing. Quilting get-togethers, or bees, provided a much-needed opportunity for a group of women to gather and meet with friends. The high level of sewing skills acquired during these years can be seen on these small quilts.

Various types of needlework were taught to little girls in the public and private schools. Quiltmaking was but one of a variety of needle arts they learned, albeit one of the most important. An 1885 text exhorts parents: "Never purchase for your child mathematical puzzles, you can teach them and amuse them by making patchwork."[3] These sentiments were echoed in other contemporary works, particularly *Godey's Lady's Book*.

Frances Lichten, author of *Folk Art of Rural Pennsylvania*, notes that a small girl often learned to quilt at her grandmother's knee: "All Pennsylvania German children were trained from their earliest days to find their excitement in work, and little maidens would sit uncomplainingly for hours in low chairs, learning to sew together the small square patches cut out for them by the grandmother."[4]

Merle Kline recalls that as a child she accompanied her mother to quiltings in Shafferstown, Pennsylvania, every Saturday during January and February, not to quilt, but to enjoy playing with her dolls while her mother quilted. This was in the first years of the present century, when little girls were still being educated in the social value and pleasurable task of quiltmaking. Merle has continued to quilt as an adult.

Although the practice of teaching sewing skills and giving lessons in patchwork to little girls has waned, the Amish value these skills and teach them to little girls. The Amish way of life continues to place a high priority on quiltmaking skills. Amish women are currently producing quilts employing the sewing skills they learned as small girls. For many Amish women, a sizable portion of their income is earned in quiltmaking activities. Because of the religious restrictions regarding color and design, Amish quilts have unique characteristics that make them readily identifiable. Amish doll and crib quilts are smaller versions of adult bed quilts.

In the nineteenth and twentieth centuries, quiltmaking offered a vocation by which women could earn money to donate to a favorite charity. As early as 1874, a reference can be found to little girls earning money through quiltmaking. In a chapter on the sewing circle in *The Schoolmaster's Trunk*, Mrs. Diaz notes, "The little girls earned their money by running errands, and picking huckleberries, and making patchwork cradle-quilts to sell."[5]

By examining how children and quilts are described in children's literature of the previous century, we can realize the important role quiltmaking and quilts played in society. The connection between quiltmaking and the virtues that lie in perseverance, patience, and family ties are evident in various children's books of the day.

Johnny Up and Johnny Down, written by Mabel Leigh Hunt, is the story of how a Quaker mother taught her son the skills of patchwork in order to refine him. She also believed that a knowledge of sewing would prove useful to him in the future. The youngster managed to finish his quilt—in the Indian Hatchet design—under duress. The quilt eventually proved helpful when he employed it to capture a rampaging ram and became a hero.

Rachel Field's *Calico Bush*, set in Maine during Colonial times, tells of a French girl, a bonded servant, who is befriended by a neighbor who gives her a gift of a partially completed quilt in the Delectable Mountains design. The symbolically positive connotations of the gift and the name of its design help her accept her new home in an unfamiliar land.

The Patchwork Quilt, by Valerie Flournoy, is the story of a little girl who lives with her grandmother. When the grandmother becomes ill and is unable to complete the family memory quilt, the little granddaughter and her mother help finish the quilt as a gesture of love and a sign of continuing family traditions.

In *The Quilt of Happiness*, by Kate Douglas Wiggin, the heroine, Rebecca of Sunnybrook Farm, conceives the idea of putting together a quilt for a lonesome woman with scraps of clothing worn by the woman's friends during happy times: " 'I can't help feeling that if we just collect scraps of happiness,' " she said shyly, " 'and cut and stitch and tack happiness into the quilt, all in secret, that Miss Roxy'd feel warmer in it, though, of course, she'll never guess why.' " The project complete, Rebecca exclaims in her usual uninhibited manner, "I'm sick to death of it! I love it to distraction, and I never want to see another as long as I live. How can anybody make 'em for fun? I could hug it, I'm so fond of it, and slap it, I'm so tired of it."[6] Many quilters can relate to those sentiments.

Katy's Quilt is set during the second half of the nineteenth century. The preparations surrounding the move to a new home in the north of Maine precipitates a rash of quiltmaking by Katy's mother, her friends, and a reluctant Katy. A gift of a crazy quilt with her name on it represents a much-needed and welcome symbol of home and friends for Katy, and she takes it with her to her new home. When a raging forest fire threatens their house, the family members soak their quilts in water and spread them on the roof to prevent it from catching fire. In this story quilts are symbolic of protection in the lives of a pioneer family.

The Patchwork Quilt, by Adele DeLeeuw, is the story of a grandmother who entertains a grandchild who is confined to bed recovering from measles. Through the vehicle of the quilt covering the bed, the grandmother relates stories of her own childhood that she recalls from the different printed fabrics in the quilt's patches.

In her 1898 book, *The Counterpane Fairy*, Katharine Pyle employs a similar device to relate fairy tales embodying various virtues to a sick boy.

Although the moral values contained in these children's books were important, we should not overlook the important aesthetic function that quilts also served. Reproductions of artworks and books with colored illustrations were unavailable to people in rural or pioneer nineteenth-century environments. Quilts provided much-needed color in many otherwise drab homes. They were also a source of pride for the women who made them, who took much pride in their handiwork.

Crib and doll quilts exercise a particular appeal at present because their small size permits them to be hung on the walls of our homes to be enjoyed as artworks. Although antique crib and doll quilts are rare and often costly, they are more affordable than other examples of Americana and even other works of art. The criteria of innovative color and design, good workmanship, and good condition apply to collecting these small treasures as surely as they do for larger quilts.

In speculating on the reasons why some of these small quilts are preserved in fine condition, partial answers might be found in examining the attitudes and life-styles of the nineteenth century. For instance, a crib quilt of the 1880s was given to Fanny Wike of Shafferstown, Pennsylvania, as a part of her wedding trousseau and was made by her aunts, the Kessler sisters. The quilt, executed in an all-white whole-cloth design, remained unused because Fanny was childless.

The unhappy fact of the high rate of infant mortality during the last century may offer an explanation for other quilts found in mint condition. Some, however, might have been made as experimental pieces, just as today's quilt makers often test ideas in a small-scale format.

Some of the finest examples of crib quilts were made with such care, with such fine fabrics, and with so great an attention to detail that it is obvious they were never intended for everyday use. They are the masterpieces in miniature, showcases demonstrating the artistry and technical skills of their makers. As such, they have been lovingly passed down from one generation to the next. We are fortunate to inherit this unique body of work—a joy and inspiration for the present-day generation.

NOTES

1. Lillian Baker Carlisle, *Pieced Work and Appliqué Quilts at the Shelburne Museum*, Museum Pamphlet Series No. 2, Shelburne, Vermont, the Shelburne Museum, 1957, p. 19.

2. Mira Bank, *Anonymous Was a Woman*, New York, St. Martin's Press, 1979, p. 23.

3. L. Thomas Frye (ed.), *American Quilts: A Handmade Legacy*, Oakland, Calif., the Oakland Museum, 1981, p. 30.

4. Frances Lichten, *Folk Art of Rural Pennsylvania*, New York, Charles Scribner's, 1946, p. 171.

5. Mrs. A. M. Diaz, *The Schoolmaster's Trunk*, Boston, James R. Osgood, 1974, p. 31.

6. Kate Douglas Wiggin, *The Quilt of Happiness*, Boston and New York, Houghton Mifflin, 1971.

🎴 142

Hexagon, Mosaic, or Flower Garden Pieced Crib Quilt. c. 1850. New York State. Silk, 37 × 32″.
Collection Mr. and Mrs. J. Stephen Huntley. Photograph by Mary Anne Stets. Courtesy Phyllis Haders.

Both the pattern and the fabrics incorporated in this example are those usually used in larger quilts. The symmetrical placement of the black hexagons adds a dramatic touch to the total design.

![143 decorative icon] **143**

Basket of Flowers with Vine Border Appliqué Crib Quilt. c. 1850–60. Origin unknown. Cotton, 33×57".
Collection America Hurrah Antiques, New York City. Photograph by Schecter Lee.

This particular piece offers an excellent example of fine quilting. The shape suggests that it was planned to fit a cradle.

![144 decorative icon] **144**

Rachie T. Strever. *Eagle Appliquéd Crib Quilt.*
c. 1850. Copake, New York. Cotton, 34×34".
Private collection. Courtesy Thos. K. Woodard
American Antiques & Quilts, New York.
Photograph by Schecter Lee.

This quilt, signed by its maker, features thirteen stars representing the original Thirteen Colonies. Eight of the stars are appliquéd in red fabric around the eagle and five are in the quilting. Adding to the joyous patriotic theme are a wreath of flowers and the birds positioned around the inner and outer circles of the wreath.

145

Rose of Sharon Appliquéd Crib Quilt. c. 1870. New England. Cotton, 44 × 42".
Private collection. Photograph courtesy Phyllis Haders.

This charming baby's quilt features flowers with centers composed of triple layers of appliqué.

146

Pieced Cotton Doll Quilt. c. 1880. Cotton, 16×16". Collection Phyllis Haders. Photograph by Mary Anne Stets.

This small, delightful quilt is a real treasure. It was probably a little girl's first attempt at quiltmaking, and was intended as a coverlet for her doll.

147

Baby's Playthings Pieced and Appliqué Quilt. c. 1880. Midwest. Wool and silk, 33 × 46".
Courtesy Thos. K. Woodard American Antiques & Quilts, New York. Photograph by Schecter Lee.

In this wonderful example, the inclusion of animals suggests that the family may have lived on a farm. Other figures may represent objects and people from the infant's everyday life. The center section is made in the crazy-quilt style, and the use of patchwork and appliqué techniques reveals the maker's needlework skills.

148

Children's Room, Stencil House. Nineteenth century. The Shelburne Museum, Shelburne, Vermont. Gift of Electra Havemeyer Webb. Photograph courtesy The Shelburne Museum.

This wonderful glimpse into the world of minatures reveals children's playthings and furnishings. The covering for the doll's cradle is a pieced quilt, and the four-poster bed is covered by a whole-cloth quilt of linen check and a canopy ruffle of printed cotton. Of special interest also is the affection obviously felt for such small treasures by their previous owner, Electra Havemeyer Webb.

🌸 149

Pieced and Appliquéd Crib Quilt Top. c. 1885. New York State. Cotton, 38 × 38″. Collection America Hurrah Antiques, New York City. Photograph by Schecter Lee.

This charming work includes a large ticking house with chimneys, birds, and figures cut from printed calico. Of special interest are the straight pieces that make up the fence and the section with the gate.

150

Diagonal Stripes Mennonite Pieced Crib Quilt. c. 1875. Pennsylvania.
Cotton, 39 × 27½". Collection America Hurrah Antiques, New York City. Photograph by Schecter Lee.

This quilt offers a fascinating collection of the textiles of the first half of the 1870s.

151

Steeplechase Pieced Crib Quilt. c. 1870. Ohio. Cotton, 42×38″. Collection Mr. and Mrs. J. Stephen Huntley. Photograph courtesy Phyllis Haders.

The interaction of shapes in this hand-dyed indigo quilt is superb, and the overall effect teases the eye. The piecing required considerable skill, for working with such curved patches is very difficult.

152

Star Everlasting Pieced Crib Quilt. c. 1880. Pennsylvania. Cotton, 38×38″. Private collection. Photograph courtesy Phyllis Haders.

For a crib quilt, the present example has an atypical, highly dynamic selection of color.

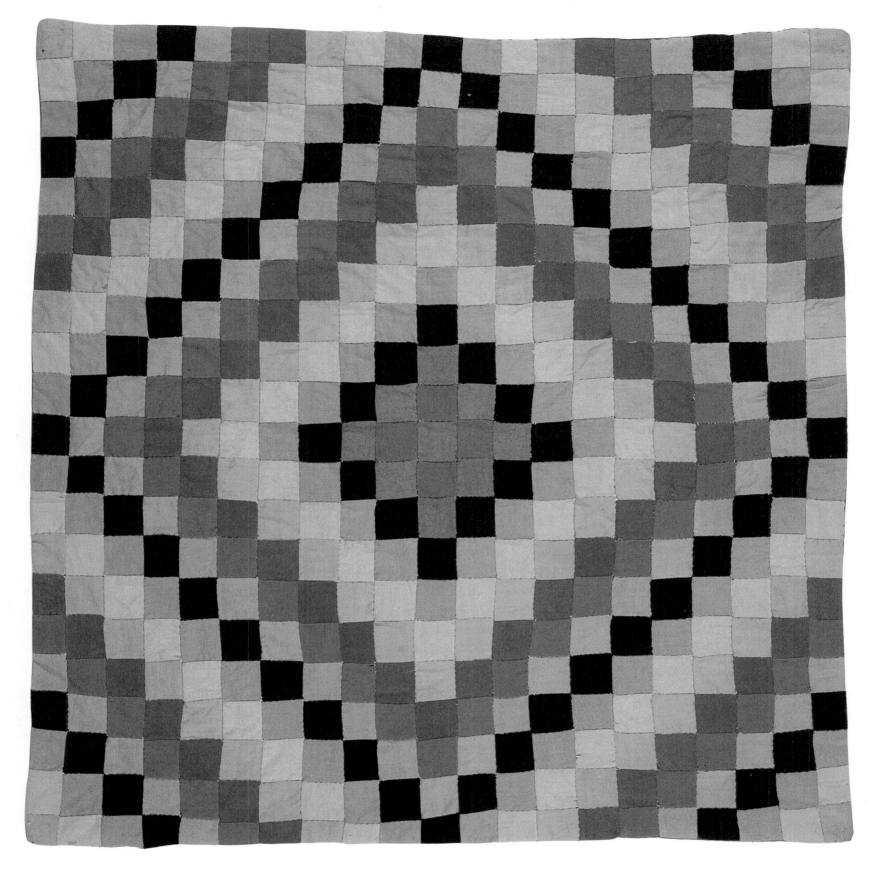

 153

Sunshine and Shadow Pieced Quilt. c. 1920. Holmes County, Ohio. Cotton, 16×16".
Collection Pat Long.

The vibrant arrangement of more than 400 three-quarter-inch squares creates a gem of color magic.

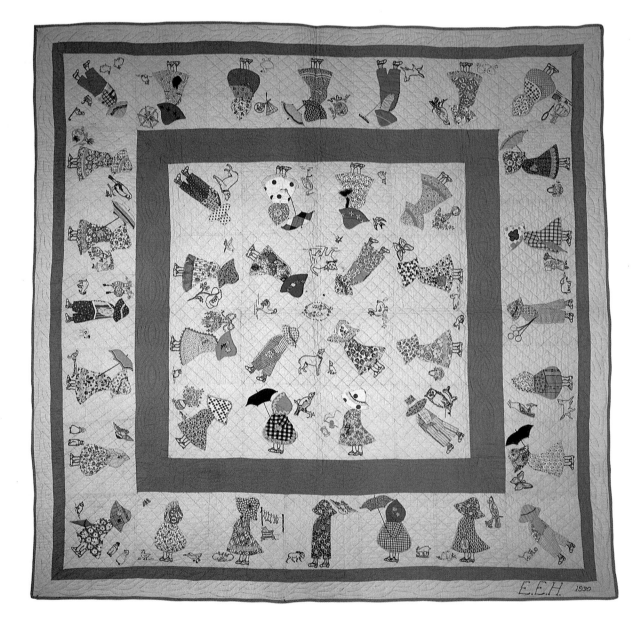

154

E. E. H. *Sunbonnet Babies* (detail of 155).

155

E. E. H. *Sunbonnet Babies*. 1930. Florida. Pieced and embroidered cotton, 79×79″. Collection Pat Long.

Dated by a quilter known to us only as E. E. H., this charming work features 40 children arranged in circles around a center. The quilt contains a wealth of interesting details and embroidery techniques. Separate but fastened-on purses and caps along with such unique eye-catching touches as braided human hair (see detail) are elements that make this quilt a special favorite of the collector's.

🌸 156

Simplicity Pieced Crib Quilt. c. 1900.
Washington County, Maryland. Cotton,
44 × 40″. Collection Pat Long.

This unique crib quilt is actually two
quilts made into one. The owner
discovered the second quilt when she
decided to ascertain the type of filling
that the maker used before quilting (see
detail). The collector is not alone in stating
that the true treasure here was the one
that remained hidden for over three-
quarters of a century.

🌸 157

Simplicity Quilt (detail of 156).

QUILTS
AT AN
EXHIBITION

QUILTS AT AN EXHIBITION

Donna Wilder

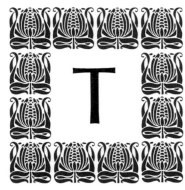

The art of quiltmaking underwent a major change between 1800 and 1900. By the mid-nineteenth century quilts were no longer assembled from discarded scraps; many fine materials were purchased specifically for quilting. Considerable freedom and creativity began to be seen in quilt-top designs. Quilt makers everywhere seemed to vie with each other in creating ever more dazzling geometric patterns.[1] Extraordinary color combinations and innovative designs echoed the changes affecting the nation. The quilters were ready to go public with their quilts.

In 1807, the first state fair, the brainchild of Elkanah Watson, was held in Pittsfield, Massachusetts.[2] (A discussion of such fairs appears in Chapter 2.) Other states followed suit, and quilts began to be regarded for more than their utilitarian value. It was not at all unusual for several hundred quilts to be exhibited—usually with other handicrafts in a separate area—often suspended from clotheslines or hung from rafters.

However, by the close of the century quilting had declined in popularity. Changing technology made inexpensive domestic goods available, so that the time and energy expended on quiltmaking could be spent on less laborious leisure activities.

A revival of quiltmaking took place around 1929, the era of the stock market crash and subsequent Depression. Women everywhere were encouraged to sew; periodicals advertised quilting kits and announced contests.[3]

Beginning in 1928 and for the next thirty-three years, the *Kansas City Star* offered its readers quilt patterns. Quilts from these patterns were soon exhibited at quilt shows; today, they are noted for excellent design, color, use of fabrics, and craftsmanship.

PRECEDING PAGE: *Maryland Album Appliqué Quilt* (detail). c. 1840. Maryland. Cotton. The Shelburne Museum, Shelburne, Vermont. Gift of Electra Havemeyer Webb. Photograph courtesy The Shelburne Museum.

In 1929, the *Indianapolis Star* printed a weekly series of twenty-six floral patterns. That same year a Flower Garden Quilt Contest was held in conjunction with the William H. Block Company to select the most outstanding quilt incorporating the firm's printed fabrics. On August 25, 1975, the *Star* ran an article about the 1929 contest and reproduced one of the entries. This resulted in an avalanche of requests for a repeat contest, which was announced in the issue of March 7, 1976.[4] One of the rules stated that entries had to be made according to the original twenty-six patterns. However, quilters added fresh imagination and innovation and incorporated unusual color schemes. The entries were shown in an exhibition jointly sponsored by the Block Company and the *Star*. A number of these quilts are still sent by their makers to other exhibitions.

Since then the contest has continued biennially. The 1987 theme was Quilt Expressions '87, cosponsored by the *Star* and Union Station—the old railroad terminus in downtown Indianapolis now renovated to house shops and restaurants—where the quilts were exhibited.

In 1933, a Century of Progress celebrated the centennial of Chicago's incorporation. In conjunction with this world's fair, Sears, Roebuck sponsored a nationwide quilting contest to promote interest in this uniquely American art.[5]

With barely five months to complete their entries, enthusiastic quilters across the country went to work to compete for the substantial sum offered for the first prize. Out of the nearly 25,000 submissions, 30 regional winners were selected to be exhibited at the Sears pavilion at the fair. The task of judging was monumental; many of the quilts were outstanding, revealing an artistic blend of colors, perfectly even tiny stitches, and creative designs. The entries ranged from traditional designs handed down since before the Revolutionary War to original patterns reflecting the fair's theme: a century of progress. Several quilt makers depicted Chicago locales or events in the city's history; others looked to the future for their inspiration.[6] The Grand National Prize was awarded to a quilt made from a traditional design (later identified as Star of the Bluegrass) submitted by Margaret Rogers Caden of Lexington, Kentucky. This fine quilt, incorporating exquisite stuffed work, was presented to Eleanor Roosevelt. Unfortunately, since 1934 it has not been traced.[7]

The 1939–40 New York World's Fair inspired a contest entitled "America through the Needle's Eye," sponsored by thirteen participating department stores in the East and Midwest. The local winning entries were shown at the fair, and the first prize went to a quilt in the Palm Leaf design submitted by Bertha Stenge of Illinois, one of the better-known quilters of the time. In 1942, she won the grand prize in the *Woman's Day* National Needlework Competition for her "Victory Quilt," which was the highlight of the exhibition at Madison Square Garden in New York. This appliquéd quilt depicted the historical events of the time with amazing accuracy.[8]

In October 1949, Stearns and Foster sponsored the Central States Quilt Exhibition. One hundred twenty-eight prizewinning quilts from that year's state fairs held in the Central States were assembled for exhibition. Many of the quilts exhibited at these state fairs followed patterns commissioned for the Mountain Mist collection of famous quilt designs.[9]

Whenever a quilt with an original pattern appeared, it—together with the design rights—was often purchased for the Mountain Mist collection. The majority of patterns in this collection were printed between 1930 and 1950. During these decades a number of major department stores nationwide mounted elaborate displays of the collection's quilts. In New York, Macy's displayed them annually in their windows. The J. L. Hudson department store in Detroit reported that in 1932 over 50,000 persons visited the store to see more than 1,000 quilts on display. In June 1985, an exhibition of the complete Mountain Mist collection was held at Cincinnati's Summer Quilt Market.

After the mid-1940s interest in quilting underwent another decline. Women were recovering from the effects of World War II, and they were also moving into the work force. Quilting was a luxury that could not often be afforded.

During the 1970s, however, quilting experienced an unprecedented renaissance inspired by the show mounted at the Whitney Museum of American Art in 1971, curated by Jonathan Holstein and Gail Van der Hoof. Entitled "Abstract Design in American Quilts," the show exerted a tremendous influence on the resurgence of quiltmaking. After the success of the New York showing, major museums throughout the country followed the Whitney's lead and organized their own extensive quilt shows with excellent attendance records. After the success of these exhibitions, quilt archives swelled as donors recognized the importance of preserving this unique genre of American folk art.

Quilt groups were soon formed, fabric and quilt shops offered classes, publications for quilters appeared, and quilt shows cropped up across the country. Once again women gathered to make quilts in order to raise funds for a worthy cause, in the tradition of the old-fashioned quilting bees. The Bicentennial celebrations heightened the growing interest, and during the two years before the event quilters from every town and municipality memorialized their heritage into quilts that would ultimately be exhibited during the Bicentennial year.

In October 1976, *Good Housekeeping* announced the Great Quilt Contest sponsored by the magazine, the United States Historical Society, and New York's Museum of American Folk Art. Fifty-one prizewinning quilts were chosen from almost ten thousand nationwide entries, and the winners were announced in the magazine's issue of March 1978.[10] Quilting had indeed found its way back into millions of homes across the country. The $2,500 first prize was awarded to the magnificent Ray of Light medallion quilt by Jinny Beyer of Great Falls, Virginia.

Quilt-block contests also became popular during this time (individual blocks with a central theme are submitted, and the winning entries are sewn together into a single quilt). The Mountain Mist collection included quilts made from these quilt-block contests, which, with the exception of 1981, continued until 1982. The winning blocks incorporate the themes of each year's contest—1974: Thirteen Colonies; 1975: State Flowers; 1976: School Days; 1977: Teen Fun; 1978: Famous Women; 1979: Nursery Rhymes; 1980: Famous American Heroes; and 1982: Movie Classics. In 1983 and 1985, Mountain Mist sponsored contests in which participants were asked to make new quilts following a Mountain Mist pattern. Cash prizes were awarded, and the eight winning quilts entered the collection. The top hundred quilts from those two contests were exhibited at the Quilt Festival in Houston. The Fairfield Processing Corporation, Poly-Fil®, has held successful quilt-block contests since 1980, when it sponsored Great Expectations, followed by Quilting through the Century in 1981, Kaleidoscope of Color in 1982, Hurray for Holidays in 1983, Geometry in Motion in 1984, The Circus Is Coming to Town in 1985, The American Heritage Sampler in 1986, and Garden Bouquet in 1987. The firm's collection of prizewinning quilts is shown at major quilting events and at major department stores. In 1985 the complete collection was exhibited at the Vermont Quilt Show in Northfield.

Often the lure of the prize is not the prime motivating factor. Usually the contestant enters to demonstrate her or his creative talents. Entrants in national quilt shows travel around the country to attend important events. One such show is Houston's Quilt Festival. In conjunction with this event, the American International Quilt Association sponsors a quilt competition for its members. Three hundred or more outstanding contemporary and traditional quilts are shown in a breathtaking display. In addition to the hundreds of antique and new quilts available for sale, there are also specially curated exhibits. Similar events, including the Continental Quilting Congress, the American Quilters Society, and the National Quilting Association Shows, and numerous state and regional shows also assemble exhibitions of outstanding quilts.

Before 1979, most exhibitions featured quilts executed in traditional patterns, techniques, and colors, and there were few opportunities for artists working with original designs, materials, and techniques. However, in 1978 a dedicated group of Athens, Ohio, quilters decided to promote interest in contemporary quilting as an art form. Their enthusiastic efforts resulted in Quilt National '79, the first such exhibition in the United States to show a jury-selected group of quilts in contemporary designs; it offered fifty-six quilts by forty-four artists. Presented biennially, the event continues to grow in scope; in 1987 it featured quilts selected from more than nine hundred entries. The expertise of these fine artists is manifested in unique works that are among some of the most innovative contemporary quilts. Quilt National opens each year at the historic Dairy Barn Southeastern Ohio Cultural Arts Center in Athens. From there it travels throughout the United States and by invitation to foreign countries.[11]

The most spectacular quilting event ever held was the Great American Quilt Festival in New York in April 1986. Organized by the Museum of American Folk Art and sponsored by Scotchgard® Products to celebrate the Statue of Liberty Centennial, it brought together quilts of all sizes and shapes, from the rarest antiques to the latest contemporary works. The highlight was the special exhibition, Expressions of Liberty, which displayed prizewinning quilts from the Great American Quilt Contest. Fifty-two quilts, one from each state and two from the United States territories, proudly symbolized the theme of "Liberty, Freedom, and American Heritage in Honor of the Statue of Liberty Centennial." Fine design, expert craftsmanship, and adherence to the contest theme were among the criteria for the selection of the winners. Moneca Calvert of Carmichael, California, won the $20,000 grand prize for her quilt "Glorious Lady Freedom," which featured meticulously pieced and appliquéd graphic designs depicting the Statue of Liberty superimposed on the American flag blended into the purple mountains, the cities, and the fruited plains. Second prize was awarded to "Spacious Skies" by Charlotte Warr-Anderson of Kearns, Utah. These two quilts are now in the Museum of American Folk Art, the Scotchgard® collection of contemporary quilts, and will travel with the other winners for three years.[12]

As a result of the mounting interest in quilts and quilt collecting and through the combined influence of concerned quilters and historians, many states have become aware of the need to document and record historically important quilts.

One of the first states to initiate such a project was Kentucky[13]; this state's ground-breaking efforts in this field are discussed in Chapter 2. Texas followed Kentucky's lead with a statewide effort to preserve the heritage and cultural contributions made to their history by women through their quiltmaking. The first stage of the continuing project culminated to coincide with the Texas Sesquicentennial in 1986. After three years of research, thousands of miles of travel, and hundreds of hours of interviewing quilt owners, 3,500 quilts either made within the state's borders or brought there before 1936 were found and documented. In April 1986, sixty-two of the finest were exhibited in the rotunda of the state capitol in San Jacinto, and an exhibit of thirty-nine examples has subsequently toured the state. Many of these quilts are reproduced in full color, and their history is documented in *Lone Stars: A Legacy of Texas Quilts, 1836–1936*, by Karey Bresenhan and Nancy Puentes.[14]

The appreciation of quilts has reached new heights today. They are now recognized as a valid art form in which fabric and needle are the artist's medium. Museums and quilt shows continue to assemble outstanding quilts of the past and present for exhibition, and innovative quilters continue to generate new enthusiasm for this unique art and to invent and create new ideas, techniques, and concepts.

NOTES

1. Patsy and Myron Orlofsky, *Quilts in America*, New York, McGraw-Hill, 1974, p. 44.

2. ———, p. 57.

3. ———, p. 63.

4. "Contemporary Quilt Carries Off Honors," *Indianapolis Star*, Section 6, p. 1.

5. Joyce Gross, "Century of Progress," *Quilters' Journal*, No. 27 (July 1985), p. 18.

6. ———, p. 2.

7. Barbara Brackman, "Prize-Winning Mystery," *Quilters' Journal*, No. 27 (July 1985), p. 9.

8. Joyce Gross, "1940 N.Y. World's Fair Quilt Contest and Exhibit," *Quilters' Journal*, Vol. 3, No. 2 (Summer 1980), p. 14.

9. Joyce Gross, "Stearns and Foster," *Quilters' Journal*, Vol. 3, No. 4 (Winter 1981), p. 9.

10. "Prize-Winning Quilts," *Good Housekeeping* (March 1978), p. 124.

11. *Quilt National Catalogue*, 1983.

12. Robert Bishop and Carter Houck, *All Flags Flying American Patriotic Quilts as Expressions of Liberty*, New York, Dutton, 1986, p. vii.

13. Jonathan Holstein and John Finley, *Kentucky Quilts 1800–1900: The Kentucky Quilt Project*, New York, Pantheon Books, 1982, 4th cover.

14. Karoline Patterson Bresenhan and Nancy O'Bryan Puentes, *Lone Stars: A Legacy of Texas Quilts, 1836–1936*, Austin, University of Texas Press, 1986, p. 6.

158

Maryland Album Appliqué Quilt. c. 1840. Maryland. Cotton, 98×101". The Shelburne Museum, Shelburne, Vermont. Gift of Electra Havemeyer Webb. Photograph courtesy The Shelburne Museum.

This quilt reveals the full sway of the maker's imagination in the combining of many motifs into a gracefully artistic, unified, yet free design. This quilt won first prize at the 1939 Maryland Fair, which is not surprising considering its spectacular color and the attention to detail.

🎕 159

Maggie Frentz. *Pieced, Appliquéd, Embroidered, and Tied Political Ribbon Flag Quilt.* 1876. New Albany, Indiana. Silk and velvet, 68 × 72". Collection Indiana State Museum and Historic Sites. (As seen in the Political and Campaign Quilt Exhibit.) Courtesy Katy Christopherson. Photograph by Nathan Prichard.

The silk bands of the flag bear the names and pictures of all the 1860 presidential contenders—Abraham Lincoln, Stephen A. Douglas, John C. Breckinridge, and John Bell—as well as the two vice-presidential candidates—Hannibal Hamlin and Edward Everett. More than 1,500 pieces of silk and velvet comprise the Yankee Puzzle design used for the background of the flag.

🎕 160

Various quilters. *Thirteen Colony Pieced and Appliquéd Friendship Quilt.* 1975. Nationwide. Cotton blends, 87 × 79". Stearns and Foster Collection.

Created for the 1975 Stearns and Foster Friendship Quilt Contest, this prizewinning quilt incorporates 30 intricate squares with historical images and motifs pertaining to the history of the thirteen original states.

The blocks were made by Marilee Abbott, Frances Albright, Candi Bailey, Mary Baker, Janet Bastendorf, Jeannie Bellarosa, Marie Brey, Mrs. Dalton Brion, Miriam Conroy. Mrs. H. D. Coyner, Mrs. H. Deascentis, Marie Dentzer, Maree Dowdey, Sally Field, Ellen Frazier, Joan Gagnon, Ruth Gibbud, Elizabeth Herrington, Elva Hicks, Ruth Hitchcock, Ruth Janesick, Mrs. Joan Lafferty, Pearl Medved, Kay Olivia, Mrs. Richard Prettyman, Mrs. Melvin Sisler, Betty Treasure, and Katherine Verney.

![161]

161

Mrs. John A. Garnett Murray. *Pieced and Embroidered Crazy Quilt*. c. 1893. Glasgow, Kentucky.
Velvet, satin, and ribbons, 64 × 64″. Kentucky Museum, Western Kentucky University, Bowling Green, Kentucky.
Photograph by John Perkins.

Special mementos were often incorporated into crazy quilts, and this example includes a painted valentine and a souvenir ribbon from the Philadelphia Centennial Exhibition. The patches have been sewed together in a variation of the Crow Foot embroidery stitch. The embroidery is chenille in some sections, and the backing is prequilted satin. The embroidered floral border on velvet is notable. This quilt was exhibited at the Columbian Exposition in Chicago in 1893.

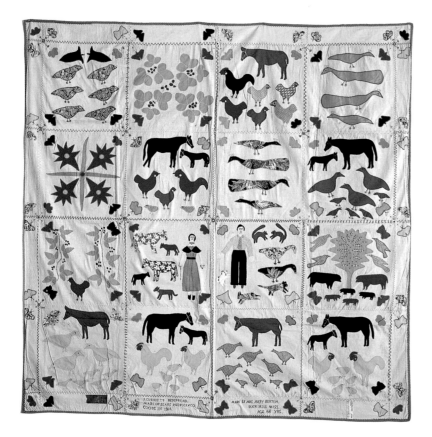

![162](lotus icon) **162**

Mrs. Avery Burton. *Curiosity Bedspread.* 1935. Duck Hill, Mississippi. Appliquéd cotton, 74×75". Collection Shelly Zegart's Quilts, Louisville, Kentucky. Photograph by Steve Mitchell.

The green ribbon attached near the bottom edge is the Award of Merit from the 1935 Sears, Roebuck National Make-It-Yourself Contest. The quilt is titled, signed, and dated in embroidery.

164

Mrs. Avery Burton. *Curiosity Bedspread* (detail of 162).

163

Mrs. Avery Burton. *Curiosity Bedspread* (detail of 162).

![ornament] 165

Various quilters. *Kaleidoscope Color*. 1982. Nationwide. Pieced and appliquéd
cotton and synthetics, 80 × 65″. Fairfield Processing Quilt Collection.

The 1982 Fairfield Processing Corporation quilt-block contest brought these dynamic prizewinning blocks to
the attention of quilters across the country. Interestingly, the contest required that all of the colors used should
be solids.

   The individual blocks were made by (left to right): Elizabeth Lucke, Bianca Hoekzma, Carol Nichols, Mary
Jo Deysach, Donna Garofalo, Irene Dillon, Evelyn Blauvet, Helen W. Rose, Louiselle Giguere, Sheryl Hinsdale
(grand prize winner), Ruth B. Campbell, Marguerite Snow, Michelle Marsicano, Victoria Johnson, Catherine B.
Spann, Pricilla L. Harding, Linda Irvine, Tracy C. Gendron, J. Karin Kerns, and Terry LeBlanc.

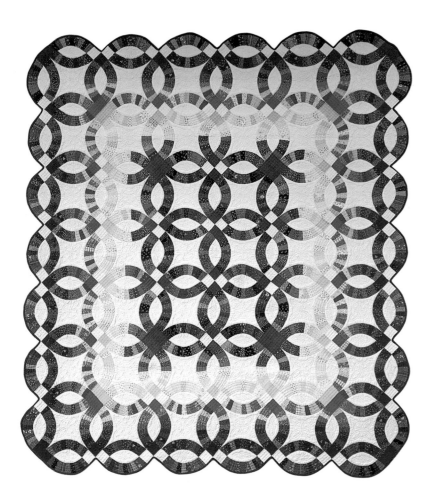

166

Mary Kay Horn. *Double Wedding Ring Pieced Quilt*. 1983. Indianapolis, Indiana. Cotton blends, 89×70". Stearns and Foster Quilt Collection.

This second place winner in the 1983 Stearns and Foster Contest clearly uses contemporary color.

167

Virginia F. Godfrey. *Indiana Seasons*. 1985. Indianapolis, Indiana. Pieced cotton and synthetics, 84×84". Collection the artist.

This elegant example won the sweepstakes award in the 1985 *Indianapolis Star* and Block's Department Store Quilt Competition. The incorporation of traditional balance with contemporary imagery provides evidence of the quilter's skill in manipulating design and color.

168

Sharon Drazer. *Floral Cameo Pieced Quilt*. Late 1980s. Drazer, Minnesota. Cotton blends, 100×84". The Stearns and Foster Quilt Collection.

This delicate, almost classically pure example offers the quilter's interpretation of one of the well-known Mountain Mist patterns.

![tulip logo] 169

Jinny Beyer. *Ray of Light*. 1982. Great Falls, Virginia. Cotton, 92 × 83″.
Collection *Good Housekeeping* magazine.

This magnificent medallion quilt was national winner of the 1982 *Good Housekeeping* Great Quilt Contest. The piece is notable for its subtle shades of blue and brown that are accentuated with imaginative quilting.

170

Various quilters. *The Circus is Coming to Town*. 1985. Nationwide. Pieced and appliquéd
cotton and synthetics, 76 × 62". Fairfield Processing Quilt Collection.

These blocks reflect all the excitement, anticipation, and enjoyment we find at the circus. Each individually designed
block was submitted to the 1985 Fairfield Processing Corporation quilt-block contest. The winning blocks incor-
porated in this quilt were made and executed by (left to right): Margaret J. Morrison (grand prize winner), Ruth
Meyer, Janelle Jones Knox, Beth J. Ide, LaVerne A. Ginn, Anna Mae Schack, Cindy Szarzynski, Thelma Ryan, Evelyn
Spillan, Jean L. Harne, Linda Denner, Helen R. Scott, Sylvia Pickell, Thelma Guzio, Mary Bowman, Priscilla Harding,
Lynn Teichman, Jo Lawson, Evelyn Stone King, and Barbara Potter.

171

Shirley Fowlkes (design) and Quilters' Guild of Dallas. *Pieced and Appliquéd Texas Motifs Quilts.*
1985. Dallas, Texas. Cotton and synthetics, 114×110". Collection Mr. and Mrs. Thomas S. Miller, Dallas, Texas.
Photograph by Bill Schultz, Chastain and Company, Dallas, Texas.

This unique pictorial appliquéd quilt took over two years, or some 4,000 hours, to make. It was jointly pieced, appliquéd, and quilted by 50 members of the Quilters' Guild of Dallas. Since its completion it has been awarded the blue ribbon at the 1985 American International Quilt Festival in Houston, and the best of show at the 1986 State Fair of Texas in Dallas.

The quilt incorporates Texas landmarks, with the larger star in the center representing the Lone Star State; it is surrounded by the governor's mansion, the sesquicentennial logo, the state capitol, the San Jacinto monument, the Texas mariner's compass, and the Alamo. The mariner's compass, which was taken from a 1955 state highway map, sets the theme for the pictorial blocks framing the quilt on the four sides. The compass points north to the top of the quilt, which contains blocks that represent North Texas. Other blocks at the bottom represent South Texas; at the right, East Texas; and at the left, West Texas. The designer, Shirley Fowlkes, is a fifth-generation Texan who was inspired to create this quilt while researching her ancestors for the Daughters of the Republic of Texas.

172

Moneca Calvert. *Hearts*. 1985. Carmichael, California. Pieced and appliquéd cotton and various blends, 73×78".
Collection The American Quilters' Society, Paducah, Kentucky. Photograph by Jerry DeFelice,
© 1986 Leman Publications.

Three sizes of hearts are set in two pattern designs, each repeating four times from the center out to the sides
and corners. This splendidly executed and sensitively colored work has received many local, state, and national
awards, including: California State Fair, 1985 (first place and second best of class); the American Quilters'
Society 1986 Annual Show, Paducah, Kentucky (first place); and the 1985 River City Quilt Show, Sacramento,
California (first place).

![173] 173

Martha Washington Quilters' Guild. *J C Penney Celebrates American Style*. 1986. McMurray, Pennsylvania. Pieced, embroidered, and appliquéd cotton and other fabrics, 66×66". Collection J. C. Penney Co., Inc., New York.

In the course of a national quilt-square contest held in conjunction with the Statue of Liberty Centennial, 1,500 J. C. Penney store managers selected quilted squares that best exemplified the themes of liberty, freedom, and our national heritage. Out of the thousands of entries, a panel of judges then selected the sixteen block designs shown here as well as four other regional quilts. The winning entries were shown at the Great American Quilt Festival in New York.

174

Judy Wasserman Hearst. *Interrelating Support*. 1986. Milwaukee, Wisconsin. Pieced and appliquéd cotton, 49×87". Collection the 4-H Center, Chevy Chase, Maryland. Photograph by Bill Lemke.

This quilt was commissioned by the Wisconsin 4-H Foundation, and it can presently be seen in the Wisconsin Room of the National 4-H Center.

Solid squares work together in this design to give strength and support to other blocks. This overall effect offers a representation of the state of Wisconsin: cities, factories, deer, (painted) cows; a tapestry of the terrain, farmland, forests, lakes, and changing seasons.

175

Carol Anne Grotrian. *Light of Liberty*. 1985–86. Massachusetts. Pieced cotton, 72×72". Private collection.

This quilt was a state winner in the Great American Quilt Contest. A fabulous work, it was conceived after the maker visited Bedloe's island, where she was fortunate enough to obtain a bird's-eye view directly over Lady Liberty's crowned head.

176

Judy Mathieson. *Nautical Stars Pieced Quilt*. 1987. Woodland Hills, California. Cotton, 88×73″. Collection the artist.

This marvelously colorful design was inspired by an 1800 watercolor by an anonymous sailor in the Greenfield Village and Henry Ford Museum. The dynamic compass motifs were inspired by those on quilts or hex signs, and the compass roses, by those on old maps. The all-cotton fabrics were hand-quilted over low-loft polyester batting.

CONTEMPORARY QUILTS

CONTEMPORARY QUILTS

Luella Doss

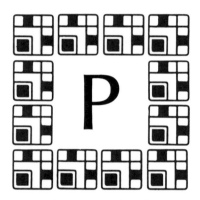

Part of the American work ethic is the belief that "a job worth doing is worth doing well." To make something from start to finish, one must first plan and design, devise and manipulate, totally immersing oneself in the task of bringing it into being. When we lose ourselves in the process of creation, we experience self-discovery.

The importance of working with one's hands was fundamental during the early years of our nation, and today all manner of arts and crafts are being created. The sterility and uniformity of mass-produced homes and furnishings have created a need for human warmth in our environment. An individual who creates in the textile medium of quilts is responding to a real cultural need. The fact that quilting is experienced on myriad levels by over a million Americans is evidence of the influence of this medium on the growth of the new American consciousness.

As Michael Kile and Penny McMorris wrote in *The Art Quilt*, "No other craft medium could engender a longing for the past and feeling of safety in the present like quilts."[1] In quilting, as in life, an important part of inner growth is an understanding and appreciation of the heritage of history, and the traditions of American patchwork, which are rich in lore and legend.

Of equal historical importance are the various techniques, dyes, styles, and designs that emerged during each era of our history. Today's quilt makers zealously study such traditions. The impetus behind the quilting renaissance is based on practical creativity that aspires to forge links between past, present, and future.

Between 1945 and the early 1960s, quilting was kept alive in tiny pockets of America. Despite the vagaries of changing tastes, it never died out, because some individuals elected to satisfy

---

PRECEDING PAGE: Judith Larzelere. *Marriage of Blue and Orange* (detail). 1980. Dedham, Massachusetts. Cotton. Collection the artist. Photograph courtesy Jan Bindas.

their personal requirements and refused to follow the dictates of a technological society that can easily manufacture bedclothes and keep us warm. However, as awareness of the creative self grew in the 1960s, articles on quilts in magazines and newspapers proliferated. Early examples that had long lain unnoticed in museum basements were brought out and shown in exhibitions.

In 1965, the Op Art movement inspired the Newark Museum to mount an exhibition of early quilts entitled "Optical Quilts." For the first time, quilts were seen primarily on their own aesthetic merits as works of art and only secondarily as stunning *tours de force* or contributions to the national crafts tradition. In 1971, the Whitney Museum of American Art's exhibition, "Abstract Design in American Quilts," ignited a blaze whose light has since shone far beyond the borders of our nation. Writing of this ground-breaking show, Janet Malcolm of *The New Yorker* stated, "I don't know when an exhibition has given me so much pleasure and so much to think about."[2] In *Craft Horizons*, David Shapira rhapsodized over the "polychrome perfection" of the quilts, calling them "tapestries of courage, stability, intransigence, and intent." To those who had categorized quilts as mere women's work, he declared, "Here is a spirit in answer to Rimbaud's almost haughty call for women to be poets. They already were."[3]

Those who have attended quilt shows and exhibitions have no doubt experienced the same emotions. In the presence of quilts one is made aware of the silent rhythms of life and the songs of the soul stitched into their fabric—a potent force of human essence evoking quilt makers of the past whose names and faces may never be known.

The air of warmth and humanity radiated by a display of quilts awoke a need in our culture. In 1972, *America's Quilts and Coverlets*, an illustrated documentary by Dr. Robert Bishop and Carleton Safford, provided another opportunity for a nation to define its roots.

Quilt exhibitions in museums and art galleries attracted unprecedented attendance for a genre previously regarded as a minor craft within the more elevated sphere of the decorative arts. In 1981, "American Quilts: A Handmade Legacy," opened at the Oakland (California) Museum, offering an opportunity to make a comparison between early and contemporary quilts; within three months 125,000 people had visited the exhibition.

Such great attention focused on the native tradition of quilts influenced a number of individuals to try their hand at making exact copies of examples they had seen. However, more often than not, producing an entire quilt proved intimidating; as relative beginners in this art, quilt makers of the 1970s were unprepared to meet so great a challenge and instead started by working on single blocks. Books and magazines reproduced scores of traditional quilt-block designs, often illustrating contemporary variations. Such encouraging suggestions, as well as the guidance offered by quilting teachers, kindled the first sparks of innovation among novices. The successful completion of a single block led to the making of others, until the maker had to decide what to do with them. Thousands of sampler quilts and pillow covers were the result.

Each block incorporated the trial-and-error attempts to master techniques unpracticed for a generation. But the experience of mastering elementary structure and technique made it possible to achieve greater creativity in this flexible medium. Quilters realized that it is possible to manipulate geometric shapes into infinite variations. They were also made aware of the greater possibilities in the choice of fabric design and the interaction of color, textures, and even possible embellishments.

The new generation of quilters realized they required more guidance, and it was forthcoming from such sources as periodicals, quilt shops, and dedicated teachers. In 1968, Bonnie Leman provided a much-needed forum with her *Quilter's Newsletter.* This was but one of many such periodicals that publish useful information and chronicle historical facts, which have found a vast readership among the nationwide network of quilters.

Quilting students also enjoyed the camaraderie they found in quilt shops; by dropping in regularly they developed new friends. Such establishments have become the twentieth-century equivalent of the old-fashioned quilting bee, where plans were made for the crafting of wedding, engagement, friendship, and baby quilts. The shop was also a place to relieve the blahs, because there was always something new to discover: fabrics, patterns, books, periodicals, and ideas.

Quilt shops stocked new devices that made the task of quiltmaking quicker and easier. The revival of quilting and the reversal of industrialization's contempt for the work of human hands has been eclipsed by the role that technology has played in encouraging the boom in today's quiltmaking. Dacron polyester, the first new quilt filler since the eighteenth century, became available to modern quilt makers. Its homogeneous structure permitted the making of a quilt without necessarily quilting every inch and provided freedom from commitment to a long-term project. The tactile pleasure afforded by working with this fluffy yet resilient material made the concept of quiltmaking even more enticing. Each manufacturer produced differing qualities: Some were softer, some were firmer, and some even fell apart too easily. In addition, some came by the yard, others were precut to standard quilt sizes, and yet others were packaged in bags already fluffed for pillow stuffing.

By the mid-1980s, quilters could choose wool, polyester, or cotton batting. A few even used silk batts, which were difficult to obtain as well as costly. To supply the need for better types of cotton batting, one variety was manufactured with an 80-percent-cotton and 20-percent-polyester content, a blend that possesses the homogeneous quality of the popular all-Dacron type but can also produce flat quilts similar to antique ones. Since many quilters wanted to vary the thickness of their quilts, battings with up to 3 inches were manufactured with the standardized quality control.

Cotton-covered polyester thread with the weight of regular cotton thread and the strength of buttonhole twist assured strong seams. Cotton quilting thread in all colors was silicon-coated to prevent knotting, thereby reducing some of the frustrations encountered in hand quilting.

New tools were introduced that facilitated all stages of quiltmaking. These included imported shears and rotary cutters for precision cutting, the latter having razor-sharp circular blades. Other accessories included line-graphed self-healing Teflon cutting boards that were impossible to cut through and 6- by 18-inch ruled and lined clear plastic straightedges to be used in conjunction with the boards. Both components were essential for cutting several layers of fabric accurately. Metal templates with sandpaper backings were manufactured, and plastic sheets for template making could also be purchased. For marking lines on quilts there were chalk pencils, soap pencils, erasable marking pens, quarter-inch masking tape, and quarter-inch rules; for quilt overlay design there were plastic precut stencils in every possible shape. Many quilt makers came to appreciate the flexibility of leather thimbles in a variety of styles. Expertise in hand quilting required short slender needles, and quilt shops carried such types as well as a platinum needle cradled in its own covered case.

One-hundred-percent cotton in prints and solids is a popular choice among quilters because of the fabric's ''hand'' and its ease in hand sewing. In the early 1970s, the productions of domestic textiles included a large proportion of polyester or polyester blended with cotton or wool, which proved a poor substitute for cotton; therefore, quilters discarded polyester knits and searched for woven cottons. Until this time the textile industry had concentrated on two main areas: home decorating and fashion. However, owing to the ever-increasing interest in quiltmaking and other needlecraft, many companies decided to cater to this new market. As a result, giant looms produced cotton fabrics in a wide range of colors, with special attention given to gradations of hue. Prints reproduced from antique examples conserved in archives and traditional stripes for borders and preprinted patchwork were designed by well-known modern quilt makers, and 72-inch-wide muslin for quilt backs also became available. Glazed cottons and new lightweight cotton sateens became favorites for whitework and trapunto. Even though the millions of quilts made during the last twenty years might not be recognizable by style, the dye colors of the fabrics furnish a clue to the decades when they were made.

Workshops, classes, and magazine features determined the latest designs and styles. Talented women and men concentrated on specific block designs and developed a specialized knowledge regarding techniques and historical periods. They shared their professional expertise with students as well as in articles for various periodicals, and many also wrote books. They were masters of their craft, and their beautiful quilts were represented in exhibitions at workshops. Their innovative variations on early blocks and designs inspired many quilts created in the 1970s and 1980s.

Many of these individuals left their careers and became quilting teachers, shop owners, authors, organizers of quilt symposiums, publishers, inventors, manufacturers of new quilting tools, patternmakers, and well-known quilt artists. Quilt artists were also teachers, lecturers, and authors, as were quilt-shop owners.

Some teachers are firm believers in maintaining direct links with traditional quilts, and such an approach usually encourages the study of early designs, adhering nonetheless to the structural boundaries imposed by block designs, balanced symmetry, and the importance of hand quilting, hand piecing, and hand appliqué to produce an authentic example. Other instructors, equally expert as needleworkers, stress the importance of structure in creative work. Concentration on such areas as the primacy of our rich quilting heritage has resulted in a solid foundation in the discipline of techniques—not only those employed in the early quilts but also those made available by modern technology. In other words, students should perfect both hand and machine work; according to their life-styles or the requirements of the project, the most appropriate techniques can be utilized.

In the 1870s, the wide adoption of the sewing machine was credited with turning women from quiltmaking to sewing clothes and items for home furnishing. A century later, computerized sewing machines do everything but place the fabric under the needle; nevertheless, the use of this device continues to be controversial. Machine quilting and appliqué have not been totally accepted in the quilt world of the 1980s.

One quilter wrote:

A famous man once said, "Only if you reach the boundary will the boundary recede before you. If you don't, if you confine your efforts, the boundary will shrink to accommodate itself to your own efforts. You can only expand your capacities by working to the very limit."

This truism was realized many times over in the process of making the "World's Largest Quilt" in 1982.[4] New ideas are always waiting in the wings—in designing and in drafting the patterns.

As the pictorial-quilt craze spread the word to even the smallest village, a number of people sensed a new trend and jumped on the bandwagon. The contemporary quilt was no longer confined to the bed; it was adaptable and capable of ornamenting a wide range of surfaces in an infinite variety of shapes and sizes. Quilts were not only hung on walls but hung from ceilings and across windows and were used to cover tables, chair seats, lampshades and lamp bases, and pillows. Quilts were also worn as clothing, including such accessories as hats and boots. Quilts adorned and enlivened the interiors of banks, libraries, corporate headquarters, shopping malls, and churches. Quilted banners lined streets during community celebrations. Traditional and contemporary quilt designs appeared on wallpaper, fabrics, carpeting, ceramic tiles, housewares, and linens. Geometric and appliqué patchwork designs were even seen in other needlework mediums, and quilt motifs were integrated into knitting, crewel, and counted cross-stitch patterns and kits. In addition, the influence of the quilt was manifested either in direct representation or in new styles of abstract art, as evidenced by certain paintings and collages.

Quilters began to organize local friendship quilt clubs, which then combined to form regional guilds, which in turn composed large state organizations. Interest was aroused in talented quilters through articles in quilt magazines, which sparked the desire to meet with and learn from recognized leaders in the field. The end result was the formation of the American Quilt Symposium. The phenomenon grew to such popularity that delegations arrived from Australia, France, Germany, the United Kingdom, and Japan.

In the October 1977 issue of *Quilter's Newsletter*, Bonnie Leman reported on the Lincoln (Nebraska) Quilt Symposium, the first extensive national event of its kind:

There was so much to see and hear and absorb, and so many old and new friends to chat with, it really took a while to come down to earth when it was over. Everyone I talked to seemed to be feeling great excitement and creative thrust. I'm sure that lots of projects are being planned and started now as a result of the meeting, and that the quilting teachers who attended will be sharing the ideas inspired by it for a long time to come.

Following the Lincoln Symposium was Hazel Carter's Continental Quilting Congress in Virginia. Soon the bulletin pages in quilting magazines included lists of such events, and by 1987 this grew to several pages in each issue filled with scores of events from quilt contests and workshops to large symposia held throughout the nation and even beyond its borders.

What was it about such symposia that made them so important? As one quilter observed:

It was overwhelming and wonderful to be surrounded by so many people who shared this obsession about quilting. To be enlightened by lecturers whose topics range from historical and contemporary quilts and/or textiles, to life prioritizing; to learn new techniques in workshops taught by people whose work I had appreciated, to attend a "show-and-tell" gathering, and to show my own work and have people applaud; to attend a quilt show/contest and be inspired, aware of the undetermined number of ideas, and amounts of energy and time in their planning and executing; to discover in the merchants mall the tools I'd been looking for—and others I never knew I needed; to purchase sought-after books; and to view a fashion show of original designs made by the participants.

Usually a quilt symposium takes two years of planning and is organized by a volunteer force. In these spontaneous gatherings, no individual's contribution is diminished by another's. Each brings unique experiences, personality, and ideas, which in turn become assets to the other participants who have come to learn. Individuals are encouraged to practice their own skills, pursue their own interests, and undergo their own experiences. The more unique the creations that quilters bring to share, the more they contribute to the inspiration of others. Such a community of interests both realizes and nurtures the ultimate quest: the search for self. These communal gatherings ensure that each participant will be respected for his or her own absolute human worth. Charles Reich suggests that "no such luxury was possible during most of man's history. It is wealth and technology that have now made community and self possible."[5]

As evidenced by the thousands of women who attend such events, there are no restrictions of time, money, or family that will keep them away once these new satisfactions and freedoms have been experienced. In 1982, Virginia Avery noted in *Quilts to Wear*:

> I've been fortunate to be invited to teach and lecture at many of these symposiums, and I am always amazed at the number of quilters—usually women—who show up; I know what planning and dogged determination lie behind each of their efforts to be there. First they have to work out the finances; paying for transportation, hotel, meals, and incidentals usually does not come out of petty cash. Women who work outside the home must arrange time off from office or shop, whether it is charged as vacation time or leave of absence. Women who are at home and responsible for husbands and children have to find a friendly mother who will pick up and deliver her young in her absence (with payment in kind at a future date). Mothers also must post reminders of schedules and appointments; and, in addition to all this, they leave refrigerators and freezers stocked with prepared meals and a list of instructions for heating and eating! I sometimes think of these quilters as indomitable ships churning steadily through unpredictable seas with a destination in mind if not in sight.[6]

Often all-night marathons are held to complete a project in time for it to be worn or exhibited at the gathering. As C. M. Penders wrote in *Lady's Circle Patchwork Quilts* (Jan. 1985, p. 67), "We assemble for the same human needs: to create, to leave something of lasting value, to enjoy one another, to grow in our craft and in our inner selves." The dashing artistic style and humorous candor of Virginia Avery, the doyenne of quilting, are welcomed at symposia everywhere. In 1978, her *Book of Appliqué* was published, and four years later she brought out *Quilts To Wear*. Her unique style of dress has become a trademark of this energetic woman, who is renowned for her mastery of the craft. By teaching, she enables others to be open and creative and to feel free to plan as they progress.

Among the greatest drawing cards to such symposia are the workshop leaders and lecturers. These prime motivators—who have developed distinct bodies of knowledge—define important approaches to design or to the philosophies of varying life-styles. One cannot overemphasize the importance of their influence or their generosity in sharing their talents and practical knowledge.

Early in 1960, Californian Jean Ray Laury was featured in many magazines with her quilts and other needlework designs. In *Quilter's Newsletter*, Bonnie Leman stated:

> Jean Ray Laury was one of the first to call my attention to quilts as art. By 1960 she was

becoming known as a stitchery artist with an especially honest and fresh view of the world. She is the author of numerous books, among them Appliqué Stitchery*(1966) and* Quilts and Coverlets *(1970), both innovators in the field at the time they were published. Over nine years ago in QN #23, we reviewed* Quilts and Coverlets, *and said in part: "The publication of a brand new book on modern quilting is a cause for celebration among quilters because it happens so seldom and especially when the book is as informational and inspirational as this one by [Ms.] Laury.* Quilts and Coverlets *offers a completely different approach to quiltmaking than the old standards we are used to. This book reflects her contemporary thinking and suggests many new and fresh ideas for today's quilt makers." Although dozens of books have been written about quilts since that time, Jean's book is still current and is now one of the standards itself.*[7]

Getting It All Together, another book by Ms. Laury, is a major contribution to quilting literature. In order to devote time to creative endeavors, many people require assistance in assigning their priorities, and this book provides clear and concise solutions to this problem. Many of Jean's quilts exemplify tongue-in-cheek commentaries on today's milieu. Others incorporate bold graphic designs that are indicative of her fresh, uncluttered approach to life.

In 1973, Beth Gutcheon's *The Perfect Patchwork Primer* was acclaimed as the most complete book ever published on patchwork instruction. Today, along with Jean Ray Laury's work, it is among the most popular and helpful of quilting manuals. Ms. Gutcheon's conversational but eloquent discussion of the meaning of quilts in the lives of our nation's citizens offers inspirational encouragement as well as an accurate appraisal of forthcoming developments.

Beth and her husband, Jeff, have become nationally known as teachers and lecturers, and are equally celebrated as contemporary quilt makers whose works are shown at major exhibitions all over the world. *The Quilt Design Workbook* (1976), which they wrote together, introduced pioneering experiments with illumination as well as their own work with geometric patchwork that created new spaces on quilt surfaces. Continuing his work with quilts, Jeff has also become involved in the wholesale and retail fabric business; this began when he started searching for unique and interesting solid and printed cottons, which he then sold to quilt shops or quilters. He ultimately went into designing his own line of fabrics.

In 1982, he wrote another book, *Diamond Patchwork*, which deals with the technique of creating three-dimensional effects on a flat surface and incorporates his background in architecture. The Gutcheons do not advocate any specific style other than self-expression. In the 1970s, their work was regarded by many as avant-garde and exemplary of new ways to manipulate design elements.

The pioneering individuals listed below have contributed stimulating concepts to the quilt genre, and their most characteristic or seminal work is also mentioned: Cheryl Bradkin for her *Seminole Patchwork*; Blanche and Helen Young for their Trip Around the World quilts; Moneca Calvert for her curved piecing techniques; Carol E. Butzke for her pictorial quilts; Helen Kelley for her Postage Stamp picture quilts and embroidered appliqués; Georgia Bonesteel for her lap quilting; Barbara Johannah for her quick piecing; Betty Boynk for her Basket quilts; Paula Nadelstern for her textured quilts depicting nursery rhymes and fairy tales; Ramona Chinn for her creativity in using leftovers from everyday life; Mary Ellen Hopkins for her unique humor and applied quick piecing; Dixie Hayewood for her crazywork; Faye Anderson for her ability to portray America's folklore in quilts; Judy Wasserman Hearst for her designs representing the changing seasons; Charlotte Patera for her reverse appliqués and interest in molas; and Marjorie Murphy for her whitework and trapunto. These are but a fraction of the hundreds of leaders who have given quilters inspiration through their innovative designs and techniques.

Learning the traditional early styles of quilting is vital to creating one's own styles. Once the structure of early examples has been mastered, individuals have the freedom to experiment. With encouragement and practice it is possible to attain greater self-expression. Inventing original work is exceptionally challenging and requires repeating experimental techniques over and over. Acceptance and encouragement of successful achievements in this area from the community of quilters helps build confidence, which is necessary when taking the risk of baring one's soul via the medium of new ideas.

Time has become one of our most precious commodities, as evidenced by the typical reaction upon seeing a quilt: "How long did it take to make?" In this computer age the options of what can be done with our time are so plentiful that it seems we need 25-hour days. Time is often seen as a form of currency that can be invested, saved, spent, wasted, lost, made up, and run out of. In America an individual's worth is measured by his or her ability to "produce"—not only with excellence but with great rapidity. As Beth Gutcheon stated:

> Now more than at any time in our history we want to connect with what is still admirable and untarnished in our history. In these times there seems to be some logic in participating in a tradition that is simple and noble and American in the way that we used to understand the word.[8]

Quilters often seem to be motivated by a strong urge to create something of lasting value, even a masterpiece in which the values and traditions of the past are incorporated within a validly contemporary work. To a generation of quilters eager to perfect their skills, Jinny Beyer offers techniques for mastering the task of intricate piecing and fine quilting. Her famous, prize-winning Ray of Light quilt inspired quilters to become meticulous. Ms. Beyer's quilts testify to the importance and joy that hand piecing and hand quilting can bring to one's life.

Without totally insulating themselves against everyday matters, many quilters state that the quilting process itself is an aid in setting one's pace, offering social and communal contacts, and developing respect for oneself and for others. Quilters are learning through practice that creativity is best nurtured, not through exhaustion, but by allowing sufficient time for leisure, and they are realizing that their work partakes of their personality.

Since its inception, the quilt revival's underlying ambition of attaining artistic excellence has been of prime importance. It is even possible that the women's lib movement might have had some influence on the categorizing of quilting as an art form. After all, if quilts are art, then their makers must be artists. In our society, artists are accorded license to be uniquely themselves, and the best achieve a high level of celebrity. Identification with the fine arts might not be so far removed from an apparent goal of the women's lib movement: to overcome self-doubt and learn to be self-sufficient, two important steps in acquiring confidence and respect. In *The Professional Quilter*, recognized quilt artist Jan Meyers observed, "As I have begun to do more teaching, I have noted a certain attitude in some workshop participants that reads something like this, 'I have only done traditional quilts. I want to learn how to design a quilt that is really original—that is ART.'"[9]

Unquestionably, quilt artists have "arrived" and are now faced with the challenge of creating even better work. Their designs have been influenced by contemporary art movements, early quilts, and acculturation in a shrinking world.

Many committed quilt artists strive for deeper understanding of design elements and experiment by working in series. Michael James follows this process with great discipline. His polychromatic works explore the interrelationship and interaction of color through the effects of light and transparency. He concentrates on simple curved shapes composed of graduated color strip piecing usually combined in block-design format. His work is arresting yet lyrical and soothing.

Nancy Crow is a colorist who employs strip piecing. She has stated that she was influenced by Seminole Indian patchwork, which is evident in her high-contrast colors that vibrate on the surface of her quilts. Like primitive drums, her symmetrically balanced design elements call and answer, sometimes in reverberating rhythm and at other times in muffled unison.

Yvonne Porcella creates energy fields with rich, vibrant colors offering strong contrasts with blacks and whites or with the static relief of delicately subdued color modulations painted on silk. She also is known for her pieced clothing designs and is a popular author, lecturer, designer, and teacher.

Nancy Halpern is recognized as one of America's most innovative quilt makers. Her abstract landscapes seem to depict nature converging with nature over architectural forms that emerge in confluence with nature. Hand-angled shapes are rendered in washes of glowing color and swim and glide in and out of a surrealistic dreaminess. She achieves this effect through the use of subtle color combinations and has been influenced by her awareness of light, weather, and the interaction of living things with the world.

Chris Wolf Edmonds first developed a reputation for her appliqué picture quilts such as "George Washington at Valley Forge" and the "Cherokee Trail of Tears," but she is equally skilled as a master of geometric and three-dimensional illusions. On viewing Ms. Edmonds's work, one is struck by an overwhelming sense of reverence. Her work has attained the level of perfection, blending mastery of technical skill with expressive power.

Based on log cabin techniques, the innovative designs of Maria McCormick Snyder are ethereal in feeling. Her inspired use of color and textured fabric creates a type of spiritual illumination that glows from the surface of her quilts.

Jan Myers's work is widely recognized for the employment of squares and graduated color, *procion*-dyed fabrics. Expanding and diminishing the size of her squares, whose rhythm is interrelated with graduated hue, she achieves the appearance of a magical gridwork. Ms. Myers's manipulation of these elements interweaves light into dark and angles into curves; she is a creator of arresting illusion.

Katie Pasquini has developed the study of the ever-enlarging mandala motifs in her quilts. Recently, her lively yet spiritual approach has resulted in active, freewheeling geometric abstractions that interplay in asymmetry. The creative freedom inherent in Terrie Hancock Mangat's often bizarre imagery somehow facilitates access to the subconscious in delightful ways. She employs her own imagery of living things in textured printed fabrics appliquéd onto a background world of energized patchwork. Small bits of cloth introduced in appliqué are then overlaid, contributing to the kinetic feeling of her surfaces.

Although each artist differs in approach and technique, their work speaks in unison about the influences of their surrounding environment and echoes in the past, present, and future. The degree to which self-expression can be identified is directly proportional to the degree to which an individual opens his or her senses to perceive. According to Abraham Maslow's theories of human motivation, our needs emerge in specific order, from the most primitive to the most complex. Neurologist Dr. A. Jean Ayres states:

> Although we may not think much about touch in our lives, the tactile system is the largest sensory system, and it plays a vital role in human behavior, both physical and mental. Touch sensations flow through the entire nervous system and influence every neural process to some extent. In addition, the tactile system is the first system to function effectively when the visual and auditory systems are just beginning to develop. For these reasons, touch is very important to overall neural organization. Without a great deal of tactile stimulation of the body, the nervous system tends to become unbalanced.[10]

The texture and softness of quilts undoubtedly aid in satisfying this earliest and most basic need. Quilts are also associated with warmth, security, and the pleasure obtained by visual stimulation. In her autobiography, Georgia O'Keeffe wrote:

> My first memory is of light—light all around. I was sitting among pillows on a quilt on the ground. The quilt was of cotton patchwork of two different kinds of material—white with very small red stars spotted all over it. I was probably 8 or 9 months old. The quilt is partially a later memory, but I know it is the quilt I saw on that day.

The fact that quilts stimulate the eye is obvious; but we need to train our eyes to perceive greater detail, to distinguish brilliance and subtle hues, to recognize lyric elements in two-dimensional design, to enjoy texture visually as well as tactilely, and to perceive pattern and motif in nature and in everyday objects. Since we are becoming ever more aware on every level, we are learning to perceive contemporary quilts as both beautiful and honest. From the heart of each quilt maker must come individual expressions of his or her reactions to the external world, and so each quilt must be vividly unique.

The quilts of the 1980s will attain fame, not for their unified focus on a small number of copyable patterns, but for their power to release the self into a creative communion with the natural world. American quilting continues its process of becoming. With over a million people involved, quiltmaking has brought about the most wide yet organized network of creative talents in any of the crafts. There are those artists who have reached a high level of public recognition, and there are those who have only today threaded their first quilting needle. To those who wonder if quilting has reached a hiatus, the answer is: It has only just begun to expand into ever-fresher areas of creativity. Quilters who have experienced the "dance" of the past and present are now striving on an upwardly spiraling, swirling path toward the future—toward spiritual heights and spaces in which the creative imagination soars. There are no limitations, only daring!

NOTES

1. Penny McMorris and Michael Kile, *The Art Quilt*, p. 46.

2. Janet Malcolm, "On and Off the Avenue: About the House," *The New Yorker* (September 2, 1974), pp. 68–73.

3. Penny McMorris and Michael Kile, *The Art Quilt*, p. 46.

4. Hazel Ross, "Making the World's Largest Quilt," *Ladies Circle Patchwork Quilt* (Fall 1985), pp. 32–33.

5. Charles Reich, *The Greening of America*, New York, Random House, 1970.

6. Virginia Avery, *Quilts to Wear*, p. 12.

7. Bonnie Leman (ed.), "Quilt Artists and Collectors Honored," *Quilter's Newsletter Magazine*, Vol. 2, No. 1 (January 1980), p. 4.

8. Beth Gutcheon, *The Perfect Patchwork Primer*, p. 21.

9. Jan Meyers, *The Professional Quilter*, No. 9 (January 1985), p. 5.

10. A. Jean Ayres, *Sensory Integration and the Child*, p. 39.

177

Nancy Crow (strip-piecing and marking) and Velma Brill (quilting). *Bittersweet XII*. 1980.
Baltimore, Ohio. Cotton and polyester, 82 × 82″. Collection The Museum of American Folk Art, New York.
Gift of Nancy Crow. Photograph by Scott Bowron.

Nancy Crow's attention to superb vibrant color demonstrates why she is celebrated in contemporary quilting circles.

 **178**

Jean Ray Laury. *Pieced and Appliquéd Bread Quilt*. 1979.
Clovis, California. Cotton, 46×53". Private collection.
Photograph courtesy Jean Ray Laury.

This charming quilt is an example of Jean Ray Laury's
individual style and exemplifies the humor that occasionally
finds its way into her work. This design was made as a gift
for a friend who baked homemade bread for the artist.
The blocks include the different types of bread that were
baked, and the ingredients and kitchen equipment used
in their preparation. The words are stamped, and some of
the details are embroidered. Jean's favorite food is fresh
bread, but as the baker herself finds hot-fudge sundaes
''irresistable,'' one is therefore featured in a block. (Jean
says she misspelled ''irresistible,'' but left it uncorrected
to show that although her friend's weakness may be
chocolate, her own is spelling.)

    For the past 25 years Jean Ray Laury has been one of
the most influential quilt and textile designers in this field.
She was one of the first to get quilts out of church bazaars
and into galleries. She is also the author of over a dozen
books, and has been accorded many one-woman shows.

179

Jean Ray Laury. *Starfire Pieced Quilt*. 1981. Clovis,
California. Cotton, 60×52". Private collection.
Photograph courtesy Jean Ray Laury.

This design uses a traditional eight-pointed star in an
asymmetrical arrangement. The positive–negative pattern
of the stars shifts between red and white, while images
emerge from a pattern of squares and triangles. The overall
impression suggests a grove of trees. The quilting parallels
the seam lines. This is an excellent example of a traditional
quilting pattern employed in a very contemporary composition.

180

Jean Ray Laury. *Four Square Pieced Quilt*. 1982. Clovis,
California. Cotton, 84×84". Collection the artist.

The title refers to the fundamental use of blocks. Design,
scale, and colors all expand from the center. Small squares
enlarge as the design grows; colors progress from yellows
at the center to yellows, oranges, and pinks on one side to
yellows, greens, and blues on the other.

181

Jean Ray Laury. *Rainbow Stars Pieced Quilt*. 1982. Clovis, California. Cotton, 114×104″. Collection the artist.

This example is representative of the designer's series of Star quilts. Here, a medallion design of stars forms the center, and stars repeat as colors move through the spectrum. The stars appear to advance and recede as they change from light to dark.

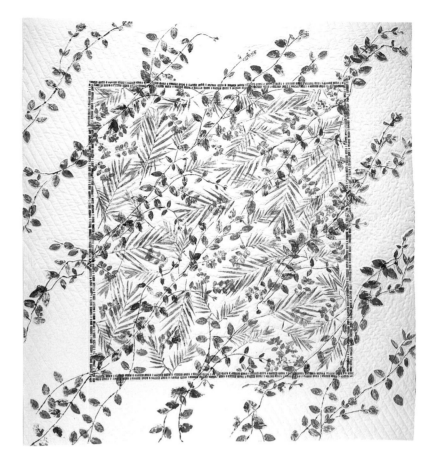

182

Gerlinde Anderson. *Sunshowers*. 1982. Riverside, California. Pieced cotton, satin, silk, velveteen, and metallic fabric, 70×60″. Collection the artist.

The quilter here expresses her impression of rain and sun. The elements struggle to obtain supremacy, and amid violent atmospheric conditions, the rain falls like arrowheads from the sky. However, the stormy conditions hold the promise of a glorious sun.

183

Margot Strand Jensen. *When the Leaves Leaved*. 1982. Aurora, Colorado. Pieced muslin, 72×68″. Collection the artist.

This is one of the few contemporary quilts in which the artist has hand-stamped the images. Margot Strand Jensen is a self-taught quilter; in this sample she wished to express her love of nature and the beauty that can be found in the "colorful clothing" of the trees' leaves.

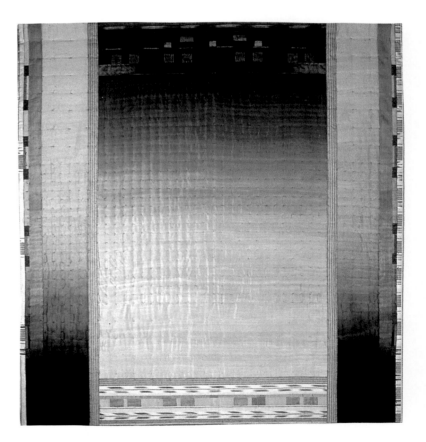

184

Ardyth Davis. *Tied Bars/Mauve-Jade Pieced Quilt*. 1983. Leesburg, Virginia. Commercial cotton ikat and silk. 92×87″. Private collection.

Since winning the 1985 Award of Excellence from Quilt National, this hand-painted and tied-silk machine-quilted fantasy has been widely exhibited during a national tour.

185

Sidney Allee Miller. *The Quilting Bee*. 1981. Galena, Illinois. Pieced cotton, 90×90". Private collection.

This quilt incorporates an idea inspired by a painting by Grandma Moses. It expresses the maker's concept of what family members would do if they attended a quilting bee: as she says, they would be "reading, working, watching, or gossiping."

⊞ 186

Tafi Brown. *Jewels*. 1982. East Alstead, New Hampshire. Pieced cotton, 72×62″. Collection the artist.

Tafi Brown is a self-taught quilter whose work has been shown in the United States, France, and Turkey. She designs houses for a woodworking company in New Hampshire. Wishing to memorialize her professional skills and accomplishments in cloth, she created this lovely quilt. (It is, incidentally a cyanotype quilt—that is, the images were reproduced by a photographic process—and such examples are relatively uncommon.)

187

Tafi Brown. *Jewels* (detail of 186).

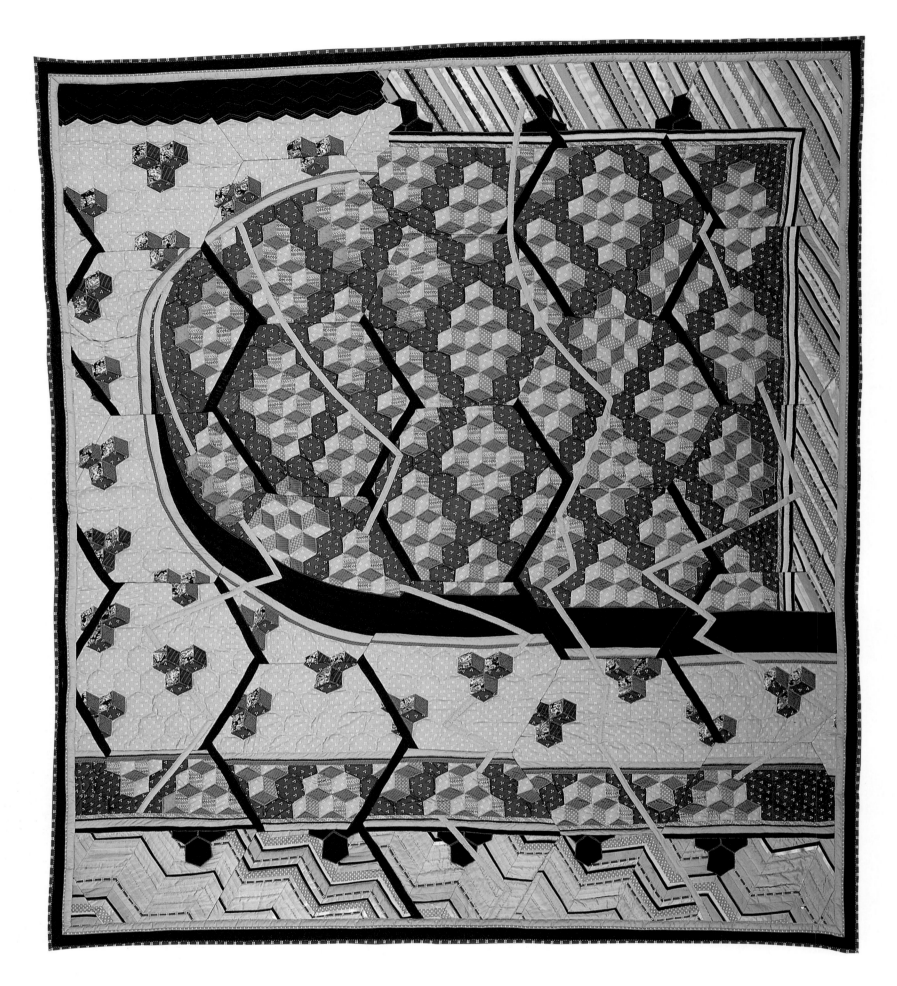

⊞ 188

Veronica Fitzgerald. *Untitled*. 1982. Oak Ridge, Tennessee. Pieced silk and cotton, 100×96″. Collection the artist.

Plums and electric blues are the main color tonalities in this unusual, asymmetrical, and illusionist design that gives the impression of ever-changing movement.

⊞ 189

Paula Nadelstern and Lynn Della Posta. *Fairy Tales*. 1983. Bronx, New York. Pieced and embroidered cotton, poly-cottons, Ultrasuede, and various blends, 72 × 72″. Private collection.

This delightful quilt was the 1983 Blue Ribbon winner of the World of Quilts contest. It represents a homage to childhood fantasies, incorporating sixteen squares each illustrating well-known children's storybook characters, from Rumpelstiltskin to the Wizard of Oz. The quilt offers an inventive use of brilliant color and design elements. It was hand-embroidered and appliquéd by Ms. Nadelstern, and machine-pieced by Ms. Della Posta.

190

Nancy Clearwater Herman. *Peacock Hallelujah*. 1983. Merion, Pennsylvania. Pieced satin and cotton, 60 × 60″. Collection the artist. Photograph by Kenneth Kauffman.

This quilt is one of a series in which patterns can be discerned that in combination create a mandala.

191

Violet S. Larsen. *Waterlily Waltz*. 1984. Portsmouth, Virginia. Pieced cotton and chintz, 36½ × 36½″. Collection the artist. Photograph by Tampte/Wilson.

By creating a hexagon set into a square with two different corners, the quilter had a beautiful star express sparkling water. The brown square suggests nests both over the water and between the waterlilies.

192

Yvonne Porcella. *In Autumn the Evening Shows Its Lavender*. 1985. Modesto, California. Pieced silk, 58 × 58″. Collection Suzanna Silverstein. Photograph by Sharon Risedorph.

Commissioned by the collector, this quilt uses a brilliant and original manipulation of fabric and placement of color that has elicited the admiration of all who have seen it at exhibitions. The fine stitching and the working of the colors along the border are worthy of special attention.

193

Yvonne Porcella. *Ginza*. 1984. Modesto, California. Pieced cotton and metallic fabric, 67 × 67".
Collection the artist. Photograph by Sharon Risedorph.

This quilt was shown at an exhibition of contemporary art held in Japan. Its vibrant colors, the clever deployment of cottons and metallics, and the careful attention to detail show why this artist is in such great demand as a teacher and lecturer. She is one of the leaders in the contemporary quilting world.

194

Yvonne M. Khin. *Around the Corner*. 1986. Bethesda, Maryland. Pieced cotton and other fabrics, 33×30". Collection the artist.

This work exemplifies a family effort; the pattern was chosen from Judy Martin's book *Scrap Quilts*, and Yvonne's husband executed the quilting.

195

Faye Anderson. *Three-Dog Night*. 1984. Denver, Colorado. Pieced cotton and lurex, 52×46". Collection the artist.

The title refers to the Eskimo practice of determining the coldness of a night by the number of sled dogs with which one needs to sleep to keep warm. The quilter's pet dogs also provide warmth and security, like a quilt. Here she has shown them playing in each of the four seasons; winter is their favorite, and is shown in the center of the quilt—where it is snowing dog biscuits. This special quilt was accorded the Judges' Choice Award at the 1985 Houston Quilt Festival.

196

Julie Berner (design) and Thekla Schnitker (needlework). *One Fine Day*. 1984. Eugene, Oregon. Pieced cotton, 40×40". Private collection.

The explosion of color in twentieth-century art and design inspired this quilt that incorporates a pattern of progressive shapes on a geometric grid.

197

Yvonne M. Khin. *Alphabets*. 1984. Bethesda, Maryland. Pieced cotton, 58×52″. Collection the artist.

The maker's skill in cross-stitch and her wish to teach her great-nephew, Stephen Axe, the alphabet are integrated here. This quilt is a unique children's teaching tool. Each letter of the alphabet incorporates images whose names begin with that particular letter; for instance the letter "P" contains a peacock, parrot, panda, penguin, potato, peach, pig, and piece of pie. It is both a beautiful and adorable work created with true imagination and obvious affection.

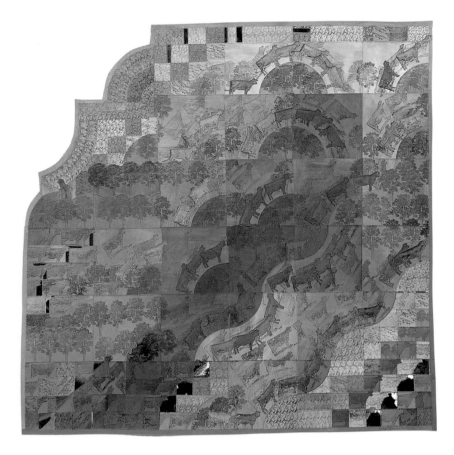

Jody Klein. *Many, Many Cows and Related Images*. 1984. Waltham, Massachusetts. Mixed mediums, 48×144". IBM Education Building, Atlanta, Georgia.

Composed of three paper-fabric laminated panels, the work was commissioned by IBM and installed in February 1984. Each panel is composed of 36 eight-inch squares and is based on a traditional quilt design. The main format is a quarter-circle cut from a square; Nine-Patch squares are also incorporated. These traditional patterns are interpreted in contemporary materials and techniques. The images include cows, trees, multiple heads of George Washington, and flowers; all of these motifs were adapted from the artist's collection of rubber stamps, which are part of a larger collection of toys and other artifacts. The triptych is incredibly well-executed and subtly colored.

The techniques by which it was made include stamping, stitching, both hand and machine stuffing (trapunto for the cows), painting, and drawing. The artist stated:

Although these pieces all incorporate my personal vocabulary of images, I am very interested in exploring other possibilities of abstract patterning related to the constructions that I have been making for the past several years. My commissioned works are designed to be site-related in color, scale, and subject, while still retaining my personal approach.

199

Therese May. *Monster Quilt #7*
(detail of 200).

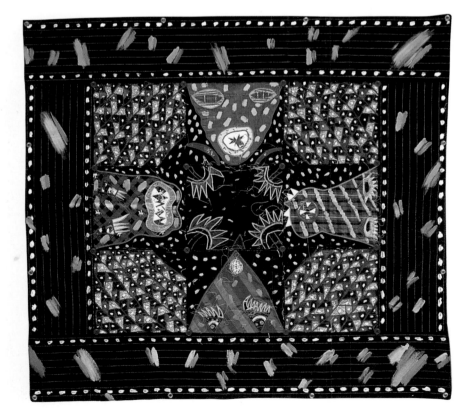

200

Therese May. *Monster Quilt #7*. 1985. San Jose, California. Pieced cotton and satin, 54×59". Collection the artist. Photograph courtesy Lynn Kellner and Sharon Risedorph.

This is just one of nine sections of an unusual quilt that gives the impression that one is viewing a modern-day avant-garde monster movie. Acrylic paint has been added to enhance the surface and threads have been allowed to hang free.

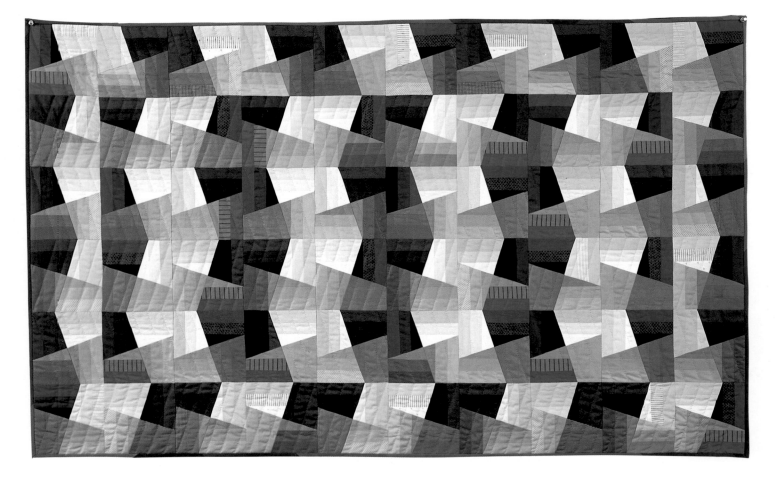

⊞ 201

Carol H. Gersen. *Autumn Night*. 1985. Exeter, New Hampshire. Pieced cotton, 36½ × 60".
Collection the artist. Photograph by David Caras.

This is the sixth in a series depicting seasonal changes; here, autumnal colors are successfully evoked by various shades of brown and blue. Machine piecing skillfully combines these colors and creates a feeling of Indian summer's warmth in this beautiful nocturne.

⊞ 202

Veronica Fitzgerald. *Untitled #1*. 1986. Oak Ridge, Tennessee. Pieced silk and cotton, 80 × 168". Collection the artist.

A former quilting teacher at the Arrowmont School of Arts and Crafts in Gatlinburg, Tennessee, the present quilter is one of today's most skillful manipulators of color, design, and texture.

⊞ 203

Soizik Labbens. *Le Chant Hindou*. 1985. Paris. Pieced cotton and chintz, 56 × 55".
Collection the artist. Photograph courtesy Bruno Jarret.

The maker writes that this abstract work was inspired by "the image of a couple of English ice-skaters dancing to the music of Rimski-Korsakov, both dressed in orange, red, and silver—it stuck in my mind and gave me the idea of color and motion." The *Chant Hindou* is "The Song of India," and it is one of the better-known arias from Rimski-Korsakov's colorful opera *Sadko*.

204

Phyllis Moore. *Lone Star Pieced Quilt*. 1985.
Lancaster, Pennsylvania.
Cotton and Dacron, 60×60″. Collection the artist.

In this recently made quilt, over 2,000 hand-pieced fabric scraps make up the border alone, which gives you some conception of the quilt's complexity.

205

Odette Goodman Teel. *Ms. Sue: Alive and Liberated*. 1986.
Massachusetts. Pieced and appliquéd cotton, 84×72″.
Private collection.

What will people think of this quilt in the future? What will be the status of women's liberation? Will there be a woman president? Women in the pulpit? Ms. Teel thinks that her quilt's interest lies in the topics she has chosen to interpret. The quilter thinks that her contribution in fabric to the women's cause will still be of interest a century from now.

206

Sharyn Craig. *Star Garden*. 1986. San Diego, California.
Pieced cotton, 79×60″. Collection the artist.

One year was spent in the preparation and completion of this quilt. Sharyn's student, Arlene Stamper, executed one of the Mariner's Compass motifs. Note the skillful workmanship that went into rendering the flowers just inside the border.

207

Moneca Calvert. *Glorious Lady Freedom.* 1986. Carmichael, California. Machine-pieced, appliqué, hand-quilted, and embroidered cotton, 72×72". The Museum of American Folk Art, New York. Photograph courtesy 3M Corporation.

Moneca Calvert won the $20,000 first prize in Scotchgard's Great American Quilt Contest for this poster-graphic contemporary adaptation of the theme of the Statue of Liberty Centennial. The judges' comments included: "a consummate piece of work," "a beautifully realized design concept," "a communication to the world of people who quilt," and "it radiates power and hope."

The maker herself stated:

> I first visited the Statue of Liberty in 1982 and wanted a design with the same visual impact as the real thing: for that reason, I wanted the figure of the statue to dominate and be as close to human size as possible. . . . I chose to do a bird's-eye view with the landscape of the purple mountains and the fields of grain receding into the horizon.

Embroidered across the bottom of the quilt is "from sea to shining sea" and "1886 to 1986."

⊞ 208

Charlotte Warr Anderson. *We Give Thanks*. 1986. Salt Lake City, Utah. Pieced and appliquéd cotton, 26 × 26″. Private collection.

The maker was asked to donate a quilt to be auctioned for the benefit of the LDS Hospital in Salt Lake City, and she thought that the quilt titled *We Give Thanks* would be a perfect choice. This beauty went for $2,600, one of the highest prices ever recorded at this auction.

⊞ 209

Penny Sisto. *Gypsies* (detail). 1986. New Haven, Kentucky. Pieced and appliquéd cotton, fur, leather, and silk. 96 × 48″. Private collection.

Penny Sisto learned quilting from her grandmother, and after making well over 500 examples, she thinks that this fabric that is hanging presently in the Church of the Epiphany reflects her trademark in the field; it expresses her strong desire to communicate her emotions and thoughts via the medium of textiles. One can't help but notice the strength projected by the faces and the colors in this unique work.

⊞ 210

Carol E. Butzke. *Bright Hopes, Bright Promise*. 1986. Slinger, Wisconsin. Pieced and appliquéd cotton, 72×72".
Collection the artist. Photograph courtesy The Museum of American Folk Art, New York.

Carol Butzke's rendering of a photograph set against a patchwork ground made her a state winner in the Great American Quilt Contest. Mrs. Butzke says of this quilt:

> *The quilted background on which the photo lies is a variation of a traditional block called Our Country. Its arms seem to link together forming a strong union, just as our fifty states join together to form a strong country.*

The skillful and subtle shadings of the brown in the clothing tones are extremely effective. One feels an emotional response to the image, which gives the impression of looking over the shoulders of this immigrant family as they gaze beyond the railing toward the distant Statue of Liberty. Ms. Butzke is a member of local quilting groups, and has been a quilter since 1980. Her work has won Best of Show, Blue Ribbon, and Viewers' Choice awards in state quilt competitions as well as received national recognition because of the present quilt, which "is dedicated to quilters, many of whom come from immigrant backgrounds."

⊞ 211

Ramona Chinn. *Converging Values*. 1986. Anchorage, Alaska. Pieced cotton, 29 × 29½″. Collection the artist.

The year 1974 saw the start of Ramona Chinn's self-instruction in the technique of quilting and its design. Twelve years later her skill and artistry allowed for this interpretation and concept of light and movement. This is but one example of her art, and it provides evidence that through hard work and perseverance, beautiful quilts can be created.

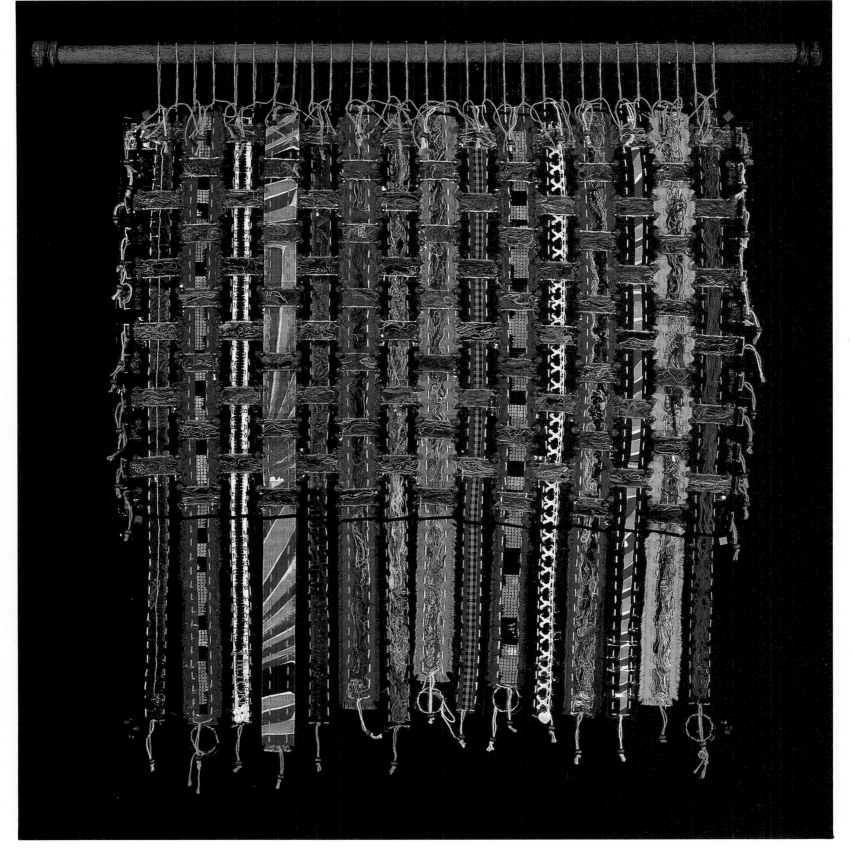

212

Ramona Chinn. *A Fiber's Fantasy*. 1986. Anchorage, Alaska. Pieced vinyl, paper, cotton, shredded fibers, and wooden beads. 24 × 20½". Collection the artist.

A challenge by the maker's friends inspired her to bring together various unrelated items from a box in executing this work. Usually, fibers are woven in fabric and are located on the outside of a quilt. However, in this unique example fabrics, paper, shredded fibers, mirrors, and other items from the box become a quilt sandwich composed of fibers woven as cloth.

🏁 213

Ellen Oppenheimer. *Broken-Arm Quilt*. 1986. Oakland, California. Pieced and appliquéd cotton, 72×72″. Collection the artist.

Although a self-taught quilter, Ellen Oppenheimer skillfully and successfully created this complicated design. The employment and juxtaposition of fabrics and colors not only is a virtuoso feat in itself, it also creates a treat for the eye.

🏁 214

Nancy Gipple. *Broken and Breaking Patterns*. 1986. St. Paul, Minnesota. Pieced leather with various fabrics, 82×144″. Collection the artist.

As she wished to express her particular love for farms, Nancy Gipple visited various fields and pastures and gathered items to make her fabric. The finished quilt exemplifies a tribute to farmers and their families, which is evidenced by the work's subtitle: "The Midwest Family Farm Blues."

![215 icon] **215**

Michael James. *Rhythm Color: Bacchanale*. Somerset Village, Massachusetts. c. 1986.
Pieced cotton and silk, 73 × 73″. Private collection. Photograph by David Caras.

Multicolored swirls of cotton and silk fabrics forming vibrant diagonals draw the viewer's eye to the twelve perfectly centered squares in this unusually fine work.

🔲 216

Patsy Allen. *Deco Tepee II*. 1986. Greensboro, North Carolina. Pieced cotton, 57 × 92½".
Collection the artist. Photograph by Steve Budman.

The present example is the second in a series. This quilt shows a sophisticated exploration of color values. The turquoise and peach squares were hand silkscreened by the artist.

🔲 217

Miriam Nathan-Roberts. *The Worms Crawl In—The Worms Crawl Out*. 1985. Berkeley, California. Pieced hand-dyed cotton, 103 × 103". Collection the artist.

This quilt is a visual treat, and offers stunning evidence of the artist's skill in manipulating cool red and gray. It is not surprising, therefore, that the piece was a first place winner in the American Quilt Society's 1986 show.

218

Judith Larzelere. *Dayglow*. 1986. Dedham, Massachusetts. Pieced cotton, 78 × 72″.
Collection the artist. Photograph courtesy Jan Bindas.

This example won second prize at Vermont's Quilt Festival in 1986, perhaps because of the surge of
visual energy radiated by the quilt. The soft subtlety and placement of color here evoke the atmosphere of
a peaceful spring day.

⊞ 219

Pamela Studstill. *Quilt #59*. 1986. Piper Creek, Texas. Pieced cotton, 52 × 52″.
Collection the artist. Photograph by Tim Tilton.

Taking an idea from one of her previous works, the quilter creates a design that draws the eye to her employment of hand-painted cottons. One cannot help but admire the fine quilting here as well as the incredibly complex design.

220

Charlotte Patera. *Tuxedo Junction*. 1986. Noreto, California. Reverse appliqué cotton, 72×72″.
Collection the artist. Photograph by Sharon Risedorph.

Named after a famous hit tune, this quilt is the ninth in a series that the maker has dedicated to the music of Glenn Miller. By following the lines and dots to the check pattern in the center, the viewer will see the "junction."

A QUILT-COLLECTOR'S PRIMER

A QUILT-COLLECTOR'S PRIMER

Celia Y. Oliver

The Shelburne Museum is widely known for a superb collection of quilts that date from the late eighteenth century to the mid-twentieth century and include every style and type of technique: whole-cloth quilts made with printed cotton or wool, or both, quilted with elaborate patterns, patterned pieced quilts from all periods, early Broderie Perse-style appliqués, elaborately patterned appliqués popular in the mid-nineteenth century, Victorian Log Cabin and crazy quilts, and twentieth-century quilts in contemporary colors with designs of the period as well as earlier, more traditional patterns. Many of the quilts are further decorated with embroidery, stencils, or even paint.

The museum quilt collection started with the private collection of Electra Havemeyer Webb, the daughter of Mr. and Mrs. H.O. Havemeyer, noted pioneer collectors who were the first Americans to seriously acquire European masterpieces. Mary Cassatt, who guided and inspired the Havemeyers in forming their collection, painted a charming and affectionate double portrait of Mrs. Havemeyer and the youthful Electra. Herself one of the earliest collectors of Americana, Mrs. Webb's interest in collecting American furniture, decorative pieces, textiles, and accessories was inspired in part by the revival of interest in traditional American handcrafts after World War I. The quilts and textiles reflect her deep regard for early American decorative art forms incorporating bold graphic patterns and clean colors. They initially were intended for decoration as well as for use in Mrs. Webb's homes. Over the years she was assisted by many well-known dealers and collectors of the day, including the quilt scholar and author of books on quilts, Florence Peto.

The scope of Mrs. Webb's Shelburne collection reflects the collecting interest of her day: primarily traditional patterns dating from the early through the mid-nineteenth century, typical of

New England and Central States (New York, Pennsylvania, Maryland, and New Jersey). Like most collectors of her time (1920–1960), Mrs. Webb had no interest in late-nineteenth-century or early-twentieth-century quilts, believing that these did not reflect the early American handcraft tradition. For this reason Victorian crazy or ''Japanese'' quilts, regional Amish and Midwestern examples, and the more modern stylized pieces from the Art Nouveau and Art Deco periods are not represented in her collection (however, subsequent donations and purchases have fleshed out the Shelburne's collection).

When first installed at the Shelburne Museum, the exhibition of Electra Webb's quilts and textiles stirred a vast amount of interest. The display was revolutionary for the time; the examples were mounted on movable racks that visitors were able to turn like the pages of a book. Nowhere else in the country was such a major collection made so immediately accessible to viewers.

Today the museum maintains a display of over one hundred quilts, rotating them from storage to display on a regular basis to ensure their preservation. While steps have been taken in recent years to apply the latest conservation methods to Mrs. Webb's examples, their basic presentation remains the same.

A collection is rarely complete, and Shelburne's is no exception. We are constantly adding to it and seeking to improve its scope and quality. We rely primarily on donations, although new acquisitions are occasionally secured through purchase. Throughout the year we receive numerous letters and phone calls from potential donors, collectors, and dealers offering us a variety of works. Every submission is carefully considered, photographs are requested, and further information is sought. The textile is then thoroughly evaluated to determine whether it merits inclusion in the museum's holdings.

How does a museum go about evaluating a quilt? Charles Montgomery, a scholar of American decorative arts, advised his students and peers ''to approach every object with an inquiring mind as well as with an inquiring eye.''[1] To evaluate a textile one must examine it carefully while asking a series of questions, the answers to which will help place the object in an artistic and historic framework. What is it? How does it look? Who made it and why? Where was it made, how and when? Obviously, the answers to some of these questions will come from the actual piece. Others will be determined from a base of information the researcher must accumulate: historical information relating to the chronology of technological advances in textile manufacture, the availability of hand-woven versus machine-made cotton and linen, the introduction of new printing techniques and chemical dyes, the evolution of pattern designs in textiles, and the popularity of various quilt patterns and construction techniques.

Evaluation of a quilt or any other artifact can be broken down into a few basic areas of consideration: aesthetic appearance, craftsmanship, history and provenance, condition, and rarity. Let us define these terms and then examine each in detail.

Aesthetic Appearance: The total effect of the quilt. A good quilt incorporates a successful combination of a good design with a pleasing choice of colors.

Craftsmanship: The maker's ability not only to execute careful and precise stitches and construction techniques but also to recognize and choose appropriate materials.

History: The maker of the quilt, where it was made, and why. This aspect is important because it places the piece into context, making it at once a beautiful bedcover and a historical document.

Provenance: The history of the quilt's ownership.

Condition: The state of a textile. This provides evidence of its use over the years. Soil and stains, frayed edges, tears, and fabric losses as well as changes to the original piece, repairs, and restoration determine not only its market value but the way it was regarded by its previous owners.

Rarity: The number of known similar pieces, taking into account all the various elements of the quilt and its history.

Aesthetic Appearance

The overall appearance of a quilt depends on the successful combination of two major factors: the overall design and the materials chosen, and the colors and patterns. Before one can subject a textile to a critique, it is important to know what one is looking at. A quilt is the end result of "quilting," a technique that joins layers of cloth or other materials by stitching through them. The basic elements of a quilt are the top, the interlining, the backing, and the edges.

Obviously, the top plays the most important role in the appearance of the quilt. The method of construction can, in part, predict the nature of the final design. Consider how these various elements combine to make a particular design successful. First, step back and look at the quilt. Take a reading of your immediate emotional response. Do you like it? When really struck by a piece, many will say, "It sings to me." I usually describe it as the quilt saying, "Take me home."

But don't take it home yet. Take your answer and ask why. Does the overall pattern or design have rhythm? Does your eye move over the design, with one element leading you to another section? Is there a sense of harmony and proportion in the design? What are the relationships of the patterns in the field to one another and to the border? Are motifs repeated and emphasized? In an overall pattern, does the design fill the space, and are the proportions effective? Whether the design is pictorial or abstract, each section of the design should balance and complement the others. The museum's pieced and appliqué Civil War quilt is an excellent example of successful design. The individual pattern elements and colors work together and move the viewer's eyes around the entire piece. The overall design of the quilt radiates from the central flower. The montage of figures in the center leads the eye around the square to the wonderful patchwork banding that creates an almost architectural barrier, or moat, between the images of hearth and home and the marching soldiers. The oversized diamonds in the border create a tension that forces the eye back to the appliquéd figures.

The aesthetic quality of the quilt depends first on how the quilter chose to integrate the pattern with the fabrics. Let us examine the three basic quilt types: whole cloth, pieced, and appliqué. The whole-cloth quilt employs only one type of fabric for the top—either plain or printed—and then relies on the textile pattern or on some type of decorative stitching for the overall pattern. The choicest whole-cloth quilts are the late-eighteenth-century and early-nineteenth-century examples made with glazed wool (often called linsey-woolsey) and quilted with elaborate patterns of scrolled vines, flowers, and hearts. Then come the so-called whitework quilts so popular in the mid-nineteenth century, which often had trapunto (padded quiltwork) patterns of floral medallions enclosed within elaborate wreaths of flowers and feathers. Originality in design and choice of fabric are very important factors in evaluating whole-cloth quilts. For instance, most whole-cloth examples made with printed patterned fabrics are merely tacked together to hold the layers. The maker of our Crystal Palace quilt chose to quilt around each figure, thus creating a three-dimensional effect.

Pieced work, or piecing, is the process of joining or seaming individual pieces of fabric together in a predetermined pattern to create a larger textile. Various techniques are employed when joining the quilt squares together to form the quilt top. The Shelburne's silk pieced quilt in the Boxed-Star pattern incorporates black velvet bands to separate the squares. The black contrasts dramatically with the brightly patterned squares and unifies the overall pattern.

The third type is the crazy quilt with its randomly joined pieces. The success of this quilt pattern relies on elaborate textiles and embroidery for overall design interest. For example, Harriet Garney Bower made her quilt in the 1890s, embroidering various flowers, figures, and designs onto the puzzlelike arrangement of pieces of velvet, brocade, and satin.

Appliqué derives from the French *appliquer*, meaning to put on or lay on. Thus, an appliqué pattern is made by placing pieces of fabric cut in predetermined shapes and sizes in a specific pattern on a larger piece of cloth called a ground. Appliqué patterns tend to be more pictorial and representational than pieced patterns because the construction technique does not depend on sewn seams and therefore allows the quilt maker greater flexibility in arranging the pattern pieces. Appliqué album quilts are highly prized, since they often allow the maker's originality and imagination to come to the fore. For example, our Oddfellows quilt was made to raise funds for a Masonic lodge in Providence, Rhode Island, immediately after the Civil War. Many of the squares employ such important Masonic symbols as the heart and hand, the beehive, and the All-Seeing-Eye. While primitive in style and craftsmanship, the Civil War quilt made in Kingston, New York, is wonderful because of its graphic simplicity and the charming combinations of motifs: Abraham Lincoln and Stephen Douglas, a checkerboard, the family pet, and various appliqué patterns popular at the time.

Many quilt designs, both appliqué and pieced, are based on a grid pattern. Pattern blocks fill each square of the grid to create an overall design. The spacing in a quilt designed on a grid can be varied and used to create interesting overall patterns. Every square can be filled with a pattern block, or the quilt can be arranged in checkerboard fashion, allowing the maker to add quilted designs in the empty squares. For example, the trapunto clipper ships add a three-dimensional quality to the museum's Trilobe Flower quilt. In addition, borders are often used to separate the pattern blocks. This technique is especially effective when the banding is more decorative than simple lines. For instance, the flowering-vine motif is used in the Oddfellows album quilt to delineate the pattern blocks and is repeated in the elaborate border.

However, the success of a quilt's appearance rarely depends solely on the choice of design. The textiles selected to create the design are also very important; their patterns and colors should heighten the interest of a design, never obscuring it. The color scheme chosen establishes the character of a quilt: Grays and browns might be considered somber; red and green, bright and cheery. Analogous color schemes, which use colors along one side of the color wheel (yellow, red, and orange or purple, blue, and green), are usually richer and warmer in feeling than monochromatic color schemes (such as shades of green or shades of red). Contrasting colors (opposites on the color wheel, such as blue and orange or red and green) create a tension that can be quite dramatic. For example, the shades of blue-violet and orange-red used in our Flying Geese quilt are almost electric, and yet the sheen of the silk brocades creates an elegant appearance.

The Op artists of the 1960s would have enjoyed the mesmerizing effect of the museum's Hexagon and Triangle quilt. The strong contrasts of the red and yellow are emphasized by the green and blue of the ombre-printed triangles. Contrasts between colors (the addition of white and black to lighten or darken) create depth, since light colors advance while dark colors recede. Log Cabin quilts depend on value contrasts for the development of their overall pattern. Our Straight Furrow quilt is successful because the bright multicolored textiles used in the light blocks offer dramatic contrast to the adjoining blocks of dark red, brown, and blue.

Variations in textile patterns create movement that attracts the eye. Our Civil War Soldiers quilt demonstrates the manner in which large-scale prints—such as geometrics and plaids—provide strong contrast and excitement, especially when pieced with textiles of small, light, airy designs. The small scattered prints often used in Log Cabin quilts can appear as a solid color when seen from a distance but surprise the viewer when seen close up.

Craftsmanship

The quality of workmanship in a quilt is critical. The quality of the stitches, seams, and appliqué edges; the assembly; the backing; the hems; and the binding all affect the overall appearance of the textile. In an article for *Quilt Digest*, Jonathan Holstein wrote:

> Art and structure are as inextricably interrelated in a quilt as they are in any object with a planned aesthetic. Just as in painting, great craft does not ensure great art, nor does a disregard of craft and conventional imagery guarantee a vital result, a successful "primitive" work.[2]

Examine the workmanship of a quilt with a very critical eye. The stitches in the seams and in the quilting should be small and even, the finer the better. Hand stitching, of course, is far more desirable than machine stitching. Seams should be straight, because the lines of a pattern are determined by straight or evenly curved seams. The hems on the appliqué edges should be carefully turned with invisible stitches. Ideally, the only stitches that should show are the decorative stitches added for special effect. Examine how the edges of the quilt are finished. Typically, the rough edges of the fabric are enclosed in a taped-on binding. The finer quilts have a bias binding made with one of the fabrics used in the pattern. A less precise quilter might have used a purchased binding or rolled the hem toward the back of the quilt.

Fine craftsmanship and careful attention to detail are readily apparent in our Foundation Rose quilt. Precise stipple quilting repeats and highlights the pattern shapes in the swag border and the rose medallions. The red piping is a special touch seen only in quilts of fine quality. Another aspect of craftsmanship is the choice of fabrics—not the patterns or colors but the quality of the goods themselves. Coarse, loosely woven textiles are certainly not as durable or attractive as tightly woven material. The materials used in the Foundation Rose quilt have stood the test of time and are still in stable condition.

Of course, the critique of a quilt's craftsmanship should be weighed against any historical information available regarding the piece, such as the maker's age or economic status. For example, the museum's Streets of Boston quilt was made by two young sisters, Angeline and Augusta Kimberley, aged thirteen and fourteen, who could not be expected to have had an older woman's expertise at needlework or to have executed a quilt with the same precision and skill.

While the design is fairly simple and the fabrics are quite ordinary, the charm of the design and the work far outweighs the imperfection of the stitches.

History and Provenance

A quilt has the potential to serve as a document of a specific culture as well as a work of art. If we can date an object and identify the maker or the region where it was made, we can learn what materials were available, what patterns were popular, and what kind of people were making quilts at that time. Any anecdote or piece of information about a textile will add to its appeal. How can such information be found? First, examine the quilt. Many quilters signed and dated their work, either on the top or on the back. But be aware that subsequent owners of the quilt, especially a daughter who inherited it, might also sign their names to the cherished heirloom. Other usually reliable primary sources are letters or documents referring to the quilt or describing it. Presentation quilts are a delight to any historian because they were specifically made to record a particular moment or event: a friend moving away or retiring, a birth, or a wedding. Consequently, each contributor signed and dated his or her square, often adding the hometown as well as a quotation.

Lacking documentation of owners' marks or written evidence, we must rely on information passed down through the family or previous owners. There are some basic questions to ask: Who made the quilt? Where did he or she live? Why was it made? What was the family's economic status? How did they earn a living? What was their life-style? Do we know anything about the maker? Did he or she have other hobbies or skills? How was the quilt passed on to the current owner? Are there any photographs of the maker and family and their home or a family genealogy?

Such detective work often brings rewards. For example, the Shelburne Museum owns a Windmill Blades quilt made in the late 1880s by Clarissa White Alford (1806–1890). Family records provided a photograph of the maker as well as information about her life in St. Albans, Vermont.

While the testimony of family and friends is helpful, it must be considered secondary information and not as reliable as information gained from the maker or a contemporary. As information is passed through each generation, names and dates are often forgotten and facts are lost, obscured, or even glamorized. Record the information supplied by the previous owners, but take the time to substantiate it. Check genealogies and town histories and—even more important—examine the quilt itself. Every textile can tell us something about its age, its maker, and even the place where it was made.

The date of a quilt often can be approximated by comparing evidence found in the quilt. Design motifs can provide good clues. The Lincoln–Douglas Debate square included in our Abraham Lincoln quilt obviously dates from the 1860s, while the clipper ship carefully stitched in quilted trapunto work on the Trilobe Flowers quilt probably would not have been incorporated in a quilt much after 1850. Quilt patterns were first advertised in women's journals in the mid-nineteenth century: with careful research one can thus document and date many patterns. Certain fabric types, such as glazed wool and calimanco, were popular only at a specific time. Identifying the printing methods used on different textiles can also provide clues to age and location of manufacture. Trends in fabric design and colors and patterns are important indications of age. For example, the umber-colored fabrics used in the Hexagon and Triangle quilts were extremely popular between 1830 and 1840.

However, bear in mind that one often can only approximate a quilt's date. Quilters often kept baskets of scraps and remnants to use in their work. In the past, people were more economical about fashion and clothing, especially in rural areas; one dress might last a woman for years, remade as fashions changed or as it was passed down through the family. Consequently, a quilt might contain fabric popular ten or even twenty years before it was actually made. A date appearing on a quilt should approximate the date of the newest textile employed.

Condition

The condition of a quilt is important in the evaluation of a piece. Not only is condition a critical element in determining the quilt's total aesthetic appeal, it also can reveal a great deal about the history of its use. The hope of every curator and collector is to find a quilt in "as new" condition, with bright true colors; perfectly clean textiles unmarred by soiling or stains; strong stable fabrics with no evidence of fraying, tears, or wear; no replacements or additions of fabric or embroidery; and no changes in the original size or shape. Any use usually leaves traces: loose stitches in seams or along appliqué edges, worn edges or replaced bindings, soils and stains, and discoloration or fading after washing owing to unstable dyes.

Many quilts were repaired through the years. Look for an edge binding that appears newer or does not match the other fabrics used in the body of the quilt. Ask questions: Are the threads all the same type? Do the dye lots appear to match? Do any of the fabrics look noticeably newer? Could there be repairs? Compare the stitches on newer-looking sections with the other stitches in the quilt. Unless many hands worked on it, as in some album quilts, all the stitches should be similar. Many early quilts were adapted to fit four-poster beds. Are the corners trimmed with the same binding as the rest of the quilt, or is it different? Crib quilts and small-size children's quilts are rare and quite popular with collectors. The relationship of the pattern size on such quilts often provides an indication of the originality of the piece. If the pattern seems too big and out of scale for a small quilt, it might have been cut down from a full-size quilt. Compare the fabric in the binding with the fabric in the rest of the quilt. If you are suspicious, check underneath the binding for fresh-cut edges.

What does all this tell us about the history of a quilt? A perfectly clean quilt with crisp, shiny fabrics or traces of pencil lines along quilting stitches might never have been used and perhaps never even was washed. Perhaps the quilt was considered an heirloom, passed down through the family unused, cherished, and carefully stored to preserve it for future generations. For example, our chintz presentation quilt was made in 1853 by the members of Rev. Benjamin Cory's congregation in Perth Amboy, New Jersey, and was presented to the minister and his wife upon his retirement. It was rarely used, and it remained in the family until it was presented to the museum in 1985.

While some quilts were designed without lower corners so that they might fit a four-poster bed, many earlier examples were adapted for such use. A change in the style of bedroom furniture could indicate a change or an improvement of the economic status of the family; for instance, a room could have been redecorated in a newer style, new furniture might have been purchased, or perhaps there was a change in the quilt's ownership. The quilt might also have been passed on to a friend or to another generation of the family. This adaptation of a quilt to fit a different type of bed than that for which it was originally made also indicates that bedcovers were valued items, reused or passed on rather than discarded.

Should a quilt not in perfect condition be collected? While some soiling, stains, and wear can be remedied with careful professional conservation treatment, others are permanently disfiguring. Be realistic about the condition of a quilt, the amount of conservation you are willing to undertake, and what the end result will be. A quilt with extensive repairs and restoration is certainly not as valuable or desirable as one in better, more original condition. However, the overall condition should be compared to the age of the textile. An older quilt is more likely to have signs of wear; we should be prepared to accept this factor as part of the quilt's history. Ultimately, the acceptable amount of wear and repair is a matter of individual choice.

Rarity

The final criterion to consider in evaluation is rarity, which is determined by relative availability. Often a piece is valued or considered interesting solely on the basis of rarity.

Typically a quilt is rare because it is unique or because few like it were made. Possibly the initial cost of materials used in it was prohibitive, and there were only a few individuals who could afford to make and own such a piece. Whole-cloth wool quilts fall into this category; the glazed wool used for the tops was imported and therefore expensive, so that few families could afford such a luxury. Late-eighteenth- and early-nineteenth-century quilts were more often pieced or plain, made with inexpensive or even hand-woven goods. However, even these pieced or ordinary plain-cloth quilts are now rare. Because they were originally considered ordinary and common, they were not treated with special care and preserved in the way that elaborately quilted wool pieces were. They generally were used until they fell apart, and today their rarity greatly affects their market value.

Other factors that aid in determining rarity are originality and uniqueness of design. The Shelburne Museum's Haskins crazy quilt is interesting because the maker—who lived in Rochester, Vermont—chose to embellish her design with appliquéd motifs inspired by her family, the world around her, and current events of the day: a mother and child, a moose and mountain lion, and a likeness of Abraham Lincoln. While the motifs incorporated in the museum's counterpane made by Mary Jane Carr are typical of those used in other needlework in the mid-nineteenth century, the combination of appliquéd patterns, cornucopias, flowering vines, wreaths, birds, and animals all enclosed by a swag border is unique. The fact that the maker signed her quilt and recorded the dates it was begun and finished makes it all the more unusual. This type of authenticated quilt, signed and dated by the maker, as well as quilts with a clear history of ownership, are rare and highly prized.

Quilts readily identifiable as having been made by a specific group of people or in a specific region are fewer in number and very desirable. Amish quilts, with their geometric patterns in clear, solid colors, and Hawaiian quilts, with their bold, naturalistic patterns, were ignored by early-twentieth-century collectors like Electra Webb, who favored more traditional Colonial patterns. Today, however, such quilts are valued as folk art and considered eminently collectible by many enthusiasts.

Final Evaluation

Now comes the hard part. After considering all the criteria we have listed and after evaluating the quilt's appearance, craftsmanship, materials, condition, history, provenance, and rarity, the separation of certain aspects of such criteria often proves difficult. For instance, while aesthetic appearance is extremely important, overall condition and craftsmanship play an integral part in that physical appearance. We might overlook a quilt in less than perfect condition if its pattern is unique and the textiles employed are considered quite rare. Many historical museums collect only artifacts with an unambiguous provenance and record of previous use. However, such factors may not be as important to a private collector. The beauty of a quilt might well outweigh an absence of historical information.

In addition to considering the quilt's merits, it is also necessary to decide if it is suitable for an individual's collection. Will it be a unique addition to the collection or will it duplicate an existing piece? If it duplicates a quilt already owned, which is the better example? Are the quilts from the same locale? Consider the collection carefully. What is its scope? Has it been assembled from a wide range of examples with no consideration of a specific theme or aim? Perhaps one is collecting single examples of each type of quilting technique or perhaps only one type— appliqué albums, for instance, or Log Cabins. Perhaps one's interest is regional.

Learn everything you can about quilts; read available books and visit public and private collections. Learn why individuals have collected quilts and why they consider a specific example important. Talk to other collectors and dealers and examine as many quilts as possible. Every quilt will teach you something if you look at it closely enough.

Whatever one's interest, it is helpful to set guidelines for the collection. These can change; they needn't be carved in stone. A collection should be continually reevaluated as examples are added or subtracted. Each collection is important and interesting because it reflects the personality of the collector. Once one decides the parameters of the collection, one can set out with a plan for acquiring the pieces needed or wanted.

NOTES

1. Charles F. Montgomery, "The Connoisseurship of Artifacts," in *Material Culture Studies in America* (compiled and edited by Thomas J. Schlereth). Nashville, Tenn., The American Association for State and Local History, 1982, p. 144.

2. Jonathan Holstein, "Collecting Quilt Data: History from Statistics," *The Quilt Digest*, San Francisco, Kiracofe and Kile, 1983, p. 64.

221

Sarah Pool and Mary J. Pool. *Appliqué Baltimore Album Quilt*. c. 1840. Baltimore.
Cotton, 106 × 107⅜". Photograph © Sotheby's, Inc., 1987.

This exceptionally important Baltimore Album Quilt, signed by the makers, is composed of a series of 25 brilliantly colored red, yellow, blue, green, and pink printed and solid calico patches in a series of 25 pieced and appliqué squares. Each contains a different pictorial or floral motif, including a depiction of a locomotive with engineer, the locomotive pulling a single passenger car with a gentleman and lady seated in the carriage. The figures and the smoke issuing from the engine are rendered in pen and ink above a swooping American eagle. There is also an impressive state house; a log cabin with two beavers on the roof, one saying "you can't come in"; the Baltimore Monument with pendant flags; a book inscribed *Album*; a majestic two-storied house; several trophies with musical instruments (including lyres and trumpets); floral wreaths; and urns overflowing with flowers and fruits. At the center there is a large spread-winged American eagle with flags and trumpets. One of the floral squares is cross-stitched "Mary J. Pool," another is cross-stitched "Sarah Pool." The entire work is enclosed within a meandering and stylized rose border; the field has diagonal line and outline stitching.

    This quilt sold for $176,000 at Sotheby's in January 1987. The price is a record in the quilt market.

222

Trilobe Flower and Trapunto Clipper Ships Pieced Quilt.
c. 1840–50. Massachusetts or Coastal New England.
Cotton, 89×78″. The Shelburne Museum, Shelburne,
Vermont. Gift of Electra Havemeyer Webb.

While the design motif of this pieced quilt is relatively
simple, interest is created by a delightful medallion composed of elaborate trapunto motifs, including wheels,
clipper ships, and floral wreaths.

223

Ann Daggs. *Central Medallion Flower Pot and Birds Appliqué
Quilt.* 1818. Rochester, New York. Cotton and linen, 84×78″.
Collection America Hurrah Antiques, New York City.
Photograph by Schecter Lee.

This quilt was signed in cross-stitch: ''Done by Ann Daggs
the 1st of May 1818.'' The quilt exemplifies a rather folksy
style for so early a date, one factor that contributes to the
opinion that it is a very important piece.

224

Garden Botanical Pieced and Appliquéd Quilt. c. 1850s.
Origin unknown. Cotton, 88×88½″. The Shelburne
Museum, Shelburne, Vermont. Gift of Electra Havemeyer
Webb. Photograph courtesy The Shelburne Museum.

Many pieced and appliquéd quilt patterns have been and
still are inspired by nature, particularly by flowers. Few,
however, offer such a creative or personal combination as
this beautiful quilt. One can almost imagine the garden
that inspired the inclusion of such pattern blocks as the
strawberry wreath, the full-blown rose and buds, and the
meadow tulip.

225

Civil War Presentation Appliqué Album Quilt. c. 1860s. Origin unknown. Cotton, linen, and wool, 83½ × 78".
The Shelburne Museum, Shelburne, Vermont. Gift of Electra Havemeyer Webb. Photograph courtesy
The Shelburne Museum.

Each of the 49 blocks in this presentation album quilt is signed by the makers. While many of the designs, such
as the oak medallion, tulips, or rose wreath, are typical of popular nineteenth-century quilt patterns, others,
like the playing puppies or rooster, were probably derived from commercial hooked rug designs; the vase of
flowers was presumably copied from a ladies' periodical or a decorator's book. The more original contributors
to this quilt chose to commemorate a special person (the seated figure of Abraham Lincoln), an event (the
Lincoln–Douglas debate), or a place (their own home).

226

Foundation Rose Variation Appliqué Quilt. c. 1850. New York State. Cotton, 87 × 90". The Shelburne Museum, Shelburne, Vermont. Gift of Electra Havemeyer Webb. Photograph courtesy The Shelburne Museum.

During the nineteenth century, the Foundation Rose was one of the most popular quilt patterns; this variant incorporates a central rose motif with eight radiating buds. While the pattern was somewhat common for the time, the quality of the appliqué and the meticulous stitching in this example are anything but common. The maker chose to outline and highlight the full-blown rose, the border swag, and the tassels with even, fine, extra-closely-laid quilting stitches, thus creating an almost three-dimensional effect.

 227

Foundation Rose Variation Appliqué Quilt (detail of 226).

228

Hexagons and Triangles Pieced Quilt. c. 1850s. Origin unknown. Cotton, 97×76". The Shelburne Museum, Shelburne, Vermont. Gift of Electra Havemeyer Webb. Photograph courtesy The Shelburne Museum.

Many quilters incorporate bold contrasting colors to create three-dimensional effects. Here, the radiating bands of yellow stand out dramatically from the ombre-patterned brown-and-green background.

![231] 231

Sarah Barber. *Rose of Sharon Appliqué Quilt*. c. 1850s. Waterville, Vermont. Cotton, 90 × 85".
The Shelburne Museum, Shelburne, Vermont. Gift of Electra Havemeyer Webb; purchased from Rupert King
(descendant of the maker). Photograph courtesy The Shelburne Museum.

Rose designs were much favored by mid-nineteenth-century quilters. Among the variations of this motif are Tea
Rose, Foundation Rose, Whig, and Mexican Rose, all descended from the Rose of Sharon, a name that finds its
origin in the "Song of Songs" from the Bible. Some scholars say that this portion of the Old Testament celebrates
wedded love, and thus the Rose of Sharon has been mainly chosen for a bridal motif on linens and bedcovers. The
present quilt, passed down through Sarah Barber's family, was often exhibited at local and state fairs, and it always
won prizes.

🌸 232

Flower Basket Reverse Appliqué Quilt. c. 1830–50. New York. Cotton, 76×76".
The Shelburne Museum, Shelburne, Vermont. Gift of Mrs. John C. Wilmerding, New York.

The technique of reverse appliqué is very difficult, and as a consequence quilts made by this technique are relatively rare. In executing such a quilt, the quilter drew the pattern onto the background material, carefully cut out pieces, and then set the patterned fabric into the inlay spaces. The background fabric was then felled down over the inlay. Careful, minute stitches and a steady hand are required to do this type of precise work.

233

Kiggins Pieced Quilt. 1852. Perth Amboy, New Jersey. Cotton, 93 × 93½″. The Shelburne Museum, Shelburne, Vermont.

This quilt was presented to Rev. Benjamin Cory by his congregation upon his retirement. Each of the 121 squares is signed by its maker, and each bears a favorite biblical verse.

234

Angeline and Augusta Kimberly. *The Streets of Boston Appliqué Quilt*. 1873. Boston, Massachusetts. Cotton, 80×76". The Shelburne Museum, Shelburne, Vermont. Gift of Mrs. Edward Craig, Venice, Florida. Photograph courtesy The Shelburne Museum.

This appliqué resembles a crazy quilt, since its jagged pieces are laid randomly onto the fabric of the white background. However, rather then being pieced together as they would have been for a crazy quilt, the pieces are appliquéd to the ground, leaving white margins between them representing the streets of Boston. The large center medallion bears the inscription "EMK 1873" and represents Boston Common. Old maps of the city inspired the use of this circle for the symbol as well as the star for Fort Independence and the double circle for the Bunker Hill Monument. The Misses Kimberly made this quilt for their sister Ellen May Kimberly of Nepaug, Connecticut.

235

Angeline and Augusta Kimberly. *The Streets of Boston Appliqué Quilt* (detail of 234).

![flower icon] 236

Star Pieced Quilt. c. 1890. New York. Cotton, linen, lace, velvet, and silk, 65 × 66". The Shelburne Museum, Shelburne, Vermont. Gift of Mr. and Mrs. Peter Paine, New York. Photograph courtesy The Shelburne Museum.

Many quilters of the late Victorian era chose to reinterpret earlier nineteenth-century patterns with elaborate fabrics. The various silks employed in this colorful example offer evidence of the multitude of luxurious materials available at the time. During the late 1800s, quilts evolved from being mere warm bedcovers to becoming decorative household accessories intended as sofa throws or lap rugs. The maker of this elegant work highlighted the colorful pattern of pieced stars with a border of black velvet and edged the quilt with a frosting of handmade linen lace.

237

Travers Family. *Presidential Wreath Appliqué Quilt.* c. 1840s. Sand Lake, New York. Cotton, 96 × 96″.
The Shelburne Museum, Shelburne, Vermont. Gift of Mrs. Webb Harris.
Photograph courtesy The Shelburne Museum.

The Presidential Wreath pattern first originated in New Jersey and subsequently found its way into the New York area. The present example was a family project. The Travers' skill is evidenced in the fine stitching as well as in the carefully executed detailing around the fine sawtooth border.

238

Flying Geese Pieced Quilt. c. 1890. Essex Center, Vermont. Silk, 64½ × 54″. The Shelburne Museum, Shelburne, Vermont. Gift of Mrs. Westcott. Photograph courtesy The Shelburne Museum.

Silk neckties provided the fabric for this beautiful, almost electric quilt. Complementary shades of blue-violet and orange-red create a dramatic tension that leads the viewer's eyes in, out, and around the pattern.

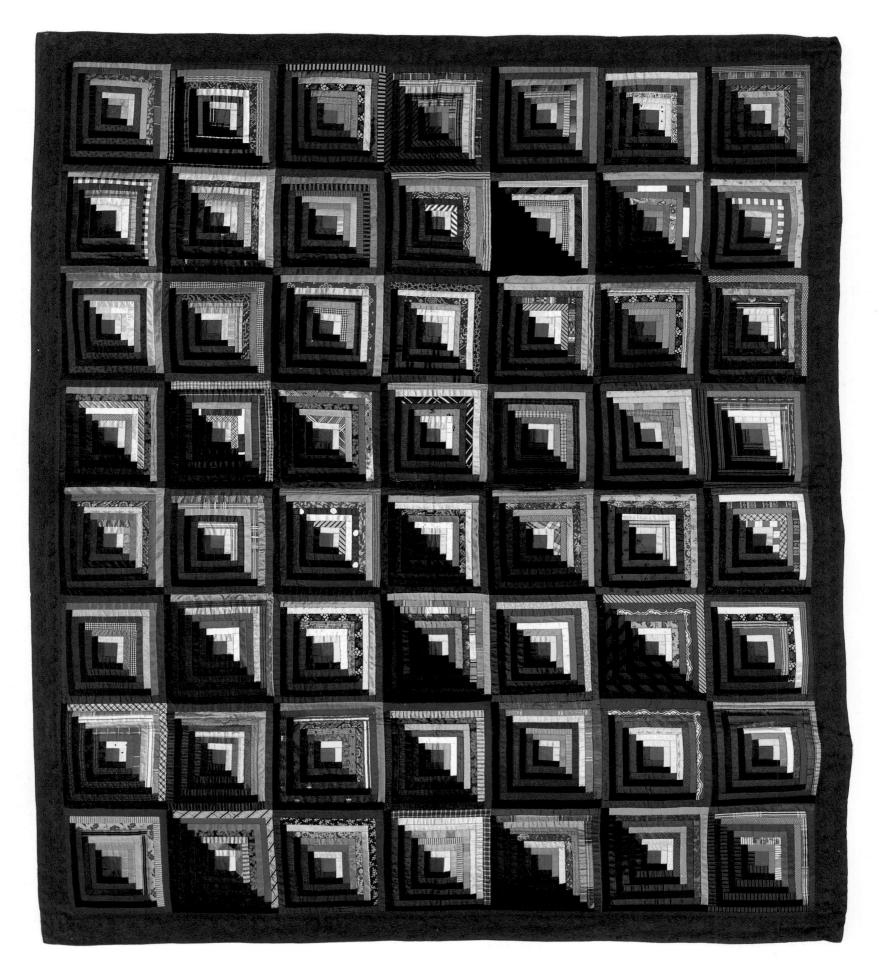

 239

Log Cabin Pieced Quilt. c. 1890. New Jersey. Silk and satin, 67½″ × 58½. The Shelburne Museum, Shelburne, Vermont. Gift of Mrs. Carl Johnson, Bogota, New Jersey. Photograph courtesy The Shelburne Museum.

Log Cabin patterns were usually made from various cotton or wool fabrics in colors chosen to highlight the strong contrast required to carry out the overall pattern. The maker of this quilt, however, employed various silks and satins to create her variant of the Straight Furrow pattern.

![leaf icon] **240**

The Waveland Quilt, Pieced Star Quilt. c. 1840. Kentucky. Cotton, 114 × 117″. Collection The Kentucky Historical Society at the Kentucky History Museum, Frankfort, Kentucky. Photograph by Nathan Prichard.

This handsome quilt exemplifies a traditional star placement, with smaller repeating stars between the points and in the corner blocks of the inside border, which is executed in a Flying Geese design. The design of the outside border is called Sugar Loaves. The quilt was originally in the collection of the Waveland Kentucky Life Museum, a state shrine. However, it has now been moved to the Kentucky History Museum for safekeeping under proper textile conservation conditions. A replica made by the Kentucky Heritage Quilt Society may now be seen at the Waveland Museum in its original setting. Twenty-two members of the quilt society worked on the reproduction, a task that tested their mathematical skills.

241

Presentation Appliqué Quilt. 1847. Origin unknown. Cotton and chintz, 108 × 90″. Collection Phyllis Haders.

This presentation quilt was made for a lay missionary and his family on the occasion of their departure for Hawaii. Each block is signed by its maker, and paper-fold, cutout appliqués were adapted from Hawaiian motifs. The large center scroll is inscribed:

> *John Noble*
> *Eliza Noble*
> *But for a being without end*
> *the vowd love we take*
> *Grant us oh God one home at last*
> *For our Redeemers sake.*
>
> *1847*

242

Presentation Appliqué Quilt (detail of 241).

243

Baltimore Album Appliqué Quilt Top. c. 1850. Baltimore, Maryland. Cotton, 88 × 88".
Courtesy Thos. K. Woodard American Antiques & Quilts, New York. Photograph by Schecter Lee.

In addition to some of the more familiar motifs found in album quilts from this area (the fire engine, monument, and heart), there are also some rare and unique blocks here, such as the middle one in the top row, and several others executed in the same manner. It is obvious that the maker of this quilt had an original style and a vivid color sense.

244

Mrs. Henry Clay (?). *Clay/Crittenden Pieced Presentation Quilt*. c. 1850. Kentucky. Chintz with polychromatic embroidered panels. 102×82". Kentucky Museum, Western Kentucky University, Bowling Green, Kentucky.

This important and historically valuable quilt is believed to have been made by Mrs. Henry (Lucretia Hart) Clay, who presented it to Mrs. John J. Crittenden as a token of the friendship between their husbands. The portrait of Clay in the central panel (see detail) appears to have been based on an 1842 painting by John Neagle. The other thirty blocks are embroidered (many with crewel wool) in salmon, light brown, and celadon. The flower designs are almost all embroidered, while some of the animals, people, and pastoral vignettes are chintz appliquéd in a technique similar to Broderie Perse. The quilting is very fine, with more than ten stitches per inch, and the motifs vary from block to block.

Crittenden and Clay were two of Kentucky's best-known antebellum politicians, and were close political allies. Henry Clay spent much of his career as a United States senator and was three times defeated in his bid for the presidency. John J. Crittenden was also a senator, and served as governor of Kentucky for two years.

🌸 245

Mrs. Henry Clay (?). *Clay/Crittenden Pieced Presentation Quilt* (detail of 244).

246

Miss A. M. Mynderse. *Garden Appliqué Quilt.* 1853. New York State. Cotton, 93 × 90″. The Schenectady Museum and Planetarium, Schenectady, New York.

The Garden design was to appliqué what the Star of Bethlehem was to pieced work—the acme of that style of quilting. The Garden had no actual pattern; rather it was a conception. No two Garden quilts are alike, although all have certain characteristics in common: a center medallion and flowers as the predominating motif. However, birds, cornucopias, fruit, and baskets are sometimes introduced. Of special interest is the fact that the quilt was signed by the maker's father, H. V. Mynderse.

247

Miss A. M. Mynderse. *Garden Appliqué Quilt* (detail of 246).

 248

Martha Hewitt. *Pieced and Appliqué Quilt*. 1855. Michigan.
Cotton, 80×72". Collection America Hurrah Antiques, New York City. Photograph by Schecter Lee.

This example is signed across the top: "Martha Hewitt Age 56 Michigan 1855." The quilt offers a unique design that incorporates a compass variation in the center, with radiating motifs of the sun, moon, stars, and rainbows surrounded by pots of flowers. At the four corners are stylized figures of soldiers holding American flags. There is a scalloped border composed of alternating colors on three sides. This rare quilt is considered to be a masterpiece of folk art.

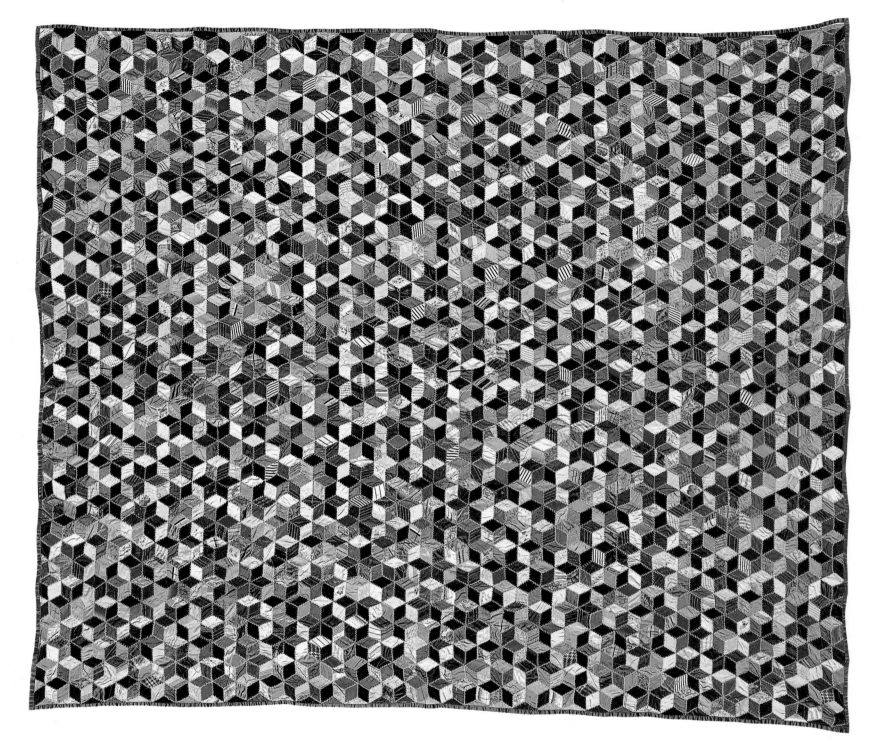

 249

Ann Johnston. *Stair Steps or Illusion Pieced Quilt*. c. 1890. Taylor County, Kentucky. Silk, taffeta, and crepe, 70×81½". Collection The Kentucky Historical Society, Frankfort, Kentucky. Photograph by Nathan Prichard.

A letter from Mrs. Elvira Johnston Wright states:

> *My aunt, Ann Johnston (1871–1964), made the quilt about 1890. She was born in Taylor County (Kentucky) and died in Oldham County. Her ancestors were pioneers in Green and Taylor Counties. Her great-great-grandfather was Thomas Wheeler Edwards, who was a representative to the Legislature from Green County in 1842. Aunt Ann's father was George Edwards Johnston (1835–1930), whose primary occupation was that of a farmer, although for several years he held an elective office in Taylor County as sheriff. Her mother was Mary Ellen Gaddie (1844–1917). Ann was one of five sisters, the only one who married and left descendants. She was an expert seamstress, and for a while worked as a milliner in Louisville. Her handwork, including this quilt, won many prizes in county fairs.*

The number of pieces in this quilt, the needlework, the colors, and the way in which the sections are balanced produce extraordinary results. The pattern can be seen as a Star pattern with six-pointed stars or as combinations of Tumbling Blocks; this creates an intriguing optical illusion. All in all, the quilt is a spectacular achievement, a work of art.

![quilt icon] 250

Salinda W. Rupp. *Pieced Sampler Quilt*. c. 1870. Lancaster County, Pennsylvania.
Cotton, 88 × 87¾". Collection America Hurrah Antiques, New York City. Photograph by Schecter Lee.

In this cotton quilt there are over 85 miniature pieced and complete quilt blocks. All are different, and each is exceptional in detail. Many represent original designs created by the maker, or they represent her own variations of classic patterns. Incorporated into this example is a very choice selection of printed textiles. This quilt is certainly one of the best of its kind because of the scale of the blocks and the skill required to stitch them, as well as the many patterns it contains.

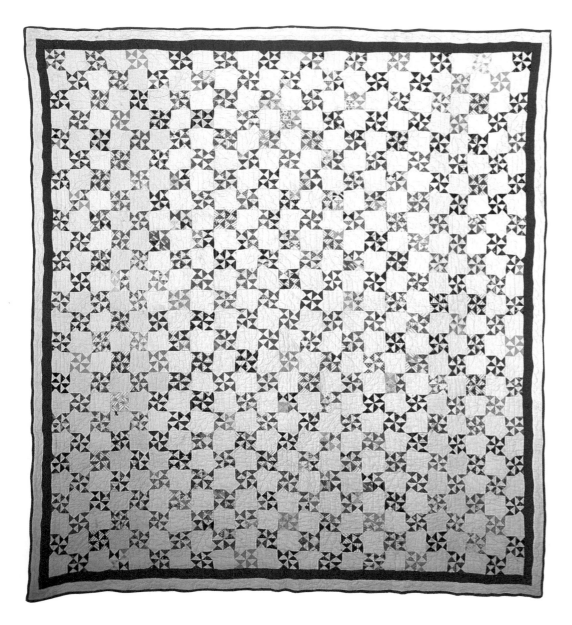

251

Rene Snider. *Windmill Design Pieced Quilt*. 1900–3. Wenatchee, Washington. Cotton, 78×70". Eastern Washington State Historical Society.

Calicos and prints were selected by Rene Snider, who lived on a homestead near Wenatchee. The 299 Windmill squares reveal the maker's special skill and her wish to create a one-of-a-kind quilt; sugar sacking was used for the white background. In 1903, after sewing in 5,083 separate pieces of fabric and attaching the brilliant red binding, the quilt was still unfinished when Mrs. Snider died giving birth to her first child. In 1928 her sister-in-law completed the quilt by using a platter from her cupboard to make the quilted oval designs and by using the outline of a spoon to create the shape of the motifs in the quilted wreath.

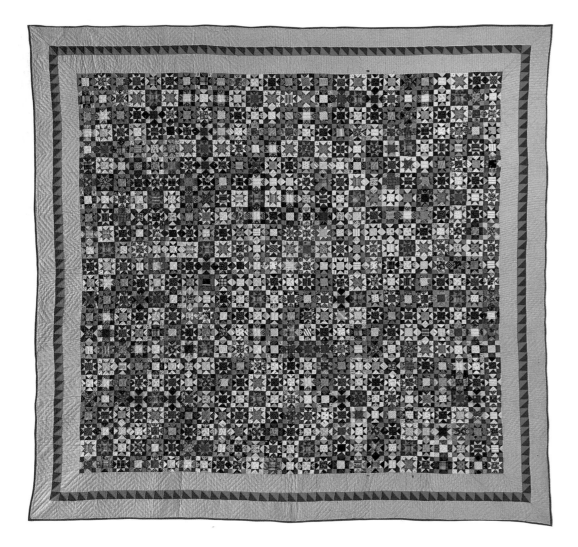

252

Pieced Star with Sawtooth Border. c. 1890. Pennsylvania. Cotton, 85×88". Courtesy Thos. K. Woodard American Antiques & Quilts, New York. Photograph by Schecter Lee.

This is meticulously composed of over 10,000 tiny pieces of colorful calico from the decade between 1880 and 1890. Probably Mennonite, the quilt is an amazing feat of stitchery.

253

Rebecca Scattergood Savery (?). *Sunburst Pieced Quilt*. c. 1840. Philadelphia.
Cotton, 125½ × 118½″. The Museum of American Folk Art, New York. Gift of C. and M. O'Neil.

The quilt top is composed of concentric octagons formed of diamonds that radiate from a central eight-pointed, yellow-and-brown print star. Rebecca Scattergood Savery is known to be the maker of several similar quilts. A great deal of skill and patience was required to cut and piece so many diamonds in exact precision on so large a surface. The quilt is undoubtedly a striking and sophisticated achievement.

LIVING WITH QUILTS

LIVING WITH QUILTS

Phyllis George Brown

 recall quilts from my early childhood in Texas, but I didn't appreciate them at the time. I can remember visiting my grandmother George's home, where she would quilt with my aunts and some friends.

"Why does Grandma spend so much time with those old quilts and all those scraps of cloth?" I wondered. It looked awfully boring. It was more fun to race around with my cousins or use one of Grandma's old quilts as a playhouse. I also thought the huge wooden quilting frame looked awkward and cumbersome in the middle of the family room. But the quilts were beautiful, and Grandma placed them all over the house: on the beds, over the back of chairs, and on couches. Each one was distinctive. There was always something special about snuggling under a warm and colorful quilt.

Through the years I acquired a few quilts, mainly gifts from my grandmother. I fell in love with their fabrics, imaginative, intricate designs, and dazzling patterns. By 1979, when I married John Y. Brown, Jr., and we returned to Kentucky after our honeymoon to start his campaign for governor, I had amassed dozens of these quilted treasures.

One of the first important quilts my husband and I bought together was a large silk one, an exquisite golden-hued beauty. It is a sampler quilt made in 1854, and each square was done by a different woman. It is too fine to snuggle under, but perfect on the wall above an old oak table that holds a collection of antique silver picture frames in our Great Room.

As fond of the quilts as I was, it wasn't until I married John that I began to appreciate their artistry and craftsmanship and to admire the women who had created all that beauty.

John and I traveled through all of Kentucky, from Pikeville to Paducah and from Monkey's

PRECEDING PAGE: *Detail from the Master Bedroom in the Home of Phyllis George Brown.* Photograph by Lee P. Thomas.

Eyebrow to McKee. On many of these trips I found opportunities to visit local craftspeople and, in so doing, to discover and appreciate the exquisite artistry that is one of the state's most valuable natural resources. It soon became apparent that rightful recognition had to be accorded these artists and their crafts. We had to find a way to focus national attention on the real treasure we had here, this legacy of needlework bequeathed to us by generations of Kentucky women.

Along with baskets, wood carvings, and weaving, I saw wonderful old quilts preserved as family heirlooms, tucked away in cedar chests, trunks, and spare cupboards. They were quietly hidden away or worn to tatters—unheralded and unrecorded. Sadly, some had been sold for a song in hard times. Hundreds of marvelous patterns, along with the delicate skill of hand quilting, had been passed from generation to generation. Daughters and granddaughters continued the craft. Church groups and rural clubs held quilting parties to create marvels of color and symmetry with stitches almost too tiny to see; unfortunately, the fruits of these hours of tedious work and years of learning often went unrewarded and unappreciated. It was vital to help these extraordinary artists by marketing their works with pride and acclaim.

Our purposes were twofold: to bring recognition to our assets by displaying and evaluating the old quilts, and to help present-day quilt makers earn a living by selling their beautiful new quilts. Thus, it was only natural for me to launch the "Oh! Kentucky" crafts movement.

We began by calling Bloomingdale's in New York and Neiman-Marcus in Dallas. We called Bullock's in Los Angeles and Marshall Field in Chicago. We organized wholesale markets in Louisville and Lexington. As a result, buyers came from across America to acquire these quilts and other Kentucky crafts for their shops. I made TV appearances on the *Good Morning, America* and *House Magazine* programs to promote Kentucky crafts and quilts. At last it appeared that the skill, artistry, and endless hours it takes to create these heirlooms were going to be given their due.

Bloomingdale's developed a theme show to publicize its sales campaign called "Oh! Kentucky—You'll Come To Love It," and decorated their New York store with our crafts. The West Coast branch of Neiman-Marcus took our country chic to their Beverly Hills store. In Chicago, the quilts sold out in two days. The money earned was turned over to the Kentucky Department of Arts, which then distributed it to fund and encourage local craftspeople.

At this same time, quilts and quilting began to be accorded feature articles in many major home-decorating magazines, crafts magazines, and even fine-art periodicals. People began to bring out family quilts from storage trunks, eyeing Grandma's handiwork with new respect. Indeed, all over America there has been a back-to-basics attitude, a renewed respect for tradition and the simple beauty of native handcrafts.

Insofar as my personal collection of quilts is concerned, I treasure each and every one. Whether hand stitched by a single maker or assembled amid the voices and warm laughter of a quilting bee, each one is a thing of beauty. I have over fifty examples, old and new, in my collection, and they are indeed used in our home. Cave Hill Place, our house in Lexington, Kentucky, was built in 1821, and it is a perfect setting for my quilts. I love to mix antiques with striking contemporary designs. There are quilts used on beds as comforters for our children, Lincoln and Pamela, and as striking wall hangings in guest rooms and along the stairway. There are four in our bedroom—one on the bed, one at its foot, and two covering a small round table (one serving as the skirt) by the fireplace. Some are framed for protection.

I store the quilts not in use in a convenient closet, which makes it easy to select different ones for any occasion. We occasionally (and carefully) use worn quilts as picnic spreads or place fragile ones under glass as conversation-piece decorations on our formal luncheon tables. At a recent luncheon for a group of women, I covered each table with a soft pastel quilt, then centered each with a delicate porcelain doll—all made in Kentucky. One Sunday at our traditional post-Derby garden party, we delicately draped quilts all along the white fence leading to the house to provide a glorious welcome for our guests. (The only trouble was that everyone wanted to buy them! I couldn't bear to part with a single one.)

Over the years I have acquired many quilts to give as gifts, sending them to family and friends all over the country. I have a number of news photos, taken during the years when I was First Lady of Kentucky, that show me either presenting a handmade quilt to the wife of a visiting dignitary or giving one as a thank-you gift abroad. My friends Olivia Newton-John and Kenny Rogers each received a Kentucky quilt as a wedding gift.

Incidentally, quilts have become gifts literally fit for a king. In one instance, a New York banker presented one made for the United States Bicentennial to King Juan Carlos of Spain. When John and I visited England, we gave a Kentucky-made baby quilt to Prince Charles and Princess Diana for the prospective heir to the throne. We weren't surprised to learn that President and Mrs. Reagan, who have often presented quilts to heads of state, also presented Charles and Diana's son Prince William with a baby quilt made by a Kentuckian.

One of the more unusual quilts in my collection is an 1874 crazy quilt made from pieces of silk that lined the top of boxes of cigars during that era; it was featured in a quilt article in *Good Housekeeping*. I also own a pair of lively pastel quilts in a Japanese-lantern pattern that I found in Kentucky; when she gets a little older they'll be perfect for Pamela's room. I treasure a multicolored quilt in primary colors, with a headboard to match, adorning the willow bed in my son's room. One of my more valuable pieces is a pre–Civil War design in red, white, and blue that has been on the wall in our breakfast room since July 1986, when we used a number of red, white, and blue patriotic quilts to enliven the decor for the Fourth of July festivities.

Another beauty is a double-sized crazy quilt pieced from scores of rich fabrics, which also contains a number of unique hand-painted patches. This unusual quilt was made in 1889 by Emma Weimer, who also did lovely hand-painted china. Mrs. Weimer's daughter told me that the quilt had never been unpacked from the trunk in her mother's attic. It was reproduced in the 1983 Kentucky Quilt Calendar. Since I grew up in Texas, naturally I own several Lone Star quilts. I also have a contemporary Amish quilt that fills me with wonder that anyone could have the ability and patience to stitch so fine a piece.

I recently began to collect quilts for my daughter, including a fantastic pastel Double Wedding Ring quilt. Every Christmas I plan to add to her collection. I also bought a Log Cabin quilt as a Christmas present for my parents.

One of my most precious acquisitions is a crazy quilt made by Jason Fenwick when he was state curator. It was assembled from small scraps of fabric (from curtains, upholstery, and bedspreads, which I chose) salvaged when the governor's mansion was being refurbished. It is only natural that I feel quite sentimental about that particular quilt, as it holds special memories for me. There are now eight quilts at Cave Hill, displayed on the wall as the works of art they are. There are others being used for the purpose originally intended, such as to snuggle up with Pamela when I read her a bedtime story.

What do I think about when I look at my quilts? Sitting here with my children, my mind turns to the women who originally made them, and I wonder who they were and how they lived.

Did they also have children who gathered in front of the fireplace, and shared these same quilts as they listened to bedtime stories? Were their imaginations also sparked by the kaleidoscope of colors and shapes? After the family was asleep, did they work on the intricate stitching by candlelight or the light of a kerosene lamp? Was that lavender floral patch part of a dress worn only to church on Sundays? Did the gingham check come from an apron worn when making bread and pies, the sturdy blue from Dad's shirt, or the little pink calico from a baby's sun dress? Did these industrious women have any idea that a century later their handiwork would become valuable collectibles or even find their way to a museum? To me, these quilts represent patches of love and fragments of life.

The lives and emotions stitched into these quilts speak to us, telling visual stories more potent than words. They brighten the grayness of everyday life. The essence of their forms, colors, designs, and patterns expresses true artistic inspiration. I believe that those who make things with their hands understand life in a different way. I look forward to bequeathing these extraordinary heirlooms to Lincoln and Pamela for them to share with their families.

For those of us who love them, every quilt is tangible fragment of history and is as precious as any old letter or faded family photograph—a vivid link to our past. As we live with these finely crafted old quilts and as we see present-day quilters create beautiful and elaborate designs, they form a link to our future —which, with God's blessing, will also be bright, honest, and finely crafted.

CARE

Even among the experts there are varying opinions regarding cleaning and caring for quilts. Some people believe they should be restored and repaired, while others believe they should be left in their original condition. All agree that good quilts should be treated with respect.

The consensus is that the handling of early and treasured quilts calls for extreme caution. Any laundering or cleaning involves elements of risk. If quilts do require cleaning, it is best to rely on professional textile conservationists who are experienced in dating and identifying fibers and knowing how to care for them (one quilt may contain dozens of different textiles in the top, another for the backing, and yet another for the batting). What follows are a number of general tips for caring for quilts:

Quilts over fifty years old or those made from fragile fabrics (silks, satins, velvets) should be cleaned only by professional textile conservators, if at all.

Quilts can be aired outdoors in clear, dry weather: They should be placed on a flat surface, protected with clean cotton sheeting, and kept out of direct sunlight. A clothesline is acceptable for a small dry quilt only if the weight of the quilt is evenly distributed and rotated and the area is sheltered from strong winds. Never hang a wet quilt on a clothesline because the weight will break the fibers and weaken the stitching.

Quilts (and other textiles) should be kept in low-humidity environments (50 percent humidity or less).

Keep quilts away from direct contact with wood surfaces, plastic, and plastic bags. If the only place you have to put them is in a wooden drawer, paint the inside of the drawer with polyurethane varnish and line it with acid-free paper, clean cotton sheets, or unbleached muslin.

Fold and store cotton quilts in thirds (top to the inside) between sheets of acid-free paper and in acid-free boxes. Do *not* use regular tissue paper.

Carefully refold quilts every several months to avoid permanent crease lines.

Wear cotton gloves when handling very old fragile quilts, as the natural oils in the fingers may leave stains.

Roll smaller quilts around cardboard tubes covered with acid-free paper. (Never place quilts in direct contact with cardboard.)

Store wool and silk quilts in clean cotton pillowcases and/or folded between clean cotton sheets.

Protect quilts from moths, but do not permit mothballs to come into direct contact with them.

Avoid storing quilts in attics or basements because of the risk of mildew.

Do not pin labels to quilts, as pins rust and/or leaves holes in the fabric.

All light is damaging, especially direct sunlight and fluorescent lights (unless they have ultraviolet filters).

In dusting quilts to remove surface soil, use the small hand-held brush attachment on your vacuum cleaner; be sure it is clean and use it at the slowest speed setting. Either wrap a clean piece of cheesecloth around the brush or place the quilt flat under a section of fiberglass screening. Vacuum through the screen, a section at a time. Beware of any sharp corners or edges on the screen and cover them with masking tape so that they won't snag the fabric. Vacuuming following these procedures may be repeated every six months or so.

IF YOU MUST CLEAN YOUR QUILT

First determine what the fibers are. Wool and silk may be dry-cleaned; cotton and linen may be washed.

Test fabrics for color-fastness before wetting them in any substantial way. This can be done by carefully placing a few drops of water on a section no longer than one inch square and located in an obscure place; then pat the section with white blotting paper to see if the color comes off on the blotter. Repeat on each patch that is different. Test individually again with the detergent solution you plan to use before wetting the entire quilt. Do not *ever* put a quilt in an automatic clothes dryer, as the agitation and the heat can be extremely damaging.

Special dry cleaners who are equipped to handle large and fragile textiles may be experienced in working with quilts. Never take a chance with your neighborhood dry cleaner. Rely on personal or professional recommendations (ask the textile curator at your local museum or a quilt-shop owner). It is difficult to anticipate what chemicals will be used in cleaning and what effect they will have on your quilt.

Be particularly cautious with quilts made up, wholly or partly, from old blacks and browns, as these colors are especially perishable because of the dyes.

Never launder silks, wools, velvets, or hand-painted and hand-dyed fabrics.

Do remember that glazed fabrics (chintz and sateen) will tend to lose their sheen after cleaning.

If you have a quilt of a manageable size that is less than fifty years old and are convinced that you know what the fabrics are, that they are color-fast and preshrunk, and that the batting material is compatible (you can find yourself in trouble if you have a cotton quilt with a wool batting), then wash it in your machine using the delicate/gentle cycle with cold water and a mild liquid detergent such as Woolite or those made especially for quilts and sold in quilt shops. Do not run the machine the full cycle; use a short cycle.

Some individuals prefer to launder in a bathtub. This must be done with extreme care and patience, as the wet quilt becomes very heavy and fibers and stitches can break. Do not scrub vigorously. Never wring out the quilt but gently squeeze out excess rinse water.

Dry all textiles flat, preferably on a layer of clean, white, soft, absorbent towels. You may have to replace the towels if they become too wet; turn the quilt over when doing so.

Never iron quilts. Synthetics can melt, and very old fabrics may shred.

Mending a quilt is up to the individual owner. An important quilt should not be allowed to fall into tatters, but sometimes replacement of fabrics or additional stitching can decrease its value as an investment. Professional advice is recommended. Some conservators will be able to replace worn patches with materials of the same age and style, or they will use a sheer fabric netting called "moline" over the threadbare areas: the original color will show through, but it will be protected.

DISPLAY

To be enjoyed and appreciated, quilts should be seen and displayed. The collector-dealer Ardis James recently said, "What's the point of collecting quilts if you keep them folded in a closet where they can't be distinguished from bathmats?"

There are quilts that are a pleasure to use on a bed or drape over the back of a sofa. There are others that you may feel deserve to be displayed on the wall as works of art and possibly even framed. Here are some suggestions for the display of quilts:

Even a large quilt can be mounted on stretcher bars. To achieve this, hand stitch a suitable fabric (a clean cotton sheet or unbleached muslin) to the four edges of the quilt. This fabric is to be wrapped around the stretcher bars; when the quilt is hung, it will not be visible. It is usually necessary to have large sizes specially ordered or constructed.

For very early quilts or fragile textiles such as silks and velvets, hang a sheet of ultraviolet Plexiglas just in front of the quilt (not touching the surface, because textiles need to breathe).

Keep away from direct or reflected light (sun or fluorescent) and heat (radiators and fireplaces).

Sew a muslin sleeve across the top of the quilt, stitch to backing only, insert a wooden dowel or curtain rod, and attach this to brackets or finials. A variation is to stitch a sleeve at the top and the bottom and insert a flat strip of wood through each.

Stitch a strip of muslin across the back and then fasten a strip of Velcro to it. Apply another Velcro strip to the wall and press the two together.

The 3M Company manufactures a product called Scotchmate Hook & Loop Fastener tape that may be stitched across the back and will hold a narrow rod.

Don't be afraid to display a quilt at an angle if the design is appropriate. Barn Raising Log Cabin quilts are dramatic when displayed in almost any direction.

If the pattern and installation allow, rotate the direction of the quilt every nine to twelve months to lessen the pull of gravity on the textile fibers.

Small quilts can be draped over a dowel on the wall or folded over a bannister.

Quilts used as table covers can be protected with lightweight Plexiglas (heavier glass or Plexiglas may leave marks); generally they should be kept away from food.

Doll and crib quilts can be professionally framed. Be sure that there is a space between the glass and the quilt for air circulation and that no nails or glue are used.

Shallow Plexiglas and ultraviolet Plexiglas cases are also available for use in displaying small quilts.

SOURCES

For more information, individual consultation, or materials to send for, the following institutions, experts, and publications are recommended.

The textile division of the Department of Agriculture in your state or in Washington, D.C. They have trained staffs in many areas, and they also issue a number of booklets on caring for textiles, removing stains, and other related subjects.

The textile curator of your local museum.

Sources of acid-free papers: TALAS (a mail-order company), 130 Fifth Avenue, New York, NY 10011; Conservation Materials, Ltd., Box 2884, 340 Freeport Blvd., Sparks, NV 89431; Process Materials, 30 Veterans Blvd., Rutherford, NJ 07070.

Ultraviolet filters: Rohm & Haas Co., 6th and Independence Mall, Philadelphia, PA 19105.

Booklets on caring for and mounting large textiles: Division of Textiles, Ms. Doris Bowan, Curator, the Smithsonian Institution, the National Museum of History and Technology, Washington, DC 20560.

Ms. Pie Galinat, 230 West 10th Street, New York, NY 10014. Specializes in restoration for museums and dealers.

Ms. Elly Seabold, Gallery of Graphic Arts, 1601 York Avenue, New York, NY 10028. Specializes in preparing and mounting quilts for hanging.

Ms. Bryce Revely, P.O. Box 15832, New Orleans, LA 70115. Specializes in restoration for museums and collectors; will work on crazy quilts.

Mrs. Patsy Orlofsky, Director, Textile Conservation Workshop, Inc., Main Street, South Salem, NY 10590. Authority on all aspects of textile conservation and restoration.

Ms. Nancy Sloper Howard, Textile Conservation Workshop, Route 2, Box 26, Winters, CA 95694. Specializes in conservation and restoration.

Ms. Tracy Jamar, Jamar Textile Restoration Studio, 250 Riverside Drive, New York, NY 10025. Experienced at dating and restoring quilts and mounting them for display.

Ms. Mary Fredrickson, Texas Conservation Center, P.O. Box 967, W.T. Station, Canyon, TX 79016. Analysis, cleaning, and restoration.

Indianapolis Museum of Art, Textiles Conservation, 1200 West 38th Street, Indianapolis, IN 46208. Dating, care, and restoration.

 **254**

Phyllis and Pamela Brown in the Master Bedroom of the Browns' Home. Photograph by Lee P. Thomas.

Romantic pastel quilts double up to cover a table here. The top quilt is done in a Dresden Plate variation; the unusual border treatment incorporates rows of pink with a scalloped edge bound in a blue that echoes not only the main colors, but also the pattern's curves. Mrs. Brown finds this cozy spot in front of the fireplace ideal for reading bedtime stories with four-year-old Pamela and her seven-year-old brother, Lincoln.

255

Sampler Quilt (detail of 256).

![256] **256**

Phyllis George Brown and Her Daughter Pamela at Home. Photograph by Lee P. Thomas.

Pictured here is the Great Room at Cave Hill, the Browns' Lexington, Kentucky, residence. On the wall is the exquisite sampler quilt that Mrs. Brown and her husband, Governor John Y. Brown, bought when they were married; a masterpiece composed mainly of silks (with an occasional piece of silk-velvet), the quilt is made up of blocks, each in a different pattern and each made by a different woman. It is dated 1854 (see detail).

257

Interior of President and Mrs. Jimmy Carter's Walnut Mountain Cabin. Photograph courtesy *Family Circle* magazine.

On the four-poster in the master bedroom of President and Mrs. Carter's vacation cabin one may see (appropriately) a Log Cabin quilt in a Barn Raising variation.

    The bed, as well as other pieces of furniture throughout the house, were designed and built by President Carter, an accomplished carpenter. Mrs. Carter is noted for her long-standing interest in American crafts, and during her tenure as First Lady she often chose handcrafted items from various states as gifts for visiting dignitaries or heads of state.

258

Interior of President and Mrs. Jimmy Carter's Walnut Mountain Cabin. Photograph courtesy *Family Circle* magazine.

Two homey quilts lie on a trundle bed in the guest room of President and Mrs. Carter's vacation cabin.

259

Home of Elizabeth Ingher. Photograph by Tatsuo Masubuchi. Courtesy Bunka Publishing Bureau, Tokyo.

A Colonial Schoolhouse quilt on the wall integrates perfectly with this charming country setting furnished with early American antiques.

260

Home of Phyllis Haders.
Photograph by Ernst Beadle.

In a room aglow with the Christmas spirit, a red and green Pennsylvania Straight Furrow quilt, a variation of the Log Cabin, shows yuletide colors. This crib quilt is displayed under a glass top on a coffee table made from an old trundle bed. On the wall is a red and white quilt made in the last half of the nineteenth century; it has an original design composed of concentric circles applied in an overlay technique.

261

Home of Phyllis Haders.
Photograph by Ernst Beadle.

This room offers a group of crisp red and green antique quilts. On the wall is an appliqué cotton quilt from around 1860 in a Spice Rose pattern with stuffed red flowers. The bed is covered by a Double Irish Chain from around 1870 that has multiple borders: a red sawtooth, a green, and a bright red binding.

262

Bedroom in Laura Fisher's Country House. Photograph by Tatsuo Masubuchi. Courtesy Bunka Publishing Bureau, Tokyo.

The quilt dealer and author, Laura Fisher, practices what she preaches: "enjoy living with your quilts." On a wall of a bedroom in her country house is a wool challis Log Cabin quilt from about 1875, executed in a Courthouse Steps variation. The Log Cabin on the bed is from the same period, but it is arranged in the Barn Raising pattern. Folded at the foot of the bed is an Evening Star quilt, and over the brass footrail is an 1880 Birds in Flight Pennsylvania cotton quilt.

 Other quilts here include an Evening Star crib quilt (on the rocking horse), a silk doll quilt in the Seven Sisters pattern, and a Basket pillow in a basket on the desk top. There is also a Log Cabin cushion on the desk stool, and a LeMoyne Star pillow nestled in the wicker armchair.

📜 263

Sitting Room of the Designer's Apartment. Photograph by Michael Dunne, courtesy Alexandra Stoddard, Inc.

Interior designer Alexandra Stoddard's New York apartment exudes a country-like feeling. Appliquéd quilts draped over antique wicker chairs create a sense of warmth and coziness. A pastel pieced quilt blends with Manuel Canovas's "Joy" chintz covering the loveseat.

📜 264

Home of Sandy Duncan. Photograph by Michael Dunne, courtesy Alexandra Stoddard, Inc.

A pink and white Basket quilt is tossed over a wicker chair in this sunny garden apartment. The hand-painted striped canvas was created exclusively for the actress by the firm of D.D. and Leslie Tillett, Inc.

📜 265

Sitting Room of Texas Home. Photograph by Hickey-Robertson, courtesy Alexandra Stoddard, Inc.

A cattle gate found on the property frames the sitting room fireplace. The pink and white quilt and the quilt pillows are from the owner's collection.

![266] 266

Girl's Bedroom in a Texas Home. Photograph by Hickey-Robertson, courtesy Alexandra Stoddard, Inc.

A Texas quilt is hung like a painting in this enchanting room. The dollhouse design hooked rug was made by George Wells.

![267] 267

Bedroom. Photograph by Keith Scott Morton, courtesy Alexandra Stoddard, Inc.

The pastel Wedding Ring quilt created by the interior designer enhances the four-poster Canadian maple bed created by her and integrates with Porthault pillows. White dotted-swiss is freely swagged as a type of canopy over the frame of the bed. The painting is by Roger Mühl.

![268] 268

Interior of a New York Apartment. Photograph by Michael Dunne, courtesy Alexandra Stoddard, Inc.

A green-and-white geometric quilt covers a wicker daybed placed at one end of a living room in a tiny New York apartment.

 269

Carolina Lily Pieced and Appliqué Quilt. c. 1860. New England. Cotton, 88 × 88″. Collection Karen Berkenfeld, New York.
Photograph by Leonard Nones, courtesy *Family Circle* magazine.

This charming pattern is known by several names and variations, including Lily, Day Lily, Meadow Lily, and sometimes
Peony. The flowers are almost always in groups of three, with some finishing details, against a white background. The
flower petals are composed of pairs of pieced red diamonds, and the stems and leaves are appliquéd. The quilt top is
made in twelve-inch blocks fitted together at an angle to form large diamonds. A green sawtooth edge border is used
on all four sides and there is a red calico print binding. Quilt stitching on the top is composed of one-inch squares,
and the borders have a diagonal pattern.

270

Yo-Yo Pieced Quilt and Patchwork Pillows in the New York Home of Gene Morin.

A Yo-Yo quilt covers a daybed in the penthouse of the antique collector, Gene Morin. This quilt—or coverlet, as it is more often called—is mostly worked in solid-color cottons, with only a few prints. The predominant colors are mauve, peach, and green, and the circles are arranged in large concentric blocks with an interesting scalloped edging. This 1920s New York State quilt measures a generous 96 × 84", with each individual yo-yo 2¼" in diameter.

Banked in the corner are a group of patchwork pillows. Note that the basket design appliquéd to the black pillow is also comprised of extremely tiny yo-yos, about the size of the pennies in the basket itself; it was made in Ohio around 1910. An interesting sidelight is that several very similar pillows from the same location and period have surfaced, and all appear to have been made by the same person; the fabrics are identical, and the only variation is the arrangement of the flowers or the arc of the basket handles. The other pillows shown here include three crazy-quilt designs in velvets and silks made round 1880 in New Hampshire. (Note that some of the New England crazy-quilt designs are not quite as elaborate as their Southern counterparts: although the sections are joined by embroidery, there are none of the embroidered flourishes within the sections.) The challis Log Cabin pillow, at left, has unusual slate-blue center squares instead of the customary red, which symbolizes the hearth. The very small pillow with the black ruffle is not patchwork, but represents an example of Amish embroidery.

271

Yo-Yo Quilt in the Home of Norma Marshall. Photograph by Tatsuo Masubuchi.
Courtesy Bunka Publishing Bureau, Tokyo.

Yo-Yo quilts are considered a novelty form, as they are made without layering, and therefore no batting or stitching is needed to hold layers together. Such coverlets are entirely composed of cloth circles, usually about three inches in diameter, with the edge of the circle turned to the middle and then gathered, thus leaving a small hole at the center. The circles are then arranged randomly—or occasionally—in patterns. In this photograph, the coverlet is used as a conversation-piece tablecloth.

 272

Judith Larzelere. *Clinging Fire*. c. 1980s. Dedham, Massachusetts. Cotton.
Photograph courtesy General Electric Research and Development Center.

Here the artist employed her skill in manipulating hot and cool colors to suggest a feeling of warmth
and restfulness. The quilt is now on display in the executive dining room of the General Electric Corporate
Research and Development Center; it is not available for viewing by the general public.

BIBLIOGRAPHY

General

"American Pictorial Quilts," catalog. Vassar College Art Gallery, January 20–February 16, 1975.

Bacon, Lenice Ingram. *American Patchwork Quilts*. New York: William Morrow, 1973.

"Baltimore Album Quilts," catalog from exhibition. Dena S. Katzenberg, curator. The Baltimore Museum of Art, Md., 1981–82.

Bank, Mira. *Anonymous Was a Woman*. New York: St. Martin's Press, 1979.

Berkshire Evening Eagle. Pittsfield, Mass.: Eagle Publishing. Excerpts of September 2, 1927, and September 14, 1929.

Binney, Edwin, III, and Gail Binney-Winslow. *Homage to Amanda: Two Hundred Years of American Quilts*. San Francisco: R. K. Press, 1984.

Bishop, Robert. *New Discoveries in American Quilts*. New York: E. P. Dutton, 1975.

Bishop, Robert, and Carter Houck. *All Flags Flying: American Patriotic Quilts as Expressions of Liberty*. New York: E. P. Dutton, 1986.

Bishop, Robert, and Elizabeth Safanda. *A Gallery of Amish Quilts: Design Diversity from a Plain People*. New York: E. P. Dutton, 1976.

Bullard, Lacy Folmar, and Betty Jo Shiell. *Chintz Quilts: Unfading Glory*. Tallahassee, Fla.: Serendipity, 1983.

Christopherson, Katy. *The Political and Campaign Quilt*. Catalog. Quilt Commentaries, The Kentucky Heritage Quilt Society and The Kentucky Historical Society, 1984.

Clarke, Mary Washington. *Kentucky Quilts and Their Makers*. Lexington, Ky.: University of Kentucky Press, 1976.

Finley, Ruth E. *Old Patchwork Quilts and the Women Who Made Them*. 1929. Reprint. Newton Center, Mass.: Charles T. Branford, 1970.

Fisher, Laura. *Quilts of Illusion*. Pittstown, N.J.: The Main Street Press, 1987.

Golden, Mary. *The Friendship Quilt Book*. Dublin, N.H.: Yankee Books, 1985.

Gutcheon, Beth. *The Perfect Patchwork Primer*. New York: David McKay, 1973.

Haders, Phyllis. *The Main Street Guide to Quilts*. Pittstown, N.J.: The Main Street Press, 1975.

Hall, Carrie A., and Rose A. Kretsinger. *The Romance of the Patchwork Quilt in America*. New York: Bonanza, 1935.

Hall, Eliza Calvert. *Aunt Jane of Kentucky*. Boston: Little, Brown, 1907. Reprint. San Pedro, Calif.: R. & E. Miles, 1986.

Holstein, Jonathan. *The Pieced Quilt: An American Design Tradition*. Greenwich, Conn.: New York Graphic Society, 1973.

Ickis, Marguerite. *The Standard Book of Quilt Making and Collecting*. 1949. Reprint. New York: Dover, 1959.

Irwin, John Rice. *A People and Their Quilts*. Exton, Pa.: Schiffer, 1983.

Johnson, Mary Elizabeth. *A Garden of Quilts*. Birmingham, Ala.: Oxmoor House, 1984.

Kakalia, Deborah U. *Hawaiian Quilting as an Art*. Honolulu: Kepola U. Kakalia, 1976.

Kentucky Quilts 1800–1900. Louisville, Ky.: The Kentucky Quilt Project. Dicmar Publishing.

Kolter, Jane Bentley. *Forget Me Not: A Gallery of Friendship and Album Quilts*. Pittstown, N.J.: The Main Street Press, 1985.

Lane, Rose Wilder. *Woman's Day Book of American Needlework*. New York: Simon & Schuster, 1963.

Lasansky, Jeannette. *In the Heart of Pennsylvania: 19th and 20th Century Quiltmaking Traditions*. Lewisburg, Pa.: Oral Traditions Project of the Union County Historical Society, 1985.

Laury, Jean Ray. *Quilts and Coverlets*. New York: Van Nostrand-Reinhold, 1970.

Lipman, Jean. *Provocative Parallels: Naive Early American-International Sophisticates*. New York: E. P. Dutton, 1975.

Lipman, Jean, and Alice Winchester. *The Flowering of American Folk Art*. New York: Viking Press.

Lipsett, Linda Otto. *Remember Me: Women and Their Friendship Quilts*. San Francisco: The Quilt Digest Press, 1985.

McMorris, Penny. *Crazy Quilts*. New York: E. P. Dutton, 1984.

Malone, Maggie. *1001 Patchwork Designs*. New York: Sterling, 1982.

Montgomery, Florence M. *Textiles in America, 1650–1870*. New York: W. W. Norton, 1984.

Nelson, Cyril I., and Carter Houck. *The Quilt Engagement Calendar Treasury*. New York: E. P. Dutton, 1982.

Orlofsky, Patsy and Myron. *Quilts in America*. New York: McGraw-Hill, 1974.

Pellman, Rachel and Kenneth. *The World of Amish Quilts*. Intercourse, Pa.: Good Books, 1984.

Peto, Florence. *American Quilts and Coverlets*. New York: Chanticleer Press, 1949.

Pettit, Florence H. *America's Indigo Blues*. New York: Hastings House, 1974.

Pettit, Florence H. *America's Printed and Painted Fabrics*. New York: Hastings House, 1970.

Plews, Edith R. *Hawaiian Quilting on Kauai*. Kauai, Hawaii: Kauai Museum Publications, 1973.

Pottinger, David. *Quilts from the Indiana Amish: A Regional Collection*. New York: E. P. Dutton, 1983.

The Quilt Digest. San Francisco: Kiracofe and Kile, 1983–85.

Ramsey, Bets, and Merikay Waldvogel. *The Quilts of Tennessee*. Nashville, Tenn.: Rutledge Hill Press, 1986.

Rowley, Nancy J. "Red Cross Quilts," published in "Uncoverings: The Research Papers of The American Quilt Study Group," vol. 3, Sally Garoutte (ed.). Mill Valley, Calif.: 1983.

Safford, Carleton L., and Robert Bishop. *American Quilts and Coverlets*. New York: E. P. Dutton, 1972.

Sommer, Elyse. *Textile Collector's Guide*. New York: Simon & Schuster, 1984.

Stevens, Napua. *The Hawaiian Quilt*. Honolulu: Service Printers, 1971.

Stewart, Charlyne. *Snowflakes in the Sun*. Lombard, Ill.: Wallace-Homestead, 1986.

Swan, Susan Burrows. *Plain & Fancy*. New York: Holt, Rinehart and Winston, 1977.

Tomlonson, Judy Schroeder. *Pennsylvania Mennonite Quilts and Pieces*. Intercourse, Pa.: Good Books, 1985.

Webster, Marie D. *Quilts: Their Story and How to Make Them*. New York: Doubleday, Page, 1915. Reprint. New York: Tudor, 1948.

Wiss, Audrey and Doug. *Folk Quilts*. Pittstown, N.J.: The Main Street Press, 1983.

Yabsley, Suzanne. *Texas Quilts, Texas Women*. College Station, Tex.: Texas A & M University Press, 1984.

Quilts: The Art of the Amish

Bishop, Robert, and Elizabeth Safanda. *A Gallery of Amish Quilts: Design Diversity from a Plain People*. New York: E. P. Dutton, 1976.

Bomann, Mieke H. "A World Apart: Kenyon's Amish Neighbors." *Kenyon College Alumni Bulletin* (June 1986).

Haders, Phyllis. *Sunshine and Shadow: The Amish and Their Quilts*. New York: Universe Books, 1976.

Holstein, Jonathan. *The Pieced Quilt: An American Design Tradition*. Greenwich, Conn.: New York Graphic Society, 1973.

Horst, Melvin J., and Elmer Lewis Smith. *Among the Amish*. Akron, Pa.: Applied Arts, 1959.

Lasansky, Jeannette. *In the Heart of Pennsylvania: 19th and 20th Century Quiltmaking Traditions*. Lewisburg, Pa.: Oral Traditions Project of the Union County Historical Society, 1985.

Pellman, Rachel and Kenneth. *The World of Amish Quilts*. Intercourse, Pa.: Good Books, 1984.

Pottinger, David. *Quilts from the Indiana Amish: A Regional Collection*. New York: E. P. Dutton, 1983.

Smith, Elmer Lewis, and Melvin J. Horst. *The Amish*. Witmer, Pa.: Applied Arts, 1966.

Tomlonson, Judy Schroeder. *Pennsylvania Mennonite Quilts and Pieces*. Intercourse, Pa.: Good Books, 1985.

Warren, Elizabeth V. "Amish Quilts," catalog from exhibition. Nassau County Museum of Fine Art, N.Y., March 17–May 12, 1985.

Hawaiian Quilts

Akana, Elizabeth A. *Hawaiian Quilting: A Fine Art*. Honolulu: Hawaiian Mission Children's Society, 1982.

Akana, Elizabeth A. "Ku'u Hae Aloha," *The Quilt Digest* (San Francisco: Kiracofe and Kile) 2 (1984): 71–77.

Barrere, Dorothy B. "Hawaiian Quilting: A Way of Life," *The Conch Shell* (Honolulu: Bishop Museum Association) 3, No. 2 (1965): 16–21.

Buck, Peter H. *Arts and Crafts of Hawaii*. (Honolulu: Bishop Museum Press) 45, Sec. V (1964): 210–213.

Campbell, Archibald. *A Voyage Round the World, 1806–1812*. Honolulu: University of Hawaii Press, 1967.

Hammond, Joyce D. *Tifaifai and Quilts of Polynesia*. Honolulu: University of Hawaii Press, 1986.

Kaeppler, Adrienne L. *The Fabrics of Hawaii (Bark Cloth)*. England: F. Lewis Publishers, 1975.

Kakalia, Deborah U. *Hawaiian Quilting as an Art*. Honolulu: Kepola U. Kakalia, 1976.

Krout, Mary H. *Reminiscences of Mrs. Mary S. Rice*. Honolulu: Hawaiian Gazette, 1908.

Leonard, Anne, and John Terrell. *Patterns of Paradise*. Chicago: Field Museum of Natural History, 1980.

Plews, Edith R. *Hawaiian Quilting on Kauai* (An Address Given to the Mokihana Club at Lihue, Kauai, March 1, 1933). Kauai: Kauai Museum Publications, 1976.

Rice, Kym Snyder. "The Hawaiian Quilt," *Art and Antiques* (May/June 1981): 101–107.

Rice, Kym Snyder. "A Cultural Crossroads: The Decorative Arts in the Early Hawaiian Kingdom, 1790–1835." Thesis, University of Hawaii 1979.

Rose, Roger G. *Hawai'i: The Royal Isles*. Honolulu: Bishop Museum Press, 67 (1980): 174–177.

Thurston, Lucy G. *Life and Times of Mrs. Lucy G. Thurston*. Honolulu: The Friend, 1934.

Tibbetts, Richard J., Jr., and Elaine Zinn (videotape producers). *The Hawaiian Quilt—A Hawaiian Tradition*. Created by Hawaii Craftsmen. Honolulu: 1986.

Baby, Crib, and Doll Quilts

Bank, Mira. *Anonymous Was a Woman*. New York: St. Martin's Press, 1979.

Carlisle, Lillian Baker. "Pieced Work and Appliqué Quilts at the Shelburne Museum." *Museum Pamphlet Series*, No. 2. Shelburne, Vt., 1957.

DeLeeuw, Adele. *The Patchwork Quilt*. Boston: Little, Brown, 1945.

Diaz, Mrs. A. M. *The Schoolmaster's Trunk*. Boston: James R. Osgood, 1874.

Field, Rachel. *Calico Bush*. New York: Macmillan, 1931.

Flournoy, Valerie. *The Patchwork Quilt*. New York: E. P. Dutton, 1985.

Fox, Sandi. *Small Endearments: 19th-Century Quilts for Children*. New York: Scribner's, 1985.

Frye, L. Thomas, ed. *American Quilts: A Handmade Legacy*. Oakland, Calif.: The Oakland Museum, 1981.

Holbrook, Ruth. *Kay's Quilt*. New York: Doubleday, Doran, 1940.

Hunt, Mabel Leigh. *Johnny-Up and Johnny-Down*. Philadelphia: J. B. Lippincott, 1962.

Lichten, Frances. *Folk Art of Rural Pennsylvania*. New York: Scribner's, 1946.

McClinton, Katharine Morrison. *Antiques of American Childhood*. New York: Clarkson N. Potter, 1970.

Orlofsky, Patsy and Myron. *Quilts in America*. New York: McGraw-Hill, 1974.

Pyle, Katharine. *The Counterpane Fairy*. 1898.

Wiggin, Kate Douglas. *The Quilt of Happiness*. Boston: Houghton Mifflin, 1917.

Woodard, T. K., and Blanche Greenstein. *Crib Quilts and Other Small Wonders*. New York: E. P. Dutton, 1981.

Quilts at an Exhibition

Bishop, Robert, and Carter Houck. *All Flags Flying: American Patriotic Quilts as Expressions of Liberty*. New York: E. P. Dutton, 1986.

Brackman, Barbara. "Prize-Winning Mystery." *Quilters' Journal*, no. 27 (July 1985).

Bresenhan, Karoline Patterson, and Nancy O'Bryan Puentes. *Lone Stars: A Legacy of Texas Quilts, 1836–1936*. Austin: University of Texas Press, 1986.

Gross, Joyce. "Century of Progress." *Quilters' Journal*, no. 27 (July 1985).

Gross, Joyce. "Stearns and Foster." *Quilters' Journal* 3, no. 4 (Winter 1981).

Gross, Joyce. "1940 N.Y. World's Fair Quilt Contest and Exhibit." *Quilters' Journal* 3, no. 2 (Summer 1980).

Gross, Joyce. "Bertha Stenge." *Quilters' Journal* 2, no. 2 (Summer 1979).

Holstein, Jonathan, and John Finley. *Kentucky Quilts 1800–1900: The Kentucky Quilt Project*. New York: Pantheon Books, 1982.

Kansas City Star, 1H (September 21, 1986).

McKee, Susan. "Contemporary Quilt Carries Off Honors." *Indianapolis Star*, sec. 6 (March 27, 1977).

Orlofsky, Patsy and Myron. *Quilts in America*. New York: McGraw-Hill, 1974.

"Prize Winning Quilts." *Good Housekeeping* (March 1978).

Quilt National Catalogue (1983).

Safford, Carleton L., and Robert Bishop. *America's Quilts and Coverlets*. New York: E. P. Dutton, 1972.

Contemporary Quilts

Avery, Virginia. *Quilts to Wear*. New York: Scribner's, 1982.

Ayres, J. Jean. *Sensory Integration and the Child*. Western Psychological Services, 1979.

Gutcheon, Beth. *The Perfect Patchwork Primer*. New York: David McKay, 1973.

Lady's Circle Patchwork Quilts (Fall 1980–October 1986).

McMorris, Penny, and Michael Kile. *The Art Quilt*. San Francisco: The Quilt Digest Press, 1986.

Myers, Jan. "From Both Sides of the Heart," *The Professional Quilter*, no. 9 (January 1985): 5. Reprinted with permission of the Flying Needle, NSCAE, May 1984.

Quilter's Newsletter Magazine (June 1971–December 1986).

A Quilt Collector's Primer

Adrosko, Rita J. *Natural Dyes and Home Dyeing*. New York: Dover Publications, 1971.

Bath, Virginia Churchill. *Needlework in America: History, Designs and Techniques*. New York: Viking Press, 1979.

Binney, Edwin, III, and Gail Binney-Winslow. *Homage to Amanda: Two Hundred Years of American Quilts*. San Francisco: R. K. Press, 1984.

Bishop, Robert, and Patricia Coblentz. *New Discoveries in American Quilts*. New York: E. P. Dutton, 1975.

Bishop, Robert, and Carleton L. Safford. *America's Quilts and Coverlets*. New York: E. P. Dutton, 1972.

Carlisle, Lillian Baker. "Pieced Work and Appliqué Quilts at the Shelburne Museum." *Museum Pamphlet Series*, No. 2. Shelburne, Vt., 1957.

Finley, Ruth E. *Old Patchwork Quilts and the Women Who Made Them*. Philadelphia: J. B. Lippincott, 1929.

Garoutte, Sally, ed. "Uncoverings: The Research Papers of the American Quilt Study Group." Mill Valley, Calif.: 1980.

Hall, Carrie A., and Rose G. Kretsinger. *The Romance of the Patchwork Quilt in America*. Caldwell, Idaho: Caxton Printers, 1935.

Hardingham, Martin. *The Fabric Catalogue*. New York: Pocket Books, 1978.

Holstein, Jonathan. *The Pieced Quilt: An American Design Tradition*. Greenwich, Conn.: New York Graphic Society, 1973.

Ickis, Marguerite. *The Standard Book of Quilt Making and Collecting*. New York: Dover Publications, 1949.

Kiracofe, Roderick, and Michael Kile, eds. *The Quilt Digest*. San Francisco: Kiracofe and Kile. Vol. 1 (1983), Vol. 2 (1984), Vol. 3 (1985), Vol. 4 (1986).

Kobayashi, Kei, ed. *Shelburne Museum: The Quilt*. Tokyo, Japan: Gakken, 1985.

Lipsett, Linda Otto. *Remember Me: Women and Their Friendship Quilts*. San Francisco: The Quilt Digest Press, 1985.

McMorris, Penny. *Crazy Quilts*. New York: E. P. Dutton, 1984.

McMorris, Penny, and Michael Kile. *The Art Quilt*. California: The Quilt Digest Press, 1986.

Montgomery, Florence M. *Textiles in America 1650–1870*. New York: W. W. Norton, 1984.

Montgomery, Florence M. *Printed Textiles: English and American Cottons and Linens 1700–1850*. New York: Viking Press, 1970.

Orlofsky, Patsy and Myron. *Quilts in America*. New York: McGraw-Hill, 1974.

Peto, Florence. *American Quilts and Coverlets*. New York: Chanticleer Press, 1949.

Peto, Florence. *Historic Quilts*. New York: The American Book Co., 1939.

Pettit, Florence H. *America's Printed and Painted Fabrics*. New York: Hastings House, 1970.

Swann, Susan. *Plain and Fancy: Women and Their Needlework, 1700–1850*. New York: Holt, Rinehart and Winston, 1977.

INDEX

Note: Folio references in Roman type refer to text pages; those in italic type refer to information in illustrations and captions.

Aesthetics, 152–153, 258–260
Albers, Josef, 28
Album Appliqué Quilt, Maryland, 193, 199
Album Pieced and Appliqué Quilt, 79
Album quilts, 22, 64, 157
Alexander, Mary, 101
Alford, Clarissa White, 261
Allen, Patsy, 250
Alphabets (Khin), 237
Amish people
   colors used by, 114–115
   crib and doll quilts, 178
   history and customs of, 111–113
   patterns among, 113–114, 116
   stitching of, 115–116
Amish Pieced Crib Quilt, Four Patch, 99
Amish Pieced Oblong or Rectangle Quilt (Yoder), 118
Amish Pieced Quilt, 119
Amish Pieced Quilt, Diamond in a Square, 29
Amish Pieced Quilt, Puss in the Corner, 98
Amish Pieced Quilt, Pyramid Tumbling Blocks, 30
Amish Pieced Quilt, Square Within a Square, 28
Amish Quilt-Seller, 117
Ammann, Jacob, 111
Anderson, Annie Burnett, 97
Anderson, Charlotte Warr, 244
Anderson, Faye, 220–221, 236
Anderson, Gerlinde, 228
Anthony, Susan B., 65
Appliqué
   aesthetics, 259
   Baltimore Album pattern, 71
   best quilts, 62
   defined, 16
   Hawaii, 136–137
   pictorial subjects, 71
Appliqué Stitchery (Laury), 220
Armstrong, Samuel Chapman, 136
Around the Corner (Khin), 236
Around the World pattern, 36, 69, 93
Arthur and Garfield Campaign Pieced Quilt, 94
Autograph quilts, 22
Autumn Night (Gersen), 240
Avery, Virginia, 219
Ayres, A. Jean, 223

Baby's Playthings Pieced and Appliqué Quilt, 185
Backing, 16
Baltimore Album Appliqué Quilt, 56
Baltimore Album Appliqué Quilt (Foote), 57
Baltimore Album Appliqué Quilt Top, 283
Baltimore Album Quilt, Appliqué (Pool and Pool), 265
Baltimore Album quilts, 22, 23, 71
Baltimore Album Quilts (Katzenberg), 22
Barber, Sarah, 273
Barn Raising variation, 272, 307
Barrere, Dorothy B., 136
Bars pattern, 28
Bars Pieced Quilt, 126
Bars with Nine-Patch Corners Amish Pieced Quilt, 118
Basket of Flowers with Floral Vine Border Pieced Quilt, 106
Basket of Flowers with Vine Border Appliqué Crib Quilt, 182
Baskets of Flowers Pieced and Appliqué Quilt, 52

Baskets pattern, 70, 220
Bear's Paw, Pieced Quilt, 92
Beck, Ida W., 58
Bell, Grandmother, 164
Bell, John, 200
Berner, Julie, 236
Beyer, Jinny, 196, 205, 221
Bias Pomegranates Appliqué Quilt, 77
Bible patterns, 67
Bible Quilt, Appliquéd, 84
Binding materials, 17
Birds in the Air design, 15
Bishop, Robert, 23, 114, 215
Bittersweet XII (Crow and Brill), 225
Black Family Album Quilt (Wilson), 26
Bonesteel, Georgia, 220
Book of Appliqué (Avery), 219
Boynk, Betty, 220
Bradkin, Cheryl, 220
Brayton, Mary, 153
Bread Quilt, Pieced and Appliquéd (Laury), 226
Breckinridge, John S., 200
Bresenhan, Karey, 48, 198
Brick or Brickyard Pieced One-Patch Quilt (Anderson), 97
Bridal quilt, 63
Bright Hopes, Bright Promise (Butzke), 245
Brill, Velma, 225
Broderie Perse Pieced and Appliquéd Quilt, 49
Broderie perse quilts, 20
Broken and Breaking Patterns (Gipple), 248
Broken-Arm Quilt (Oppenheimer), 248
Broken Bars Amish Pieced Quilt, 118
Broken Dishes Amish Pieced Quilt, 109, 121
Broken Star or Carpenter's Wheel Pieced Quilt, 89
Brown, John Y., Jr., 294, 303
Brown, Pamela, 302, 303
Brown, Phyllis, 293, 302, 303
Bruce, Sophronia Ann, 96
Bunyan, John, 68
Burton, Mrs. Avery, 202
Bussey, Augusta Elizabeth Duvall, 159
Butzke, Carol E., 220, 245

Caden, Margaret Rogers, 195
Calico Bush (Field), 179
Calimanco quilts, 20
Calvert, Moneca, 197, 208, 220, 243
Campbell, Archibald, 135
Carlisle, Lillian Baker, 177
Carolina Lily, Pieced and Appliqué Quilt, 310
Carpenter's Wheel or Broken Star Pieced Quilt, 89
Carr, Mary Jane, 263
Carter, Hazel, 218
Carter, Jimmy, 304
Cassatt, Mary, 256
Centennial Quilt, Pieced and Appliquéd, 25
Centennial Quilt, Pieced and Appliquéd (Knappenberger), 47
Center Square quilts, 15
Central Medallion Flower Pot and Birds Appliqué Quilt (Daggs), 266
Chant Hindou, Le (Labbens), 241
Charity quilts, 22
Cherokee Trail of Tears (Edmonds), 222
Chester Dare Embroidered and Appliquéd Crazy Quilt (Miller), 162
Children's Room, Stencil House, 186
Chinn, Ramona, 220, 246, 247
Chipyard pattern, 93
Christopherson, Katy, 72

Church Amish Women Quilting, 116
Circus is Coming to Town, The, 206
Civil War Presentation Appliqué Album Quilt, 267
Clark, Edward B., 67
Clark, Ricky, 73
Clarke, Mary Washington, 19, 62
Clay, Henry, 72, 107, 284, 285
Clay, Mrs. Henry, 284, 285
Clay/Crittenden Pieced Presentation Quilt (Clay), 284
Cleveland, Grover, 165
Cleveland-Hendricks Political Pieced and Embroidered Crazy Quilt, 165
Clinging Fire (Larzelere), 313
Cobweb and Stars Amish Pieced Quilt, 123
Cohan, George M., 65
Colonial Schoolhouse quilt, 305
Comforts, 18
Commemorative Pieced Quilt, 46
Commemorative quilts, 21–22, 157
Concentric Kaleidoscope-like Design, Pieced and Appliqué Quilt, 40
Constitution, 53
Converging Values (Chinn), 246
Cook, Captain James, 134
Cooke, Mrs. C. M., 145
Cory, Benjamin, 275
Counterpane Fairy, The (Pyle), 179
Courthouse Steps variation, 307
Cows: Pieced Pictorial Patchwork, 48
Coxcomb with Rose Border Pieced and Appliqué Quilt (Hart), 76
Cradle Quilt, Log Cabin Amish Pieced (Horn), 120
Craft Horizons, 215
Craig, Sharyn, 242
Crane, Walter, 154
Crazy Patch Slumber Throw (Bussey), 159
Crazy quilt, 18
   aesthetics, 259
   construction of, 152
   frugality and, 68–69
   history of, 152–155
   materials, 155–157
Crazy Quilt, Pieced (Hotchkiss), 172
Crazy Quilt, Pieced (Laury), 173
Crazy Quilt, Pieced and Embroidered, 49, 172
Crazy Quilt, Pieced and Embroidered (Holland and Ross), 163
Crazy Quilt, Pieced and Embroidered (Layman), 170, 171
Crazy Quilt, Pieced and Embroidered (Murray), 201
Crazy Quilt, Pieced and Embroidered (Steinbock), 168, 169
Crazy Quilt, Pieced and Embroidered (Willis), 167
Crazy Quilt, Pieced and Embroidered Floral Album, 161
Crazy Quilt, Pieced, Appliqué, and Embroidered (Marvin), 151, 166
Crazy Quilt, Pieced, Embroidered, and Painted (Grandmother Bell), 164
Crib and doll quilts, 129, 176–180
Crib Quilt Top, Pieced and Appliquéd, 186
Crittenden, John J., 284
Croly, Jane, 158
Crossed-T's Pieced Quilt, 96
Crow, Nancy, 22, 222, 225
Crow Foot embroidery stitch, 201
Crowns and Kahalis (Na Kalauna Me Na Kahali) *Appliqué Quilt,* 142
Crowns (Na Kalauno) *Appliqué Quilt,* 149
Crystal Palace, 43
Cube quilts, 15
Curiosity Bedspread (Burton), 202

Curved piece quilts, 71
Cushman, Elizabeth Diltz, 35

Daggs, Ann, 266
Dallas, George M., 46
Davis, Ardyth, 228
Dayglow (Larzelere), 251
Deco Tepee II (Allen), 250
Delaunay, Robert, 123
Delectable Mountains pattern, 68
DeLeeuw, Adele, 179
Della Posta, Lynn, 233
Diagonal Stripes Mennonite Pieced Crib Quilt, 175
Diamond Amish Pieced Quilt, 126
Diamond in a Square Amish Pieced Quilt, 29, 127
Diamond in the Square (Nine-Patch) Pieced Quilt, 125
Diamond Patchwork (Gutcheon), 220
Diamond patterns, 28, 70
Diaz, Mrs. A.M., 179
Diltz, Hanson Penn, 35
Display, 299–300
Doll quilt, see Crib and doll quilts
Doll Quilt, Pieced Cotton, 184
Dorcas Magazine, 152, 157
Double Hearts motif, 122
Double Irish Chain, 306
Double Nine-Patch Amish Pieced Quilt, 122, 124
Double Wedding Ring design, 16
Double Wedding Ring Pieced Quilt, 40
Double Wedding Ring Pieced Quilt (Horn), 204
Douglas, Stephen A., 290
Drazer, Sharon, 204
Druckman, Nancy, 23
Drunkard's Path design, 16, 129
Duncan, Sandy, 308

Eagle Appliquéd Crib Quilt (Strever), 182
Eagle Pieced and Appliquéd Quilt, 78
Eastlake, Charles, 153
Edge of the Rainbow (Lihilili Anuenue) Appliqué Quilt, 143
Edmonds, Chris Wolf, 222
E.E.H. (quiltmaker), 190
Eight-Pointed Star Pieced and Appliquéd Trundle Quilt, 38
Elgin, Carrie Diltz, 35
Embroidered quilts, 20–21

Fabrics, 17–19
Fairy Tales (Nadelstern and Della Posta), 233
Feathered Star with Streak O'Lightning Border Mennonite Quilt, 130
Feed sacks, 18–19, 78
Fenwick, Jason, 296
Fiber's Fantasy (Chinn), 247
Field, Rachel, 179
Finley, Ruth, 63
Fisher, Laura, 307
Fitzgerald, Veronica, 232, 240
Flag quilt (Hawaii), 142
Flag Quilt, Friendship, Pieced and Appliqué, 52
Flag Quilt, Political Ribbon, Pieced, Appliquéd, Embroidered, and Tied (Frentz), 200
Flags Pieced Quilt, 78
Floating Diamond Amish Pieced Quilt, 126
Floral Album Crazy Quilt, Pieced and Embroidered, 161
Floral Cameo Pieced Quilt (Drazer), 204
Floral Vine Border with Basket of Flowers Pieced Quilt, 106
Flournoy, Valerie, 179
Flower Basket Reverse Appliqué Quilt, 274

Flower Garden, Hexagon, or Mosaic Pieced Crib Quilt, 181
Flower Garden Pieced Quilt (Mitchell), 91
Flower Garden Pieced Quilt or Grand-mother's Flower Garden (Diltz, Elgin, and Cushman), 35
Flower patterns, 68
Flying Geese pattern, 15, 70, *281*
Flying Geese Pieced Quilt, 279
Folk Art of Rural Pennsylvania (Lichten), 178
Foote, Hannah, 57
Foster, Stephen, 65
Foundation Rose Variation Appliqué Quilt, 268, 269
Four-Patch Amish Pieced Crib Quilt, 99
Four-Patch pattern, *40*, 69–70
Four Square Pieced Quilt (Laury), 226
Fowlkes, Shirley, *207*
Framed Center Design of a "John Hewson" Appliquéd Quilt, 42
Franklin, Benjamin, 42
Frentz, Maggie, *200*
Freycinet, Louis de, 135
Friendship Flag Quilt, Pieced and Appliqué, 52
Friendship Medley quilts, 65
Friendship Quilt, Pieced, Embroi-dered, and Tie-Quilted (Williams), 80
Friendship quilts, 64, 65, 157, *170*, *171*
Friendship Quilt, Thirteen Colony Pieced and Appliquéd, 200
Friendship/Sampler Pieced Quilt, 82
Fuqua, Evelyn, 18

Gallery of Amish Quilts, A, Design Diversity from a Plain People (Bishop and Safands), 114
Garden Appliqué Quilt (Mynderse), 286
Garden Botanical Pieced and Appliquéd Quilt, 266
Garden Island Appliqué Quilt, 142
Garden of Eden and the Garden of Elenale (Na Kihapi Nani Lua 'Ole O Edena A Me Elenale) Appliqué Quilt, 145
Garfield, James, 53
Garfield and Arthur Campaign Pieced Quilt, 94
George Washington at Valley Forge (Edmonds), 222
Gersen, Carol H., *240*
Getting It All Together (Laury), 220
Ginza (Porcella), 235
Gipple, Nancy, *248*
Glorious Lady Freedom (Calvert), 243
Godey's Lady's Book, 155, 157, 178
Godfrey, Virginia F., *204*
Good Housekeeping magazine, 21, 196
Grandmother's Flower Garden or Flower Garden Pieced Quilt (Diltz, Elgin, and Cushman), 35
Grandmother's Flower Garden Pieced and Embroidered Quilt (Montgomery), 90
Grandmother's Garden design, 16
Grant, U.S., 53
Graveyard, Pieced, Appliquéd, and Embroidered Quilt (Mitchell), 74
Graveyard quilt, 63
Greenaway, Kate, 155
Grotrian, Carol Anne, *210*
Gutcheon, Beth, 220, 221
Gutcheon, Jeff, 220
Gypsies (Sisto), 244

Haders, Phyllis, *306*
Hall, Eliza Calvert, 72
Halpern, Nancy, 222
Hambrick, Martha Ann Brown, *100*
Hamlin, Hannibal, 200
Hammond, Joyce, 136
Hand-Pieced Amish Quilt, 128
Hand quilts, 64
Harper's Bazaar, 154, 156, 157
Harrison, Benjamin, 95
Harrison, Caroline, 19
Hart, E.J., 76

Harvest Star pattern, 122
Harvest Sun pattern, 122
Haskins, Mrs. Samuel Glover, 160
Haskins Quilt, The (Haskins), 160
Havemeyer, Mr. and Mrs. H. O., 256
Hawaiian Appliqué Quilt, 140, 148
Hayes, Rutherford B., 163
Hayewood, Dixie, 220
Hearst, Judy Wasserman, *210*, 221
Hearts (Calvert), *208*
Henderson, Sarah, 39
Hendricks, Thomas, 163, 165
Herman, Nancy Clearwater, *234*
Hewitt, Martha, 23, *287*
Hewson, John, 17, 42
Hexagon, Mosaic, or Flower Garden Pieced Crib Quilt, 181
Hexagonal patterns, 69
Hexagonal Star Quilt, Pieced (Alexander), *101*
Hexagons and Triangles Pieced Quilt, 270, 271
Hints on Household Taste (Eastlake), 153
Hired Man's quilts, 123
Holland, Anna Lou, 163
Holly Berry Appliqué Quilt, 75
Holstein, Jonathan, 196, 260
Honeycomb or Mosaic Pieced and Appliqué Quilt (Bruce), 96
Hopkins, Mary Ellen, 220
Horn, Mary Kay, 204
Hotchkiss, Mary Lou, *172*
Houses and Weeping Willows Pieced and Appliquéd Quilt, 88
Hunt, Mabel Leigh, 179
Hussey, Mary, 148

Imperfection, 75
In Autumn the Evening Shows Its Lavender (Porcella), 234
Indiana Seasons (Godfrey), 204
Ingher, Elizabeth, 305
Interrelating Support (Hearst), 210
Ivey, Virginia Mason, 63, 71–72, *107*

Jackson, Andrew, 72, 107
Jacob's Ladder pattern, 99
James, Ardis, 299
James, Michael, 22, 59, 222, 249
J.C. Penny Celebrates American Style, 209
Jensen, Margot Strand, 228
Jewels (Brown), 230, 231
Johannah, Barbara, 220
"John Hewson" Appliquéd Quilt, Framed Center Design, 42
Johnny Up and Johnny Down (Hunt), 179
Johnston, Ann, *289*
Jones, Stella, 136
Joseph's Coat Mennonite Pieced Quilt, 85
June, Jennie (Jane Croly), 158

Kaikahi, Ioela, *145*
Kaikainahaole, F. C. M., *145*
Kaleidoscope Color, 203
Kamehameha III (k. of Hawaii), 139
Ka Na Kani Lehau (The Rain that Rustles Lehua Blossoms) Appliqué Quilt, 144
Kaomi Malie (Press Gently) Appliqué Quilt, 144
Katy's Quilt, 179
Katzenberg, Dena S., 22
Ka Uhi Wai O Kaala (Mist of Mt. Kaala) Appliqué Quilt (Hussey), 148
Kaui O Maui (Maui Beauty) pattern, 143
Keepsake quilts, 65
Kelley, Helen, 220
Kentucky Pinwheel Pieced and Appliquéd Quilt, 102
Kentucky Quilts and Their Makers (Clarke), 19, 62
Kentucky Quilts 1800–1900, 72
Khin, Yvonne M., 236, 237
Kiggins Pieced Quilt, 275
Kile, Michael, 214
Kimberly, Angeline, 260, 276
Kimberly, Augusta, 260, 276
Kit quilts, 21
Klee, Paul, 118
Klein, Jody, *238–239*
Kline, Merle, 177, 178

Knappenberger, G., 47
Kopp, Joel, 23, 72
Kopp, Kate, 23
Kretsinger, Rose, 21
Kuu Hae Aloha (My Beloved Flag) Appliqué Quilt, 133, 138–139, 146, 147
Ku-U-Hae Appliqué Quilt, 142

Labbens, Soizik, *241*
Lady of the Lake pattern, 68
Lady of the Lake Pieced Quilt, 92
Lady's Circle Patchwork Quilts (journal), 219
Lancaster County quilt, 28
Langford, Margaret O'Sullivan, 90
Larcom, Lucy, 178
Larsen, Violet S., 234
Larzelere, Judith, 213, 251, 313
Laury, Jean Ray, 173, 219–220, 226, 227
Layman, Mrs. Newton (Mattie), 170, 171
Le Chant Hindou (Labbens), 241
Legacy or Sampler Quilt, Pieced and Appliquéd, 83
Legacy quilts, 65
Lei Mamo (Mamo Lei) Appliqué Quilt, 141
Leman, Bonnie, 215–216, 218, 219–220
Lemon (LeMoyne) Star pattern, 51, 70, 74
Lemon (LeMoyne) Star Pieced Quilt (Shanks), 102
Leverett, Sarah Sedgwick, 15
Lichten, Frances, 178
Lightning Streak, 99
Light of Liberty (Grotrian), 210
Lihilili Anuenue (The Edge of the Rainbow) Appliqué Quilt, 143
Lilioukalani (q. of Hawaii), 139
Lincoln, Abraham, 200, 261, 263, 267
Lincoln (Nebraska) Quilt Symposium, 218
Linsey-Woolsey quilts, 19
Lipman, Jean, 15
Literary themes, 68, 92, 155
"Lizzie's Quilt": Fans Amish Pieced Quilt, 131
Log Cabin Amish Pieced Cradle Quilt, 120
Log Cabin design, 15, 69, 70–71, 153, 307
Log Cabin Mennonite Pieced Quilt Windmill Blades Variation, 27
Log Cabin Pieced Quilt, 34, 255, 272, 280
Log Cabin Pieced Quilt, and Tumbling Blocks, 31
Log Cabin Pieced Quilt, Barn Raising or Sunshine and Shadow Variation, 33
Log Cabin Pieced Quilt, Barn Raising Variation, 32
Log Cabin Pieced Quilt, Streak O'Lightning Variation, 32
Lone Star or Star Variation Pieced Quilt (Vanzant), 41
Lone Star Pieced Quilt (Moore), 242
Lone Stars: A Legacy of Texas Quilts, 1836–1936 (Bresenhan and Puentes), 198

Maile, Koolau K., *145*
Malcolm, Janet, 215
Mamo Lei (Lei Mamo) Appliqué Quilt, 141
Mangat, Terrie Hancock, 222
Mann, Bruce, 72
Many, Many Cows and Related Images (Klein), *238–239*
Mariner's Compass Pieced and Appliquéd Quilt, 87
Marriage of Blue and Orange (Larzelere), 214
Marvin, Florence Elizabeth, 151, 166
Maslow, Abraham, 223
Masonic Ribbon Pieced and Embroidered Quilt, 54, 55
Materials
  aesthetics and, 258–259
  contemporary, 216–217
  crazy quilts, 155–157
  crib and doll quilts, 177
  described, 17–19
  frugality in, 68–69

Hawaii, 137
  innovation in, 194
Mathieson, Judy, *211*
Maui Beauty (Kaui O Maui) pattern, 143
May, Therese, *238–239*
McIntyre, Fannie, 18–19
McMorris, Penny, 214
Medallion quilt, 205
Memory quilt, 172
Mennonite Pieced Crib Quilt, Diagonal Stripes, 175
Mennonite Pieced Quilt, Joseph's Coat, 85
Meyers, Jan, 221, 222
Miller, Annie Hines, 162
Miller, Eleanor Bingham, 72
Miller, Sidney Allee, 229
Minimalist painting, 15
Mist of Mt. Kaala (Ka Uhi Wai O Kaala) Appliqué Quilt (Hussey), 148
Mitchell, Bette McCarney, 91
Mitchell, Elizabeth Roseberry, 74
Monster Quilt #7 (May), *238–239*
Montgomery, Charles, 257
Montgomery, Mrs., 148
Montgomery, Sue Cheatham Smith, 90
Moore, Phyllis, *242*
Morin, Gene, 311
Morris, William, 153, 154
Morton, Levi P., 95
Mosaic design, 15
Mosaic, Hexagon, or Flower Garden Pieced Crib Quilt, 181
Mosaic or Honeycomb Pieced and Appliqué Quilt (Bruce), 96
Mountain Mist pattern, 204
Mourning quilts, 15
Ms. Sue: Alive and Liberated (Teel), 242
Murphy, Marjorie, 221
Murray, Mrs. John A. Garnett, 201
Museum of American Folk Art, 197
My Beloved Flag (Ku'u Hae Aloha) Appliqué Quilt, 133, 138–139, 146, 147
Mynderse, A.M., 286

Nadelstern, Paula, 220, *233*
Na Kalauno (Crowns) Appliqué Quilt, 149
Na Kalaunu Me Na Kahali (Crowns and Kahalis) Appliqué Quilt, 142
Na Kiphapi Nani Lua 'Ole O Edena A Me Elenale (The Garden of Eden and the Garden of Elenale) Appliqué Quilt, 145
Nathan-Roberts, Miriam, 250
Nautical Stars Pieced Quilt (Mathieson), *211*
New Yorker, The, 215
Nine-Patch blocks, 130
Nine-Patch Corners with Bars Amish Pieced Quilt, 118
Nine-Patch Diamond in the Square Pieced Quilt, 122, 124
Nine-Patch pattern, 69, 70, 98
Nine-Patch Postage Stamp Miniature Pieced Quilt, 37
Nine-Patch Variation Pieced Quilt (Hambrick), 100
Niumalu or Nawilili Beauty Appliqué Quilt (Montgomery), 148

Oak Leaf motif, 122
Oblong or Rectangle Quilt, Pieced Amish (Yoder), 118
Ocean Waves Amish Pieced Quilt, 128
Ocean Waves pattern, 70
O'Keeffe, Georgia, 223
Old Patchwork Quilts and the Women Who Made them (Finley), 63
One Fine Day (Berner and Schnitker), 236
One-patch patterns, 69
Op Art, 15, *128*, 215, 260
Oppenheimer, Ellen, *248*
Optical-illusion patterns, 71
Orndorff, Drucilla, 81
Orndorff, Jessie Bailey, 81
Our Acre and Its Harvest, 153
Owsley, William, 102

Pasquini, Katie, 222
Patchwork Quilt, Pieced Pictorial, Cows, 48
Patchwork quilts, 62, 179
Patera, Charlotte, 221, *253*
Patriotic quilts, 21–22
Pattern quilts, 21
Patterns, *see* Quilt patterns; *entries under name of specific patterns*
Paulet, George, 139
Paxton, Joseph, *43*
Peacock Hallelujah (Herman), *234*
Pellman, Kenneth, 114
Pellman, Rachel, 114
Penders, C. M., 219
Pennsylvania Straight Furrow quilt, 306
Peterson's Magazine, 153, 154
Peto, Florence, 256
Pictorial subjects, 71
Pieced and Appliqué Quilt (Hewitt), 287
Pieced Sampler Quilt (Rupp), 289
Pieced Star with Sawtooth Border, 290
Piecing, 15, 70, 71, 259
Pilgrim's Progress (Bunyan), 68
Pine Trees pattern, 70
Pinwheel design variation, *121*
Pinwheels with Sawtooth Border Pieced Quilt, 86
Political Ribbon Flag Quilt, Pieced, Appliquéd, Embroidered, and Tied (Frentz), 200
Political themes, 68, 94, 95
Polk, James K., *46*
Pomegranates (Bias) Appliqué Quilt, 77
Pool, Mary J., 23, *265*
Pool, Sarah, 23, *265*
Porcella, Yvonne, 222, *234, 235*
Postage stamp quilts, 15, *36, 69, 93,* 220
Prairie Star Pieced and Appliquéd Mennonite Quilt, 122
Presentation Appliqué Quilt, 282
Presentation quilts, 64, 65
Presidential Wreath Appliqué Quilt (Travers Family), 278
Press Gently (Kaomi Malie) Appliqué Quilt, 144
Professional Quilter, The (Meyers), 221
Provocative Parallels (Lipman), 15
Pryor, Nannie Elizabeth, *86*
Puss in the Corner Amish Pieced Quilt, 98
Pyle, Katharine, 179
Pyramid Tumbling Blocks Amish Pieced Quilt, 13, 30

Quilt Design Workbook, The (Gutcheon and Gutcheon), 220
Quilt Digest, 260
Quilter's Guild of Dallas, *207*
Quilter's Newsletter, 216, 218, 219–220
Quilting bee, 17
  Amish people, 113, 115, *116*
  contemporary, 216
  crib and doll quilts, 178
  society and, 64–66
Quilting Bee, The (Miller), 229
Quilting materials, *see* Materials
Quilt #59 (Studstill), *252*
Quilt patterns, 194–195
  aesthetics, 258–260
  Amish people 113–114, 116
  Bible themes, 67
  block constructions, 69–70
  building themes, 68
  crazy quilts, 154–156
  crib and doll quilts, 177
  curved shapes, 71
  flower themes, 68
  Hawaii, 137–139
  household utensil themes, 68
  literary themes, 68
  Log Cabin patterns, 70–71
  love and courtship themes, 68
  nature themes, 67–68
  political themes, 68
  square dance themes, 68
  star patterns, 70
  trades themes, 67
Quilts and Coverlets (Laury), 220

Quilts and quilting, 62–73, 153, 261–262
  cleaning, 297–299
  construction of, 15–17
  defined, 15
  evaluation guidelines for, 257–264
  frugality in materials, 68–69
  Hawaii, 136–137
  history of, 14–15, 21, 194–196
  preservation, 72–73
  superstitions about, 63–64
  types of, 19–22
  values of, 22–24
Quilts, Coverlets, Samplers, Hooked Rugs (Bishop), 23
Quilts of Tennessee, The (Walkvogel and Ramsey), 72
Quilt top, 15

Rainbow Monogram and Initial Appliquéd and Embroidered Quilt (Beck), *58*
Rainbow Stars Pieced Quilt (Laury), 227
Rain that Rustles Lehua Blossoms (Ka Na Kani Lehau) Appliqué Quilt, 144
Ramsey, Bets, 72–73
Ray of Light (Beyer), 205, 221
Red Cross Quilt, 65, *81*
Red Cross Quilt, Pieced, Appliquéd, and Embroidered (Orndorff and Orndorff), *81*
Reich, Charles, 219
Religious groups, 73
Religious themes, 82, 84, 85
Representation of the Fairground Near Russellville, Kentucky, 1856, A (Ivey), 71, *107*
Representation quilts, 21
Rets, Janett, 154
Rhythm/Color: Bacchanale (James), 249
Rhythm/Color: Spanish Dance (James), *59*
Rice, Mary Sophie, *142*
Robbing Peter to Pay Paul Quilt, 71, *102*
Roosevelt, Eleanor, 195
Rose of Sharon Appliquéd Crib Quilt, 183
Rose of Sharon Appliquéd Quilt (Sears), *84*
Rose of Sharon Appliqué Quilt (Barber), *273*
Rose Wreath with Tulips and Kentucky Flowerpot Corners Appliqué and Pieced Quilt with Trapunto Stitching (Henderson), *39*
Ross, Christine Holland, 163
Rowley, Nancy J., 65
Rupp, Salinda W., 289
Ruskin, John, 153

Sacking materials, 18–19, *48,* 68
Safands, Elizabeth, 114
Safford, Carleton, 215
Salvage, 68
Sampler or Legacy Quilt, Pieced and Appliquéd, 83
Sampler Quilt, 302
Sampler Quilt, Pieced and Appliqué, 105
Sampler quilts, 22, 65
Savery, Rebecca Scattergood, *291*
Schnitker, Thekla, *236*
Schoolhouse Amish Pieced Quilt, 130
Schoolhouse Pieced and Appliquéd Quilt, 88
Scott, Sir Walter, 68, 92
Scrap quilts, 93
Sears, Eunice, 72
Sears, Jane Neale, *84*
Sears, Roebuck Company, 21
Seminole Indian patchwork, 220, 222
Sewing machine, 67, 115
Shanks, Margaret, *102*
Shapira, David, 215
Ship's Wheel or Prairie Star Pieced Quilt (Sutherlin, Pryor, and Cora), *86*
Ships Wheel pattern, *122*
Shipyard pattern, 69
Shoo Fly pattern, 70

Shoo Fly Pieced Quilt, 44, 45
Shunk, Francis R., *46*
Signature quilts, 22, 65, 172
Simplicity Pieced Crib Quilt, 191
Sisto, Penny, 244
Snider, Rene, 290
Snowflake pattern, *104*
Snyder, Maria McCormick, 222
Solomon's Puzzle Amish Pieced Quilt, 129
Specialty materials, 19
''Spectrum'' (Yarrall), 15, *36*
Spice and Rose pattern, 306
Spider's Web, Pieced Quilt (Langford), *90*
Square Within a Square Amish Pieced Quilt, 28
Stair Steps or Illusion Pieced Quilt, 288
Star Everlasting Pieced Crib Quilt, 188
Starfire Pieced Quilt (Laury), 226
Star of Bethlehem design, 16
Star or Lone Star Variation Pieced Quilt (Vanzant), 41
Star patterns, 70, 86
Star Pieced Quilt, 277
Star Quilt, Hexagonal, Pieced (Alexander), *101*
Star Quilt, Pieced, The Waveland Quilt, 281
Star Quilt, Pieced, with Appliqué Bouquets (Trabue), *103*
Stars and Cobweb Amish Pieced Quilt, 123
Steinbock, Anna Marie, *168*
Stenciled quilts, 20
Stenge, Bertha, 195
Stewart, Susan, 19
Stoddard, Alexandra, *308*
Storage, 295–296
Stowe, Harriet Beecher, 65
Streak O'Lightning Border with Feathered Star Mennonite Quilt, 130
Streak O'Lightning design, 15
Streak O'Lightning Variation, Log Cabin Pieced Quilt, 32
Streets of Boston Appliqué Quilt, The (Kimberly and Kimberly), 276
Strever, Rachie T., *182*
String quilting, *41,* 69
Studstill, Pamela, *252*
Stuffed-work quilts, 20
Sugar Loaves pattern, 281
Sunbonnet Babies (E.E.H.), *190*
Sunburst design, 15
Sunburst Pieced Quilt (Savery), *291*
Sundheimer, Lizzie, *131*
Sunshine and Shadow Pieced Quilt, 189
Sunshine and Shadow Variation or Barn Raising Variation, Log Cabin Pieced Quilt, 33
Sunshowers (Anderson), 228
Sutherlin, Mary, *86*

Tapa fabric, 134, 135
Teel, Odette Goodman, 242
Templates, 15, 16–17, 69, 70
Testimonial quilts, 157
Texas Motifs Quilts, Pieced and Appliquéd, 207
T form pattern, *96*
Thematic quilts, 21–22, 67–68
Thirteen Colony Pieced and Appliquéd Friendship Quilt, 200
Three-Dog Night (Anderson), 236
Thurston, Lucy, 135
Ticks, 18
Tied Bars/Mauve-Jade Pieced Quilt (Davis), 228
Tilden, Samuel, *163*
Tippecanoe Pieced Quilt, 95
Tithing quilts, 22
Tobacco Sacks Pieced Quilt, 48
Trabue, Fannie Sales, *103*
Trapunto Quilt, Pieced, 50, 51
Trapunto quilts, 20, 39
Travers Family, *278*
Triangles or Thousand Pyramids Pieced Quilt, 97
Trilobe Flower and Trapunto Clipper Ships Pieced Quilt, 266
Trip Around the World pattern, *36, 69,* 220

Trip Around the World Pieced Quilt (Willoughby), *93*
Triple Bars Amish Pieced Quilt, 126
Trundle Quilt, Eight-Pointed Star Pieced and Appliquéd, 38
Tumbling Blocks and Log Cabin Pieced Quilt, 31
Tumbling blocks design, 15
Turnham, Sally, 66
Tuxedo Junction (Patera), *253*

Updegraph, Mary E., *56*

Van der Hoof, Gail, 196
Vanzant, Ellen Smith Tooke, 41
Vasarely, 15
Virginia Ivey Appliqué and Figural Stuffed-Work Quilt (Ivey), 63, 71–72, *107*

Wade, Fairfax, 154
Walkvogel, Merikay, 72–73
Washington, Martha, 42
Waterlily Waltz (Larsen), *234*
Watson, Elkaneh, 66, 194
Waveland Quilt, The, Pieced Star Quilt, 281
Weaver, Jane, 153
Webb, Electra Havemeyer, 256–257, 263
Webster, Marie, 16, 21
Wedding Ring (Double) Pieced Quilt, 40
Wedding Ring quilt, 309
Weddings, 63, 64, 65
We Give Thanks (Anderson), 244
West, Dorothy, 72
Western Kentucky University Folklore and Folklife Archives, 69
Wheeler, Candace, 154
When the Leaves Leaved (Jensen), 228
Whitework quilts, 20, *51, 71,* 72
Whitney, Eli, 18
Whole-Cloth Pieced Quilt, Crystal Palace, 43
Whole-Cloth Quilt, Pieced, 42
Whole-cloth quilts, 17
Wiggin, Kate Douglas, 179
Wike, Fanny, 180
Williams, Mrs. J. P., *80*
Willis, Elizabeth Thomas, *167*
Willoughby, Jewell, *93*
Willow Oak Appliqué Quilt, 61, 104
Wilson, Sarah Ann, 23, 26
Windmill Blades Variation, Log Cabin Mennonite Pieced Quilt, 27
Windmill Design Pieced Quilt (Snider), *290*
Windmill pattern, 70
Woman and Her Quilts, A, 117
Woman's Day, 195
Women's liberation movement, 221
Woodard, Thomas K., 23
World of Amish Quilts, The (Pellman and Pellman), 114
Worms Crawl In-The Worms Crawl Out (Nathan-Roberts), 250

Yankee Puzzle pattern, 70, *200*
Yarrall, George W., *36*
Yoder, Mahala, *118*
Young, Blanche, 220
Young, Helen, 220
Yo-Yo Quilt, 311, 312

Zegart, Shelly, 72